Multiculturalism in a Global Society

21ST-CENTURY SOCIOLOGY

SERIES EDITOR: Steven Seidman, State University of New York at Albany

The *21st-Century Sociology* series provides instructors and students with key texts in sociology that speak with a distinct sociological voice and offer thoughtful and original perspectives. The texts reflect current discussions in and beyond sociology, avoiding standard textbook definitions to engage students in critical thinking and new ideas. Prominent scholars in various fields of social inquiry combine theoretical perspectives with the latest research to present accessible syntheses for students as we move further into the new millennium amidst rapid social change.

Multiculturalism in a Global Society

PETER KIVISTO

Blackwell
Publishing

Editorial Offices:
108 Cowley Road, Oxford OX4 1JF, UK
  Tel: +44 (0)1865 791100
350 Main Street, Malden, MA 02148-5018, USA
  Tel: +1 781 388 8250

First published 2002 by Blackwell Publishers Ltd, a Blackwell Publishing company

Library of Congress Cataloging-in-Publication Data

Kivisto, Peter, 1948–
    Multiculturalism in a global society / Peter Kivisto.
        p.   cm. – (21st-century sociology)
    Includes bibliographical references and index.
    ISBN 0-631-22193-X (hbk. : alk. paper) – ISBN 0-631-22194-8 (pbk. : alk. paper)
      1. Multiculturalism.   I. Title.   II. Series.

HM1271 .K58 2002
305.8—dc21

                                                2002019090

A catalogue record for this title is available from the British Library.

Set in 10 on 12 pt Photina
by Ace Filmsetting Ltd, Frome, Somerset
Printed and bound in Great Britain
by TJ International, Padstow, Cornwall

For further information on
Blackwell Publishers, visit our website:
www.blackwellpublishers.co.uk

To Stanford M. Lyman

Scholar, teacher, friend and keen observer of our multicultural world

Contents

Figures, Maps, and Tables

Figures

Maps

Tables

Acknowledgments

A number of people helped me to write this book, and I would like to take the opportunity to thank them. Several individuals provided me with especially sage advice along the way, particularly as I wrestled with getting a handle on the vast literature on multiculturalism and transnationalism that has appeared on the scene in recent years. These include Richard Alba, Martin Bulmer, Herbert Gans, Harry Gouldbourne, Tariq Modood, Ewa Morawska, Janusz Mucha, Joane Nagel, Alejandro Portes, John Solomos, and Rudy Vecoli. In addition, friends at my home institution not only supplied valuable insights at various junctures, but also provided needed encouragement: John Guidry, Rick Jurasek, Mike Kirn, and Rocky Sexton. Readers of the entire manuscript are to be thanked. Kevin Fox Gotham's comments were most helpful. Thomas Faist was especially helpful in preventing me from making a number of factual errors in connection with the European scene. But more than that, Thomas was the most important sounding board I had throughout the entire process, and for that I am most appreciative. I would like to thank Steven Gold for his contribution to this project. Steve provided me with an extraordinarily detailed commentary and analysis of my first draft, which proved to be invaluable in preparing the final version of the manuscript.

Once again Jean Sottos, our departmental secretary, played a key role in assisting me with word-processing, preparing charts and tables, and other related nitty-gritty tasks. Despite the chaos that frequently characterizes our office, she always did so with great aplomb and grace.

Thanks to Steve Seidman, 21st Century Sociology Series editor, for asking me to sign on to this project. I am very happy to be part of such a fine series. Thanks also to my editor, Susan Rabinowitz. Working with Susan proved to be a distinct pleasure: she is a perceptive critic, with a clear sense of how to make a book better and how to get the best out of her authors. Since Susan was away on maternity leave during part of the time I was writing, I was most fortunate to be able to work closely with the highly capable Ken Provencher for several months and found that to be a rewarding experience.

Once again, the usual suspects at home helped to make this possible. My wife, Susan, is always my main source of inspiration and my biggest cheerleader. For that, I cannot begin to repay what I owe her. My children, Sarah and Aaron, in their own quiet ways continue to be sources of support.

This book is dedicated to my teacher, Stanford M. Lyman, the person who got me interested in the study of ethnic relations over a quarter of a century ago at the New School for Social Research. Stan's scholarly contributions to this field, his role as a mentor, his passion, wit, and loyalty all had a profound impact on my intellectual development. This book is a small effort aimed at repaying the debt I owe him.

Introduction: Multicultural Societies and Globalization

In recent years, the words "multiculturalism" and "globalization" have captured the imagination of scholars and the public alike. These two commonly used, and frequently misunderstood, terms are increasingly employed as people attempt to make sense of some of the most fundamental and dramatic changes that have reconfigured economic arrangements, challenged political systems, and recast issues related to cultural identities during the past half-century. For those living in what will be the focus of this book, the advanced industrial liberal democracies, two things are abundantly clear about the present. First, their societies are considerably more ethnically diverse – and thus multicultural – than they once were. Second, these societies are now more interconnected and interdependent than ever before, the consequence of globalization trends that, though as Karl Marx was aware, were evident as early as the nineteenth century, nonetheless have become far deeper and more far-ranging in their impacts since the Second World War. The purpose of this book is to explore the contours and the implications of these developments.

We live in a world that is at once local and global – and increasingly the distinction between the two is difficult to make, as the use of the term "glocalization" by sociologists such as Ulrich Beck (2000: 45–50) and Zygmunt Bauman (1998) suggests. Whether or not one finds this particular term useful, it is clear that the dramatic increases in capital flows, labor migrations, the revolution in communication technologies, and the greater ease in long-distance travel have resulted in the dual processes that theorist of modernity Anthony Giddens (1990: 21–7) has referred to as "distanciation" and "disembedding." With these terms he points to the fact that contemporary social relations are no longer necessarily linked to particular places. Instead, we have entered a world in which social relations are less tied to "local contexts of interaction" and we are witnessing their "restructuring across infinite spans of time-space." Postmodern geographer David Harvey (1989) has made a similar point in his discussions of the implications of "time-space compression." Such ideas have informed a growing body of scholarship concerned with the process and the significance of globalization. Without delving into these particular theoretical formulations, suffice it to say that what both Giddens and Harvey are addressing is the fact that we have entered an era in which our received notions about such things as distance/ proximity and place/space are necessarily being reconceived.

The implications of the profound economic, political, and cultural changes that have reconfigured the modern world-system during the past half-century are far-reaching, complex, and in many respects not well understood. It is the task of this book to look at one of those particularly difficult to comprehend, but extraordinarily important implications: the role of globalization in its varied manifestations in defining the contemporary salience of what Arjun Appadurai (1990: 297) has referred to as "ethnoscapes." By this term, he means the social landscapes created by ethnic group affiliations. In exploring the major ethnoscapes of the advanced industrial societies, we will focus on the three interrelated ties of blood: ethnicity, race, and nationalism (henceforth I will use the term ethnicity as a shorthand to encompass all three of these terms; a section of the next chapter entertains a discussion of my understanding of the relationships among the three terms). In turn, the reciprocal role that ethnicity plays in redefining global markets, culture in its varied guises, and received notions of the centrality of the state and the significance of citizenship will also be explored.

The renewed and reconfigured salience of ethnicity in recent decades has manifested itself in two main ways: by the migration of newcomers into various nations throughout the world, and as a result of the resurgence of nationalism among long-established minority groups within existing states.

The Turbulence of Migration

Nikos Papastergiadis (2000) has described the first phenomenon as the "turbulence of migration." By this he refers to the fact that millions of people in the world are on the move, and more specifically, they have exhibited a willingness to leave their countries of origin for other places around the globe, whether they be in neighboring nations or in distant lands (Hammar & Tamas 1997). Given the fluidity of international migratory patterns, it is not surprising that we do not have precise figures on the number of people who can be defined as migrants. Estimates range from anywhere between 80 million and 125 million international migrants (Castles & Miller 1993: 3; Faist 2000a: 3).

These numbers need to be put into perspective. In the first place, as Thomas Faist (2000: 4) has noted, even the higher of these figures repre-

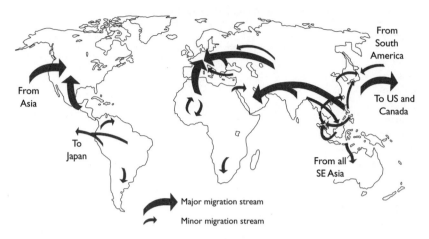

Map I   Major world migration patterns in the 1990s
Source: Population Reference Bureau, Population Bulletin, July 1997.

sents only about 2 percent of the world's population. In other words, the vast majority of people do not opt to leave their nations of origin. Secondly, these people have tended to come from a relatively select number of nations on earth. Figure 1 provides a glimpse into the origins and destinations of major and minor migration streams during the last decade of the twentieth century. Some nations (e.g., Mexico and Turkey) have witnessed large-scale emigration, while many other nations, including some of the poorest in the world, have sent relatively few to other nations. From the point of view of immigrant-sending countries, the impact on their societies varies widely, and because this topic has not received the kind of scholarly attention it deserves, there are unfortunately serious gaps in what we know about the implications of mass emigration on such nations. The advanced industrial nations are not the only immigrant-receiving countries. For example, in some Middle East nations such as Bahrain, Kuwait, Saudi Arabia, and the United Arab Emirates, migrant laborers from Asia and poorer neighboring countries constitute a significant majority of the work force, sometimes reaching levels between 60 percent and 90 percent. Little research on these migrants has been done, in no small part due to the unwillingness of the rulers of some nations to permit an open inquiry into the lives of their foreign workers. We will not be examining these migrants, but will instead concentrate on those settling in the advanced industrial societies.

In a report published by the Population Reference Bureau, Philip Martin and Jonas Widgren (1997) contend that the level of international migration at present is at a record high, and they predict that in the foreseeable future, the level will likely increase. Moreover, they note, some of the world's wealthi-

Table 1   Immigrants in advanced industrial nations

Country	Number of immigrants
Australia	4,000,000
Austria	512,000
Belgium	900,000
Canada	4,000,000
France	3,600,000
Germany	5,000,000
Italy	800,000
Netherlands	692,400
Sweden	490,000
Switzerland	1,200,000
United Kingdom	1,894,000
USA	21,000,000

Source: ILO/IOM/UNHCR, 1994.

est countries are experiencing significant demographic changes as a consequence of the surge of immigration. Table 1 reports on the number of immigrants in major advanced industrial nations. Seven nations, including the United States, Canada, Germany, France, the United Kingdom, Italy, and Japan, are home to around a third of the world's migrant population.

In order to suggest something of the flavor of the significance of the immigration of peoples from less-developed countries of the South to the most advanced industrial nations of the North, consider as illustrations the following examples that will be addressed in further detail in the chapters that follow.

● In the late 1920s, sociologist Robert Park (1950: 151) predicted the demise of Chinatowns in the United States. In the short term, Park was correct in describing the decline of the Chinese population in America, for his prediction was made with the realization that between 1880 and 1924, immigration laws had prevented the Chinese from entering the country legally. Thus, a group that was overwhelmingly male benefited neither from newcomers from their homeland nor from a capacity to reproduce in sufficient numbers to grow. Thus, in his view, the Chinese American community was destined to disappear. However, since 1965, when a new immigration law opened America's gates to mass migration once again, the Chinese population has risen dramatically to reach all-time high levels. Historic Chinatowns in major cities such as New York City, San Francisco, and Los Angeles have been unable to contain all of the newcomers and have thus spilled out of their original boundaries (sections of New York's Little Italy, for example, are now *de facto* part of Chinatown), while new suburban Chinatowns in places such as Monterey Park, California, which is the only city in the United States with a majority Chinese population, and in the Flushing section of New York City have become the homes of middle-class immigrants (Fong 1994).

- Taking advantage of their status as Commonwealth citizens, and responding to the job prospects that arose in the postwar reconstruction of Britain, black Caribbeans and residents of the Indian subcontinent residing in British colonies or former colonies migrated in significant numbers to Britain during the 1950s and 1960s. Though as a percentage of the overall British population their numbers were low, their concentration in particular locales and in particular occupational niches (for example, public transportation) led many whites in Britain to conclude that they were being overrun by nonwhite immigrants. Very quickly, the newcomers confronted the unvarnished racism of a nation unprepared for settlers of color in their midst. Race riots broke out in several cities, while an unofficial political slogan of the Conservative Party in a contested parliamentary election in Smedley was, "If You Want a Nigger for a Neighbor, Vote Labour." The political demagogue – and at the time cabinet official – Enoch Powell warned ominously of the "rivers of blood" that would flow if immigration was not curtailed. Thus, as they attempted to gain a foothold in their new homeland by finding jobs, raising families, and in various ways learning to adjust and adapt to their new home, the immigrants were forced to concentrate considerable amounts of time, energy, and meager financial resources on finding ways to combat the racism of a nation where there "ain't no black in the Union Jack" (Gilroy 1987).

- The Maghreb nations of northwest Africa, especially Algeria, Morocco, and Tunisia, supply the largest number of contemporary immigrants to France. Their presence raises not only issues about race and, as with the British example, the legacy of the colonial past, but also about religion. The ideal of French republicanism suggests that anyone who is or becomes a French citizen is French. This implies openness to newcomers and to their cultural heritages. However, as *L'affaire du foulard* (translated as "the headscarf debate") vividly illustrated, the republican ideal does not necessarily support diversity. The controversy involved Muslim schoolgirls who insisted on wearing the *hijab*, or headscarf, to school in accordance with Islamic practice, and school administrators who contended that this was impermissible because it violated the principle of *laïcité*. The administration maintained that insofar as state-sponsored education is secular, schools could not allow religious expressions that might be construed as acts of proselytizing or promoting a particular religious belief. In 1994, this position became official governmental policy when the Education Minister François Bayrou issued a blanket ban on headscarves. The clash of cultures evident in this dispute pushed to the forefront of contemporary debates questions about the extent to which the French are actually prepared to wrestle with multiculturalism (Wieviorka 1995a).

- The resurgence of violence linked to neo-Nazi skinhead groups in Germany has prompted the German government to initiate several initiatives to combat what many perceive to be a growing threat to minority groups, be they immigrants, Jews, or both, insofar as about half of Jews living in Germany today are recent immigrants from Eastern Europe. The dilemma for Germany is that the economy is heavily reliant on foreign workers, who comprise about 10 percent of the nation's population. Without their presence, the overall population of the nation would actually decline. At the same time, disaffected and often unemployed Germans, particularly in the eastern part of the nation, where the communist regime left the region in economic ruin, have been drawn to the ranks of right-wing extremism. Government estimates put the number of extremists at around 50,000, of which about 9,000 are considered to be violence prone. At the beginning of the twenty-first century, these groups were responsible for around 14,000 anti-immigrant and anti-Semitic crimes, including 750 that can be categorized as violent crimes. The social democratic government of Gerhard Schröder has undertaken a number of actions designed to combat this growing threat. These include a variety of public displays intended to symbolize solidarity with victims, implementing tougher laws against extremists, establishing websites to challenge neo-Nazi propaganda efforts in cyberspace, and initiating court proceedings to ban the National Democratic Party since its xenophobic message has made it a magnet for right-wing skinheads (AP Worldstream 2001).

Nations Without States

But immigration is only one key ingredient contributing to the potent role of contemporary ethnicity and ethnic group relations. The other involves the persistence of historically rooted ethnic divisions based on what Walker Connor (1994) describes as "ethnonationalism," which involves the claims by various ethnic groups to a national identity distinct from the nation-state in which they are located. In other words, those movements working to advance the interests of what Montserrat Guibernau (1999) has described as "nations without states" have increasingly mobilized to promote nationalist agendas. In so doing, they have called into question the ability of existing states to contain these attempts to dismantle and reconfigure existing nation-state boundaries. As will be seen in the case studies, contemporary indigenous peoples in settler states evidence a distinctive yet parallel form of ethnonationalism (Pearson 2001).

Of particular significance is the fact that these nationalist challenges to existing state configurations are occurring in democratic regimes. It is worth noting that when speaking of the advanced industrial states we are simultaneously speaking about liberal democratic political systems which place a premium on the rule of law and on valuing individual (though not necessarily group) rights. Thus, the question arises about the capacity and the willingness of states to consider the possibility of granting greater autonomy (such as rights to limited self-government and control over educational and cultural policies), or in some instances outright independence, to various regions. Indeed, at the core of the debates over contemporary nationalist movements is which of these two possibilities – autonomy or independence – ought to be the ultimate goal. Linked to the matter of goals is the issue of means. Must nationalist movements operate within the parameters of the legal system of a state they find in some ways to be illegitimate and repressive, or are extralegal activities permissible? Expressed in the bluntest possible terms, should nationalist campaigns be waged at the ballot box or with bullets? Consider, if you will, the following examples that will be analyzed in greater detail in subsequent chapters, and it is clear that depending on the particular movement, each of these options is currently being embraced.

- A new Scottish Parliament convened in 1999, one of the major consequences of a policy undertaken by the Labour government of Tony Blair known as "devolution." This term refers to the process of shifting power from the center of the British state to the regions that have demanded greater autonomy. It marked the first time that a Scottish Parliament has assembled since the Act of Union between Scotland and England in 1707. The main political force backing the nationalist campaign has been the Scottish Nationalist Party (SNP). For many in the SNP devolution is not an end, but the first step in the move to total independence. In other words, psychologically they no longer consider themselves to be British, and they want to translate that sense of identity into concrete political practice by affecting the break-up of Britain (Nairn 1977). They do not think it desirable to forge an identity that is at once Scottish and British. Instead, they envision Scotland as part of Europe, without the need for the intermediary identity associated with Britishness. Others in Scotland disagree – particularly those affiliated with the Labour Party, but even many in the SNP – contending that while they want to rectify centuries of English domination, promote Scottish culture, and improve the Scottish economy, think this can best be accomplished by remaining a part of Britain (Nairn 1999). This debate has taken place at the ballot box and in the court of public opinion. It has not been advanced by recourse to violence.

- Nationalism in Northern Ireland provides a stark contrast to that in Scotland. In the first place, it reflects a society divided nearly in half along religious grounds, with the majority Protestant population seeking to remain a part of the United Kingdom, while the Catholic minority seeks to reunite with the rest of Ireland – the outcome of the movement's failure earlier in the twentieth century to remove the British from all of Ireland (O'Brien 1972). During the 1960s, the Northern Ireland Civil Rights Association emerged to press for an end to Protestant discrimination against Catholics in areas such as housing and employment, influenced in no small part by the civil rights movement in the United States. But British intransigence, combined with the revival of militant groups such as the Irish Republican Army, resulted in an escalation of the conflict and the beginning of a long period known as "the Troubles." Three forces were pitted against each other: militant republicans from the Catholic community, militant loyalist organizations from the Protestant camp, and the British military. Armed with what Michael Ignatieff (1997) has called the "warrior's honor," republicans and loyalists alike have waged campaigns of terror, including bombings and assassinations. The result is that over a period of 30 years, 3,600 people have been killed, most of them civilians. After years of efforts to find a negotiated settlement to the conflict, in 1998 both sides in the conflict entered into the Belfast Agreement under the auspices of the combined efforts of the British and Irish governments. Whether this effort to institutionalize and manage the conflict will ultimately succeed remains at the moment an open question.
- In Canada, the nationalist Parti Québecois has waged a political campaign since the 1960s designed to loosen the ties of a province with a French-speaking majority from the rest of Canada. Parallel to the Scottish case, members of the nationalist movement are divided about whether the goal is to obtain greater autonomy or complete independence. To date, the province remains a part of Canada, but the French-speaking population in the province is as deeply divided as the Scottish about the desirability of remaining within the Canadian confederation. Given the uncertainty about the future of Quebec's status, many English-speaking Canadians have left the province. Efforts on the part of the federal government to recognize Quebec as a distinct society while simultaneously preserving the unity of the nation have not succeeded. It has not managed to articulate a resolution to the conflict that is acceptable to the majority of the Francophone community in Quebec and to the citizens of Canada's other provinces. It has, however, succeeded in eliciting hostility from some other provinces that resent the idea that one province would be singled out for distinctive treatment (Thomson 1995). Making the situation more complex is the fact that Montréal, the largest city in Quebec, has been the recipient of a large influx of non-Francophone

immigrants. These newcomers are not enthusiastic about the independence movement, and as a result have been the victims of nativist hostility by some militant sectors of the Francophone community.

- According to historians Eric Hobsbawm and Terence Ranger (1983), one can speak about the ideologies underlying contemporary nationalism as the product of "invented traditions." By this, they mean that the past is manipulated in the interest of current political concerns. Nowhere perhaps is this idea of invention more evident than in the case of Italy's Lega Nord (Northern League). The organization is committed to fighting for the secession of the more modernized and affluent region of northern Italy from the more economically and politically underdeveloped regions of southern Italy. In attempting to define Italy as an artificial construct that brings together two distinct peoples, the Lega Nord has been accused – quite accurately – by critics of promoting a Social Darwinian-inspired form of racism that depicts southern Italians as inherent inferiors. In response, they claim that the people of the north have been the victims of cultural oppression, the consequence of their "annexation" to Italy in the 1860s. The organization has argued for the creation of a new republic of the north that it dubs "Padania," and it has produced various trappings of an independent state such as a flag, national anthem, and capital (Venezia). In advancing its cause, it has identified with the idea of a new Europe of Regions and seeks to articulate a vision of Padania independent of Italy, but embedded within the European Union (Lega Nord 1996).

Overview of the Book

The topic of this book is the power of ethnic identity in the twenty-first century, in a novel world that Manuel Castells (1997) has aptly characterized temporally as the "information age" and spatially as the "network society." In order to appreciate the protean character of ethnicity in this new global age, and its capacity to take varied shapes and forms while producing an equally varied array of outcomes, I will examine a number of case studies from the major advanced industrial nations in the world.

However, the purpose of this book is not simply to offer journalistic accounts of various contemporary manifestations of the significance of ethnic identities, allegiances, and interactions. Rather, I intend to provide a way of interpreting these particular manifestations in a comparative framework. In order to accomplish this task, it is first necessary to engage in an extended discussion of the theoretical issues that inform current scholarly debates about ethnic phenomena. Chapter 1, "Ethnic Theory in a Global Age," sifts through some of the central concerns of contemporary theorists of ethnicity. The chapter begins by deconstructing three crucial terms: race, ethnicity, and nationality. It then proceeds to explore the ways the role of ethnicity in contemporary social life has been portrayed by modernization theory – represented in particular by the work of Talcott Parsons – and by Marxist theory. This leads to a discussion of current theoretical efforts to rethink modes of inclusion and exclusion, focusing on assimilation, cultural pluralism, transnational immigration, and multiculturalism.

Chapters 2 and 3 are devoted to sustained case studies of the three major settler states in the world: the United States, Canada, and Australia. The populations of each of these nations consist of substantial majorities who are either immigrants or the offspring of immigrants. In each of them, the comparatively small indigenous populations – the American Indians in the US, First Nations peoples in Canada, and the Aboriginal peoples of Australia – lost their lands to the colonial conquest of Europeans and live today as marginalized and disadvantaged groups. The ethnic composition of each of these nations is exceptionally heterogeneous.

Chapter 2 is concerned with, as the title indicates, "The United States as a Melting Pot: Myth and Reality." It begins with an overview of the formative period of the American republic and of the period known as the Great Migration, between 1880 and 1930, that is intended to provide a historical context in which to assess the present. This background will set the stage for the following sections, wherein the central factors shaping the nature of intergroup relations in the post-civil rights era and in a period of mass immigration are analyzed. Specifically, we shall inquire into the particular circumstances of each of the major panethnic groups that comprise what David Hollinger (1995) has referred to as the "ethnic pentagon." These include European-origin whites, African Americans, American Indians, Latino Americans, and Asian Americans. The chapter concludes with a discussion of the content of a peculiarly American multicultural vision and the discontents such a vision has provoked.

Chapter 3, "Canada and Australia: Ethnic Mosaics and State-sponsored Multiculturalism," offers a comparative portrait of two other large settler states that, unlike the US, remain part of the British Commonwealth. Again, brief historical sketches will serve to put into context current developments. Of particular importance in the Canadian case is the fact that two groups claim to have "charter group" status: the Anglophone and Francophone communities. The significance of this fact is discussed in terms of the self-defined ideal of Canada as a mosaic – and thus as a society that fosters the perpetuation of a pluralist or multicultural vision of itself. The implications of this vision, at a time when Québecois nationalism threatens the integrity of the nation-state and when new levels of immigration have produced a considerably more diverse society, will be explored. Australia, which remained far more ethnically homogeneous than Canada until recently, will afford an instructive comparison. The federal governments of both nations have played instrumental roles in forging explicit multicultural policies. The chapter will conclude with an analysis of the nature of those policies, the reasons they came about, and their implications.

Chapters 4 and 5 turn to those western European nations that have not historically defined themselves to be immigrant-receiving nations, but have experienced significant levels of immigration during the second half of the twentieth century. The result is that they are at present characterized by an ethnic heterogeneity previously unknown. At the same time, nationalist movements have arisen in some of these nations that, parallel to the situation in Canada, call into question the long-term viability of existing nation-state arrangements.

Chapter 4 looks at "John Bull's Island: Britain in a Postcolonial World." The first sections of the chapter are concerned with three nationalist political movements that have had a significant impact on the post-Second World War United Kingdom: the irredentist struggle in Northern Ireland led by the Irish Republican Army, the campaign for Scottish independence promoted by the Scottish Nationalist Party, and the parallel independence movement in Wales. We will attempt to discern whether or not, as Tom Nairn (1977) has argued, these movements signal the "break-up of Britain." These particular movements will be compared to parallel movements elsewhere in western Europe. The second half of the chapter turns to the impact of immigration. While the primary focus will be on groups from various Commonwealth nations that began to enter Britain in significant numbers after 1950, we will also look briefly at the presence of the Irish and other European immigrants. Chiefly from the Indian subcontinent, the Caribbean, and Africa, the new Commonwealth immigrants changed the racial composition of Britain and added to the religious pluralism of the nation as well. The conclusion of the chapter will look at the implications of immigration for both the immigrants and British society.

Chapter 5 offers a comparison and contrast between the two largest nations of continental western Europe: "Germany, France, and Shifting Conceptions of Citizenship." These two countries have become major immigrant-receiving nations. In both instances, considerable ambivalence about and resistance to the presence of newcomers has resulted, and has fueled the rise of extremist right-wing organizations that have sought to repatriate immigrants and, in their more violent and illegal manifestations, have engaged in assaults, arson attacks, and murders in an effort to terrorize immigrants. At the same time, many progressive elements in each country have come to the support of immigrants.

Despite these parallels, the two nations offer an interesting study in contrasts. Germany, with a longstanding conception of a "blood and soil" version of citizenship, has been ideologically ill-equipped to deal with newcomers, and thus the presence of immigrants – particularly from Turkey and the former Yugoslavia – poses difficult questions about the willingness or ability of the nation to include them as genuine members of German society. In contrast, the republican ideals of France – embedded in their idea of citizenship based on the principle of *jus solis* – suggest that anyone can become a citizen of the nation merely by embracing its values and swearing allegiance to it. As recent history amply attests, as a result of the presence of the new immigrants, not so much from other places in Europe, such as Portugal, but particularly from north Africa, the reality of the situation diverges considerably from the ideal. Indeed, the racialization of French society as a result of immigration raises challenges about inclusion quite similar to those evident in Germany. Given the fact that the European Union is developing policies pertaining to immigration and citizenship that are to be uniformly implemented by the member nations, the role of this suprastate organization in shaping the futures of immigrants in both countries will be considered briefly.

Chapter 6, "Multicultural Prospects and Twenty-first Century Realities," attempts to tie the preceding case studies together in a succinct summary. It is intended to distill from them a general sense of the shared problems and the possibilities confronting the liberal democracies of the advanced industrial nations as they experience unprecedented levels of immigration and the challenges of nationalist minorities in a global era. Since much hinges on the capacity of these nations to reconceptualize and revitalize received notions of citizenship, the book concludes with a brief disquisition into the crucial historical choices of the twenty-first century.

Ethnic Theory in a Global Age

How do sociologists theorize ethnicity? What are the conceptual tools that they use to make sense of the tenacity and the fluidity of ethnic identities and communities in the contemporary world, and how do they account for the gamut of ethnic relations between and among groups? Given the fact that sociologists since the nineteenth century have concerned themselves with ethnic phenomena, it's not surprising that there is no unequivocal answer to each of these questions. Especially in the twentieth century, and at an accelerated pace after mid-century, a considerable amount of sociological energy has been expended in attempting to articulate useful theoretical formulations to help us shed light on the topic (see as illustrations Glazer & Moynihan 1975; Francis 1976; Banton 1987; Yinger 1994). Many theories pose serious challenges to competing theories, and it is clear that not only is there no consensus among sociologists today, but that a unified theoretical position is a chimera.

I will make no effort to present anything resembling a comprehensive portrait of the range and scope of ethnic theory. Rather, the purpose of this chapter is to choose selectively from a range of ethnic theories in an effort to distill from them a useful framework for analysis. One of sociology's perennial issues involves the extent to which we can generalize from the concepts and theories we use. Are they meant to apply everywhere and anywhere, or do they have a somewhat more limited utility? In terms of our concerns, suffice it to say that what follows is intended to be of relevance to certain places around the world, specifically those nations that can be characterized economically as advanced industrial and politically as liberal democracies. This is not to suggest that elements of the chapter's discussion are not relevant in other settings. They well might be. However, it is useful to keep in mind the particularities of the nations that will be our focus.

Analytic Distinctions: Ethnicity, Race, and Nationality

At the outset it is important to define what we construe to be our subject matter. Wsevolod Isajiw (1979: 25) has offered a particularly succinct and useful definition of the ethnic group, which he characterizes as "an involuntary group of people who share the same culture or the descendants of such people who identify themselves and/or are identified by others as people belonging to the same involuntary group." Note the following about this definition. There is an objective component to it insofar as an ethnic group is the result of the existence of various combinations of such cultural markers as a shared history, language, religion, sense of tradition, system of values, folklore, and the like. It also has a subjective quality insofar as it requires identification, by members of the group and/or by others.

With this operational definition, we turn to the contested debates that characterize efforts to delineate the most appropriate way that three terms – ethnicity, race, and nationality – ought to be viewed in relation to one another (Banton 2001: 185–7).

Against race

The most contested relationship is that between the concepts ethnicity and race. Three different potential relationships have been posited. The first position contends that ethnicity and race should be treated as being analytically distinct. The second is a modification of the first insofar as it wants to maintain a distinction, while at the same time conceding that in some circumstances ethnicity and race overlap. The third position disputes both of these stances, suggesting instead that ethnicity ought to be viewed as the overarching term, with race being seen as a subset of ethnicity.

Among the theorists who opt for the first position are Michael Omi and Howard Winant. In their influential book, *Racial Formation in the United States* (1994), they seek to preserve an analytic distinction between the two terms, contending that the dynamics of interethnic relations are distinct from those of race relations. Focusing on the particular history of the United States, the authors use the term ethnicity in referring to European-origin immigrant groups, while race is used in referring to African Americans and Native Americans (and implicitly Latinos and Asians). In making this distinction, they argue that race is a social fact. In doing so they open themselves up to the charge that they have essentialized race. In other words, by treating race as being constituted by one essential characteristic – biologically determined differences – they portray it as an unchanging given. This conceptual problem arises despite Omi and Winant's assertion that race should be construed as socially constructed.

From this perspective, race tends to acquire an obdurate reality quite unlike the presumed fluidity associated with ethnicity. Omi and Winant highlight the fact that voluntary immigrants to the United States have had very different historical experiences compared to both the victims of the slave trade and the victims of colonial conquest. On this basis, they believe, ethnicity ought to be distinguished from race. A problem with their argument is that it offers a historicist account on behalf of an analytical distinction. It conflates analytical categories with everyday applied uses of the terms. It is true that most of the voluntary immigrants to the US (those from Europe) are described in everyday discourse today as ethnic, while the offspring of African slaves and American Indians are depicted as racial groups. But such was not always the case. In fact, many European immigrants were defined racially in the late nineteenth and early twentieth centuries. The key point here is that Omi and Winant fail to offer a distinction between ethnicity and race that is based on clear analytic distinctions rather than on commonsense understandings of ordinary people.

In one recent attempt to offer a more sustained rationale for such an analytical separation, Eduardo Bonilla-Silva (1999: 902–3; see also 1997) contends that the distinction is justified, in the first place, due to different histories rooted in the emergence of the modern capitalist world-system. He sees race as the earlier of the two terms, being the product of "colonial encounters" dating to the fifteenth and sixteenth centuries, while ethnicity "is connected to the history of nation-state formation," and as such only emerged in the late eighteenth century. Bonilla-Silva furthers his case by contending that race is about power relations, while ethnicity is not. In addition, race is to be seen as imposed from the outside by hegemonic groups as a rationale for excluding groups, while ethnicity involves the groups themselves attempting to stake out boundaries that are designed to promote a sense of distinctiveness.

Stephen Cornell and Douglas Hartmann (1998: 25–34) have offered a careful articulation of the second position. While they assume that in most instances the difference between ethnicity and race will be maintained, they envision some situations in which the terms are overlapping. Central to their position is the suggestion that ethnic groups are predicated on such shared notions as imputed common origin, with the associated assumptions of shared historical experiences and symbolic identity markers, while racial groups are defined in terms of presumed physical or biological differences. In making this distinction, their starting point is the same as that of Omi and Winant and Bonilla-Silva.

The problem with this stance is that all racial groups are always defined in part on the basis of the criteria Cornell and Hartmann list as characteristic of ethnic groups. Moreover, ethnic markers are not necessarily free from physical associations (e.g., the stereotypical images of blond Scandinavians versus swarthy Mediterranean groups). The other factors Cornell and Hartmann point to involve whether or not differences in power (including the power to construct one's own identity rather than having it imposed externally) and status characterize intergroup relations. Here they are in agreement with Bonilla-Silva. They contend that power differences are typical in shaping social relations among racial groups, but that this is not necessarily so for ethnic groups. This distinction, too, is empirically problematic.

Suffice it to say that since all ethnic group formations constitute attempts at social enclosure, defining simultaneously the "us" and the "them," one would be hard pressed to find empirical examples of two ethnic groups in any society that cannot be distinguished in terms of their respective levels of power and status in that society. Take, for example, Belgium's two main ethnic groups, the Flemish and Walloon communities. While the balance of power between the two has in fact shifted over time, one cannot understand the character of intercommunal relationships in that nation without taking into account differences in the respective political power and economic clout commanded by each group at various periods of the nation's history. Indeed, the tensions in that country at the moment that are threatening to split it in half are the result of two groups that have failed to arrive at a situation in which both communities agree that real equality exists between them.

The third position constitutes an alternative to the first two by proposing that ethnicity ought to be viewed as the more general term, capable of encompassing all of the groups that the theorists advancing the other two positions choose to locate under the race rubric. At the same time, the potent impact of race as a marker of identity need not be lost, because race can be incorporated as one of the potential characteristics of ethnicity – similar, for example, to the potential role of religion. Such an approach would ensure that race is not essentialized, but instead is seen as socially constructed, and thus as flexible and subject to historical modification. One need only point to the fact that in practice many groups that in Bonilla-Silva's framework would be seen as ethnic groups – including such European-origin immigrants to the United States as Italians and Poles – were viewed at certain historical junctures as distinct races. As recent research by scholars such as David Roediger (1991) and Theodore Allen (1994) indicates, for these groups the processes of incorporation into the fabric of mainstream society and upward social mobility involved *becoming* white.

Another problematic feature of efforts to treat ethnicity and race in essentially either/or terms is related to the history of racialist thought, which is predicated on the idea of innate biological differences. This position became especially common in the nineteenth century with the rise of pseudoscientific accounts of the presumed inherent inequalities of races, seen for example in the work of Arthur de Gobineau (1915 [1853–5]). Influenced by Social Darwinian thought, such ideas in the early part of the twentieth century had a profound impact on the eugenics movement and on Nazi political ideology – as well as on the thinking of some early figures in the history of sociology such as Franklin Giddings, Edward Alsworth Ross, and others who played significant roles in the anti-immigration agitation that led to the draconian National Origins Act of 1924 that effectively put an end to mass immigration for the next four decades (Hawkins 1997).

However, at the same time sociology and related social sciences began to question the biological determinism of such thinking. This was particularly evident in the writings of several members of the Chicago School of Sociology, most notably W. I. Thomas and Robert E. Park (Kivisto 1990; Lal 1990). It also became the hallmark of the cultural anthropology of the influential Columbia University scholar Franz Boas, who trained a generation of America's most important anthropologists, including Ruth Benedict and Margaret Mead. Although critics have contended that at least some of these figures failed to make a complete break with biological accounts of racial inequalities, most agree that their work represents a significant departure from biological determinism and moved the social sciences in the direction of a social constructionist account of race (Bash 1979; Jenkins 1997).

During the past half century, except for such retrograde polemicists as Richard Hernnstein and Charles Murray, in their controversial *Bell Curve* (1994), and J. Philippe Rushton, in his *Race, Evolution, and Behavior* (1999), the social sciences have achieved a consensus that race is a social construct. Indeed, even most conservative intellectuals were critical of such efforts to return to Social Darwinian thought, dressed up in these works under the guise of sociobiology. Insofar as a consensus has been achieved in repudiating this type of thought, it then becomes the case that phenotypical differences cannot be seen as relevant to group identities (being irrelevant, for example, to matters related to intelligence and moral character), *except* when such differences are socially defined to be of significance – in situations, in other words, where meaning is imposed on such differences.

Thus, the question arises: can (and should) an analytic distinction between ethnicity and race be maintained? Paul Gilroy (2000: 1) has recently challenged the distinction by seeking to stake out an alternative approach that "considers patterns of conflict connected to the consolidation of *cultural lines* rather than color lines and is concerned, in particular, with the operations of power, which, thanks to ideas about 'race,' have become entangled with those vain and mistaken attempts to delineate and subdivide humankind." John Lie (2001: 2) simply responds to the question by stating, "I eschew the term race because of the biological unity of the human race." In somewhat more blunt language, Orlando Patterson (1997: 173) answers the question in the negative, contending that, "The term *race* itself must be abandoned . . . and

the distinction between 'race' and ethnicity should be abandoned as mean-
ingless and potentially dangerous."

I don't propose to abandon the term "race," but I do agree with the general thrust of Gilroy's, Lie's, and Patterson's arguments, which is that we
ought to use ethnicity as an umbrella term. Ethnicity refers to social boundaries that are constructed on the basis of what are presumed to be shared
genealogies; cultural features such as language, religion, customs, traditions,
values, symbols, a shared history and folklore; and a shared geographic origin (Barth 1969; Francis 1976; Schermerhorn 1978; Yinger 1994). On this
basis, I concur with Susan Olzak (1992: 24) when she writes that "*race* is a
specific instance of ethnicity, defined by membership based on what are *assumed to be* inherited phenotypical characteristics." I also agree with Steve
Fenton's (1999: 4) contention that "The term 'ethnic' has a much greater
claim to analytical usefulness in sociology because it is not hampered by a
history of connotations with discredited science and malevolent practices in
the way the term 'race' is."

However, race is used in everyday language, and it is the task of sociology
to make sense of how people define situations and to determine what the
implications of those definitions are for social relations. For this reason it
would be unwise to follow Patterson's suggestion to take a pledge to refrain
from using the term. Instead, it would be wise to follow Mara Loveman's
(1999: 891) proposal that at the same time that we discard race as a category of analysis, we refocus our interpretive lenses by studying race as a
"category of practice." An important part of this project would involve the
examination of racism as ideology, the racism of everyday life, institutional
racism, and racialist social movements – all facets of the racialization of ethnicity (Mac an Ghaill 1999; Bonilla-Silva 2000; Memmi 2000; Winant
2000).

Nation and people

The relationship between ethnicity and nationality should be conceptual-
ized differently than that between ethnicity and race. A nationality group
refers to a collectivity predicated on claims regarding a sense of peoplehood
linked to a notion of a nation. Nationalism refers to an ideology of statehood,
and as such advances territorial claims designed to justify existing nation-
states or to provide rationales for calls to create new nation-states or to re-
cover lost ones (Breuilly 1982; Smith 1986; Kedourie 1985; Gellner 1983;
Hobsbawm 1990).

Scholars such as John A. Armstrong (1982) and Anthony Smith (1991) have
examined the historic roots of the "collective memories" and "nostalgic
myths" that underpin the sociocultural dynamics of contemporary national

identities, pointing to cases with considerable continuity between past and future. Other scholars, such as Liah Greenfeld (1992) and Philip Gorski (2000), have amplified this notion of the *longue durée* of nationalism. However, the general consensus among scholars today is that nationalism, and thus contemporary notions of nationality, are distinctly modern in their origin and character, dating to no earlier than the eighteenth century. This debate need not concern us for our purposes. In either event, nationalism ought to be seen as the product of what E. J. Hobsbawm and Terence Ranger (1983) have referred to as the "invention of tradition," emphasizing in their choice of words what they take to be the conscious manipulation of myths, legends, and histories by nationalists who forge, in Benedict Anderson's words, "imagined communities."

Craig Calhoun (1997: 4–5) provides a laundry list of characteristic features of the rhetorics of nationality. Borrowing from and adapting his list, I would identify the following as being of central importance: (1) definitions of boundaries (territorial, population, or both); (2) notions of national integrity and indivisibility; (3) a concept of self-sufficiency, autonomy, and sovereignty; (4) a sense of a common culture (including such features as language, values, beliefs); (5) beliefs about the roots of the nation's identity being located in the distant past; and (6) a conviction that the members of the nation share a common descent, history, and right to be involved in the affairs of the nation.

As this list suggests, there is clearly a family resemblance between ethnic and nationalist groups. This should not be surprising given the philological roots of the word *ethnos*, which is the Greek term for "nation." But what exactly is the relationship? Are they synonyms or is there some other relationship linking them? Calhoun (1997: 40) offers a commonly employed understanding by locating ethnicity in an intermediary position between kinship and nationality. From this perspective, nationality refers to a politicized form of ethnicity. In other words, while territorial claims and a political agenda are inherent in the definition of nationality, such is not necessarily the case for ethnicity. In this scenario, nationality groups constitute a subset of ethnicity groups. For example, while Italian immigrants and their descendants residing in Canada today comprise an ethnic group, the separatist demands of the Parti Québecois transform French Canadians into a nationality group. The latter case is an example of ethnic nationalism, or, as noted earlier, what Walker Connor (1994) had described as "ethnonationalism."

However, it is also possible to consider national identities in pluralist societies that are not the politicized expression of any particular ethnic group, but rather as constituting a unique form of corporate loyalty distinct from the "ethnonational bond" (Connor 1993). In these situations, notions of citizenship and patriotism offer a sense of a more universal identity within the nation that transcends the particularistic identities of ethnicity. In other words, ethnonationalism is not the only form that nationality identity can take; it can also take the form of civic nationalism. One possible outcome of the development of civic nationalism is that national identity will ultimately undermine and replace ethnic identities. People will come to see themselves as individuals and citizens, not as members of ethnic groups. Another possibility yields an alternative to the either/or character of the first. Here civic nationalism coexists with ethnicity, but in a context where the salience of the former is greater than the latter, thereby ensuring that the forces of unity are greater than the forces of separatism. This version of civic nationalism plays a role in important evolutionary models of social change in modern societies, witnessed for example in the work of Talcott Parsons, to which we turn in the following section.

Rethinking Modernity's Straight Path

When the new global ethnic formation first began to take shape during the years immediately after the Second World War, Talcott Parsons, sociology's preeminent social theorist during this period, articulated a theoretical vision of modernity that synthesized the thinking of theorists whose work dated from the nineteenth century up to the early decades of the twentieth (Nielsen 1991). He was the inheritor of a historical legacy that was based on the fundamental assumption that the evolution of modern industrial societies signaled the demise of certain forms of solidarity and the rise of new forms – predicated in no small part on the idea that individuals would be increasingly free from the ascribed particularistic identities characteristic of traditional or premodern societies and would enter a world based on individual achievement and universal values (Parsons 1967, 1971, 1975).

The dichotomous typologies of these early social theorists captured their sense of the master trends shaping large patterns of civilizational change. These include Henry Sumner Maine's characterization of a shift from status to contract; Herbert Spencer's distinction between militant society and industrial society; Ferdinand Toennies' contrast between *Gemeinschaft* and *Gesellschaft*; Ludwig Gumplowicz's focus on a change in the basis of social conflict from *Rassenkampf* (race conflict) to *Klassenkampf* (class conflict); and the theorist with the greatest impact on Parsons' thought, Emile Durkhiem's analysis of the move from mechanical solidarity to organic solidarity. Despite their differences – and there were many – these and other social theorists during the formative period of sociology shared a conviction that the future spelled the replacement of ascribed identities by achieved ones, and the substitution of particularistic values and group affiliations with universalistic ones. They anticipated, to borrow the felicitous phase of Benjamin Nelson (1949), the transition "from tribal brotherhood to universal otherhood." Parsons distilled, refined, and revised this evolutionary perspective during the course of his career.

Parsons launched his career with *The Structure of Social Action* (1937), a book that was intended to reveal what he considered to be a remarkable theoretical convergence among his immediate predecessors. He argued that despite the overt differences that characterize their respective works, the key figures in the formative period of social theory had managed – without being aware of it – to articulate a shared vision of the characteristic features that contributed to establishing order and promoting the directions of change in modern societies. They provided the basis for the establishment of a unified vision of social theory (Camic 1989). Critics of Parsons have accused him of glossing over the profound differences among his predecessors. Undeterred by such accusations, throughout his subsequent career Parsons continued in an ecumenical spirit, seeking to bring various competing theoretical camps into the large tent he called functionalism or structural functionalism. In these efforts, Parsons proved himself to be the consummate theorist of modernity (Robertson & Turner 1991). As such, a brief examination of his understanding of the main contours and components of modernity and their implications for ethnicity can serve both as a synecdoche for the work of earlier theorists and a backdrop for the work of ethnic theorists addressing the middle-range arena of what would become the hegemonic theory of ethnicity: assimilation theory.

Intent on developing a general theoretical framework that might be appropriated by all of the social sciences, Parsons' work operates at a level of high abstraction. Key to his distinctive contribution to theory is his wedding of functionalist theory to evolutionary thought. It constitutes the foundation for his grand narrative of modernity (seen particularly Parsons, 1971 and 1977; see Vidich & Lyman, 1985: 78–9 on this point).

In a manner reminiscent of Durkheim, Parsons first distinguishes modern from premodern societies by noting the heightened complexity of the former in contrast to the latter. Secondly, he points out that a more complex society is one with greater adaptive capacity (Parsons 1977: 230). In other words, modern societies are better able to respond to external changes and problems compared to their predecessors. In describing what is involved in the evolutionary change from premodern to modern society, Parsons identifies four processes of evolutionary development: differentiation, adaptive upgrading, inclusion, and value generalization. Differentiation can be seen as Parsons' term for what Durkheim refers to as the division of labor. Adaptive upgrading is "the process by which a wider range of resources is made available to social units"; inclusion involves the incorporation of "new units, structures, and mechanisms within the normative framework of the societal community"; and finally, value generalization means that societal values are "couched at a higher level of generality" (Parsons 1971: 27). As should be obvious, Parsons presents a remarkably positive portrait of the evolutionary forces shaping modern societies.

The major implication of these four interrelated trends for ethnicity is that they individually and corporately signal the increased capacity of the nation-state – or in Parsons' terms, the "societal community" – to bring ethnic groups into full societal membership. In other words, the general societal trend of modern societies entails the incorporation of ethnic groups. Here Parsons is in general agreement with the earlier theorists noted above. However, from his perspective, incorporation does not necessitate the disappearance of ethnic groups into the societal whole. Indeed, Parsons seems to assume that ethnic pluralism or multiculturalism will characterize modern societal communities for the foreseeable future.

However, the significance attached to particularistic ethnic identities progressively gives way to a more universalistic basis for national solidarity, namely that based on citizenship. As Parsons (1971: 92) saw it, "The most important new basis of inclusion in the societal community has been *citizenship*, developing in close association with the democratic revolution. Citizenship can be dissociated from ethnic membership, with its strong tendency toward nationalism and even 'racism,' which provides a sharp ascriptive criterion of belonging." In other words, ethnic groups can coexist with a citizenship based on civic nationalism, provided that the salience of ethnicity declines. In particular, in order to avert intercommunal conflict based on ethnic differences, a shared sense of citizenship must be sufficiently powerful to override the divisive potential of ethnic group allegiances. In making this claim, Parsons offers a macrotheoretical explanation for, as we shall see below, Milton Gordon's (1964) contention that pluralism should be seen as possible in a society where assimilation is occurring.

In the midst of the civil rights movement in the United States, Parsons (1967: 422–65) examined the implications of citizenship for African Americans by posing as a question, "Full Citizenship for the Negro American?" In answering this question, Parsons offered accounts of two interrelated topics. First, he sought to explain why blacks had been denied for so long the fruits of full citizenship. Why had their historical experience proved to be so different from that of other – and especially European-origin – ethnic groups in America? Parsons' answer focused more on cultural factors than political or economic ones. The fact that until the middle of the twentieth century, blacks were overwhelmingly concentrated in the south, a region that maintained its agrarian character long after the rest of the country had industrialized, was of primary importance to his argument. The increasingly anachronistic values that undergirded the caste-like quality of race relations in the south were antithetical to the larger society's thrust toward a more inclusive vision of citizenship. The migration of blacks out of the south and the belated modernization of that region signaled the erosion of premodern value patterns. It is interesting to note that this line of argument was used by Parsons decades earlier in attempting to explain the triumph of Nazism in Germany. Here, too, he emphasized cultural factors – the feudalistic, militaristic, and authoritarian elements of German society – that conspired to put a brake on Germany's transition from a premodern to a modern nation (Parsons 1993; see Brick 2000 on the "shift away from economics" in Parsonian theory).

Secondly, Parsons attempted to account for the forces promoting full incorporation into the societal community. While economic factors associated with the increased demand for labor in industrial societies could be seen as contributing to the process of inclusion, changes in culture are once again posited as more crucial. Predicated on the idea of the sovereignty of the individual, cultural changes, of which changes in law are a manifestation, have resulted in the progressive emancipation of individuals from all particularistic solidarities. These have been replaced by a situation characterized as "diffuse enduring solidarity," by which he means that rather than being attached intensely to one ascribed group, such as an ethnic group, individuals will increasingly choose to embrace a variety of loyalties (Parsons 1975: 58).

The inclusion made possible by the expansion of citizenship rights and by the enhanced salience of civic nationalism in place of the ethnic (WASP) nationalism of an earlier era did not necessitate the version of assimilation associated with the image of the melting pot – with its implication that the final outcome entails the eradication of distinctive ethnic group identities. Instead, as noted above, Parsons thought that inclusion made possible ethnic pluralism, which, he contended, was "coming to be increasingly characteristic of modern societies." The United States, always the empirical focus of his theoretical discourses, was viewed as the exemplar of the changes that could be expected in all modern and modernizing societies.

Anticipating Herbert Gans's (1979) discussion about the emergence of "symbolic ethnicity," which reflected on the significance of an ethnic nostalgia for the past that is devoid of behavioral consequences, Parsons describes the symbolic markers differentiating ethnic groups as being increasing empty of content. Likewise, anticipating Mary Waters' (1990) work, he depicted ethnic identification as becoming increasingly optional, by which he meant that ethnicity became increasingly a matter of voluntary commitment on the part of individuals rather than an ascribed identity capable of being corporately enforced (Parsons 1975: 64–5).

Parsons also considered the possibility that events could conspire to reverse, for a time, the general linear movement toward inclusion. Reflecting Durkheim's influence on his work, he notes the possibility that periods of rapid social change might produce "anomic social disorganization and alienation," and that as a result one could expect to see an intensification of "groupism" or "de-differentiation" (Parsons 1975: 68–70). In this way, he accounted for the possibility of periodic ethnic revivals, which he thought were likely to take an exclusively cultural form, but which may also on occasion include an explicitly political dimension. He also recognized that the darker side of rapid change could involve various manifestations of ethnic conflict. However, in the overarching Parsonian grand narrative of historical change, it is clear that such reversals amount to no more than temporary setbacks.

Critics and proponents of Parsonian social thought agree on one thing: he had a profound impact on sociology between the Second World War and the Vietnam War. Not only did his version of modernization theory shape sociological agendas for analysts of the advanced industrial nations, but it also shaped the thinking about expected developments in the less-developed nations as well, many of which had entered the postcolonial era (Apter 1969). Thus, although Parsons framed his theory in terms of societal communities already fully immersed in modernity, his grand theory presumed that modernization was a global phenomenon that would diffuse from the most advanced to the least advanced nations. Nonetheless, Parsons' own work remained bound up within the confines of the nation-state itself as the proper unit of analysis. Though his theory implied globalization, it would be a latter-day Parsonian, Roland Robertson (1992), and not Parsons himself, who articulated a theory of modernization as a truly global phenomenon. Indeed, Robertson is one of the key theorists associated with the development of globalization theory.

Rethinking Marxist Expectancy

Karl Marx was not included among the key social thinkers singled out by Parsons for inclusion in *The Structure of Social Action*. However, he too should be seen as an advocate of modernization theory. Nowhere in his writings is this more evident than in Part I of *The Communist Manifesto* (1967 [1848]: 19), wherein Marx and his colleague Friedrich Engels, in a tract intended to urge the working classes to embrace a revolutionary movement designed to overthrow capitalism, offer midstream a remarkable paean to capitalism. Industrial capitalism, they argued, had proven in its relatively short history to be the most dynamic, productive, and innovative economic system in history and it had already created wonders surpassing the those of the ancient world. Capitalism was portrayed as playing a progressive role in effecting a break from traditional society and setting industrial societies on the path of modernity. Marx wanted to overthrow capitalism because, due to its class character, he was convinced that it could not deliver on its potential for creating a postscarcity society. However, he was an unabashed enthusiast of urban industrial society and modern civilization.

The reverse of this enthusiasm was a disdain for tradition and for those locales in any society where tradition was best preserved. Thus, his unflattering description of the "idiocy of rural life" was a reflection of his assessment of rural life as a bastion of tradition. Marx's view of history as progress was predicated on the potential for the working class to achieve a sufficient level of class-consciousness to make possible an organized struggle against the bourgeoisie. In other words, not only was the proletariat seen as exploited by the hegemonic class in capitalism, but it was also seen as having a historic mission: replacing capitalism with communism, and in so doing, creating a classless society. For this to be possible, inherited particularistic identities had to be transcended, and in this regard, ethnic identities were viewed as one of the major impediments to the development of a class-conscious proletariat.

Marx did not preoccupy himself with this topic because he assumed that capitalism itself would prove to be a solvent dissolving ethnic and other tradition-based identities and affiliations. From this perspective, class contestation defined the grand narrative of social change in capitalism, with ethnicity being reduced to an epiphenomenon. However, it was subsequently clear to Engels (1959: 458) that ethnicity could serve at least for the foreseeable future as a powerful drag on working-class mobilization. Thus, in a letter to Friedrich Sorge, the central factor he pointed to in accounting for the failure of socialist organizing in the United States was the divisiveness of powerful ethnic loyalties and the reality of ethnic tensions and conflicts (see a full discussion of the relationship between immigration and socialism in the US in Lipset & Marks 2000: 125–66).

Ethnicity was far from a short-term problem in the development of class-consciousness. Twentieth-century Marxists would be forced to continue contending with its obdurate persistence and would offer a variety of attempts to reconcile this empirical reality with the expectation of ethnic consciousness progressively yielding to class-consciousness. The work of Oliver Cox (1948, 1987) can be seen as a paradigmatic instance of classical Marxist thought (despite Cox's protestations to the contrary). Critical of mainstream race relations scholarship for its presumed lack of attentiveness to economic considerations and class structure, he argued that racism could be explained by capitalism. Cox's Marxism led him to privilege class in a manner that treated race as a subterfuge that served the capitalist class by diverting attention from the more fundamental reality of class exploitation (Burman 1995: 75–7; Wieviorka 1995a: 83–4). In simple terms, race could be used by the ruling class as an effective divide-and-conquer strategy.

One can find similar reductionist efforts in the work of more recent orthodox Marxists, such as in the work of scholars associated with the British journal *Race and Class* and in the work of British Trotskyist Alex Callinicos (1993: 52–7), who contended, for example, that the violence in Los Angeles that erupted in the wake of the decision to free the white police officers accused of beating motorist Rodney King ought to be seen as "class rebellion, not a race riot."

British sociologist Robert Miles's (1982, 1989, 1993; see also Phizacklea & Miles 1980) theoretical project amounts to a sustained effort to avoid this reductionist tendency, while simultaneously preserving what he considers to be the core of Marxist analysis, namely the privileging of the capitalist mode of production as an explanatory concept in accounting for contemporary manifestations of racism. Like Cox before him, Miles is critical of what he refers to as "the race relations" approach of mainstream sociology. He urges the abandonment of "race" and "race relations" as theoretical concepts, contending that they freeze as a social fact what is in reality a social process, that of "racialization." In place of race and race relations, he proposes a perspective focused on "the determination and effects of different modalities of racism within the historical matrix mapped by the evolution of the capitalist mode of production and by the associated rise of the nation state" (Miles 1993: 21; see Thompson 1989 for a similar line of argument).

Critics are suspicious of Miles's claim that he has actually managed to avoid reducing race to class (Solomos 1986; Anthias 1990; Solomos & Back 1995). In his theory, racism must be understood in terms of the class determination of the capitalist mode of production. Implicitly this appears to suggest that racism is an epiphenomenon or a subterfuge hiding more basic, underlying class divisions. By rooting his analysis in a variant of historical materialism, Miles ignores the role of culture in generating and sustaining racism.

Labor migration constitutes the major empirical focus underpinning his approach. As such, one might question the extent to which it is possible to generalize from this perspective. Whatever explanatory value his theory might have in accounting for the racism encountered in Britain since the influx of immigrants from the Caribbean and the Indian subcontinent that began in the 1950s, can it explain the enduring nationalist conflicts in Northern Ireland, Scotland, and Wales? Can it explain ethnic conflict in the nations of eastern Europe, that until recently stood outside of the capitalist orbit? How useful is such an approach in analyzing such Third World conflicts as Rwanda's genocidal battles between Tutsis and Hutus?

Perhaps the greatest irony surrounding contemporary Marxist theorizing about ethnicity is that, rather than expecting, as Marx did, that ethnicity would ultimately "melt into air" as a consequence of the modernizing thrust of capitalism, it seeks to account for the persistence of the ethnic factor. Marx, quite simply, assumed that the erosion of ethnic ties would be one of the positive unintended consequences of capitalist development. Theorists such as Miles no longer share Marx's expectation. At the same time, they resist efforts to treat ethnicity and ethnic conflict as both analytically and empirically distinct from class and class conflict. What we see in this and the preceding section is that while Marxist approaches to ethnicity have privileged the economic at the expense of culture, the reverse was the case for Parsonian social theory.

Rethinking Modes of Inclusion and Exclusion

Modernization theory and Marxism operate at the level of what C. Wright Mills (1959) called "grand theory." At a somewhat more grounded level of analysis, within the subfield of race and ethnic studies, theories of the middle range have shaped research agendas. As noted earlier, none have been of greater consequence than assimilation theory, a theory that explicitly informed modernization theory and implicitly informed Marxist thought. Thus, we begin our analysis in this section with a discussion of assimilation.

The rise of assimilation theory

The United States has been the central empirical referent of theorists of assimilation, beginning with the earliest articulation by the Chicago School of Sociology. Robert Park (1950), the head of that department during its heyday, is generally credited with presenting the outline of an ecological version of assimilation theory, where he suggested that when two groups find themselves forced to interact due to the migration of one or both groups, the relations between the groups proceeds through a four-stage "race relations cycle": (1) contact; (2) conflict; (3) accommodation; and (4) assimilation. Commentaries on Park's four-stage process noted its affinity with modernization theory, with its implicit assumption that change would occur gradually, progressively, and inevitably (Lyman 1972; Kivisto 1990; Lal 1990). While Park clearly had in mind the voluntary immigrants that came from Europe en masse to the United States in the late nineteenth and early twentieth centuries, he saw this process as applying to racial minorities as well. Indeed, he drew a parallel between the migration of agrarian workers from Europe and elsewhere to urban America and blacks leaving the American south for northern cities: both primarily were peasants entering an urban industrial milieu. Thus, the impact of the migration was the same for all groups, whether it was the trans-Atlantic migration of Europeans, the trans-Pacific migration of Asians, or the movement of blacks out of the rural south and into the urban north. In this respect, Park challenged the biological racism of his era. All groups were capable of being assimilated by the working of the race relations cycle.

Stanford Lyman (1972) has referred to what he calls the "Aristotelian character" of Park's theory, by which he meant that by not delineating a time frame for the working out of the cycle, Park produced a nonfalsifiable theory. Empirical indications that the process was not working in the way it was expected to were dealt with by introducing the notion of accidents, events that intervened to slow down or even stop the process temporarily. The assumption was that these accidents could impede, but not terminate, the eluctable workings of the cycle. Racism thus could be construed as an accident that could be overcome by "enlightened" racial thinking.

But what did assimilation actually entail? On this score, Park's work was not entirely unambiguous. At times, the endpoint of assimilation would appear to be the amalgamation brought about by the dismantling of the last barrier between groups: intermarriage. Intermarriage spelled the end of distinct ethnic group boundaries and the emergence of a new sense of collective identity. In the American context, this means that Italians, Swedes, Africans, Jews, and so forth would not, in the end, become hyphenated Americans, but rather simply Americans. This, in short, was the theoretical articulation of the melting pot ideology.

A major cottage industry dedicated to measuring the social distance among various ethnic groups in America arose at the instigation of Park's colleague, Emory Bogardus (1933, 1959). A measure of the acceptance of various groups in America, the social distance scale examined the gamut of tolerance, ranging from, at the one end, questioning whether members ought even to be admitted to the country to, at the other end, whether or not individuals find it acceptable that their child would marry a member of the group. The latter is amalgamation, which in this scenario constitutes the final stage in the process of assimilation.

Park (1950) was aware that amalgamation had not occured in the United States and that in fact it was not likely to occur any time soon. Thus, in a study of the racial polyglot territory of Hawaii, he noted the tenacity of ethnic identities. Furthermore, near the end of his life, his reappreciation of the potency of racism led him to a far more pessimistic assessment of the foreseeable future for black Americans. In short, he evidenced a keen appreciation of the continuing impact of prejudice and discrimination on preventing the incorporation of various groups into the fabric of the larger society.

Elsewhere Park's use of the term assimilation was meant, if not to distinguish it from amalgamation, at least to suggest that assimilation did not necessarily entail amalgamation. In a book co-authored with Herbert A. Miller and W. I. Thomas (though the latter's name does not appear on the title page), Park focused particular attention on acculturation, which concerns the acquisition of the values, attitudes, beliefs, language, and behaviors of the host society (Park & Miller 1921). Actually, acculturation can mean two things. It can mean that newcomers adapt to the mores and folkways of the white Anglo-Saxon Protestant majority. In this sense of the term, acculturation means Anglo-conformity. However, it can also imply a reciprocal or dialectical process wherein not only are the newcomers transformed, but so is the host society as a consequence of their presence. Park's writings waver between these two versions of acculturation.

Despite the impact of his thought on not only the members of the Chicago School, but on American sociology in general, it should be remembered that Park never articulated a fully developed systematic statement on assimilation. He never resolved the lack of precision about what is meant by assimilation. Nevertheless, assimilation theory would prove to be the hegemonic theory in the study of ethnic and race relations from Park's lifetime until the late 1960s.

Assimilation did receive a fuller conceptual treatment several decades after Park's work, in Milton Gordon's highly influential *Assimilation in American Life* (1964). The purpose of the book was twofold: to add conceptual rigor to the term "assimilation" and to offer an assessment of, as the subtitle of the book indicates, the role of race, religion, and national origins in the United States at the middle of the twentieth century. Here we will concern ourselves only with the first of his concerns.

Gordon (1964: 71) identifies seven types of assimilation: (1) cultural or behavioral assimilation – or in other words acculturation; (2) structural assimilation, which involves the entrance into the organizations and institutions of the host society at the "primary group level"; (3) marital assimilation – or amalgamation; (4) identificational assimilation, which means the creation of a shared sense of peoplehood at the societal level; (5) attitude receptional assimilation, which refers to the absence of prejudice; (6) behavioral receptional assimilation, which refers to the absence of discrimination; and (7) civic assimilation, where interethnic conflicts over values and power are overcome by the shared identity of citizenship. Gordon refers to this list not only as types, but also as stages, implying some idea about the sequencing of assimilation. However, he hedges his bets here, except insofar as he is clear about which type of assimilation is most crucial to the process: structural assimilation. Once it occurs, he contends, all of the others will inevitably follow. As Gordon (1964: 81) summarized it, "Structural assimilation, then, rather than acculturation, is seen to be the keystone of the arch of assimilation."

The fall of assimilation theory

One of the intriguing features of Gordon's thesis involves his effort to locate cultural pluralism within a theory of assimilation. Heretofore cultural pluralism had served as something akin to the theoretical loyal opposition to assimilation. The term was popularized by the philosopher Horace Kallen (1924) in his critique of the demand of nativists for the 100 percent Americanization of immigrants. Such a demand, he argued, was antithetical to democratic ideals, which he contended were best realized by the persistence of ethnic group life. Kallen's thesis was less a theory and more a plea for tolerance and the acceptance of diversity. It was concerned less with what is than with what ought to be.

The term gained renewed currency with the publication – at virtually the same time that Gordon's book appeared – of Nathan Glazer and Daniel Patrick Moynihan's *Beyond the Melting Pot* (1963), which argued that ethnic groups in America, rather than disappearing, have continued to persist over time, often as interest groups shaping politics and culture at both the local and national levels. A study of five large ethnic groups in New York City, the book was meant to illustrate that, as the authors put it, "The point about the melting pot . . . is that it did not happen" (Glazer & Moynihan 1963: v). Indeed, it is true that no ethnic group in America has disappeared (Higham 1975: 234).

By the 1970s, assimilation theory had lost its hegemonic status, replaced by cultural pluralism. The notion that an ethnic revival was underway among European-origin groups – dubbed by the polemicist Michael Novak (1972) as the "unmeltable ethnics" – gained currency. Related to this view was a substantial body of empirical research that pointed to the persistence, rather than the erosion, of ethnicity. The most important exponent of this position was the sociologist Andrew Greeley (1971, 1974; Greeley & McCready 1975), who relied heavily on National Opinion Research Center surveys to examine a wide array of attitudinal and behavioral topics, all of which were intended to ascertain the extent to which ethnicity still mattered. It is important to note that this research did not focus on racial minorities who had experienced high levels of prejudice and discrimination, and thus had not managed to assimilate because of externally imposed barriers. Instead, the focus was on those groups that appeared to many to be headed, as Richard Alba (1985) put it, into "the twilight of ethnicity."

The remarkable feature about this research was that although the findings in support of ethnic persistence were mixed at best, and crucial issues that would cast the persistence argument into question, such as intermarriage rates, were largely ignored, nonetheless it served to bolster the cultural pluralist paradigm. Greeley's findings really pointed to little more than the obvious fact that assimilation had not yet reached its end stage. But no serious social scientist actually made such a claim, and thus the research was directed to challenging a straw man. In no small part, the appeal of cultural pluralism had to do with political and cultural currents in the larger society, which reflected a renewed appreciation of diversity, a concern with one's roots, and a challenge to a view of assimilation that equated it with Anglo-conformity. The consequence of this theoretical shift was that sociologists would seriously entertain the question posed by Nathan Glazer (1993): Is assimilation theory dead?

The resuscitation of assimilation theory

A growing number of scholars, particularly by the 1990s, began to answer Glazer's question in the negative (Kazal 1995). Assimilation theory may have been wounded, they contended, but it was not dead. Historical sociologist Ewa Morawska (1994) was not alone in arguing "in defense of the assimilation model." Key to her thesis is the claim that assimilation offers a more useful framework for exploring levels and modes of ethnic group incorporation into the larger society than does its main challenger, which she refers to as the ethnicization approach (her term for cultural pluralism, or for what above was referred to as the persistence of ethnicity model). A reconsideration of assimilation should, she contends, avoid treating it unproblematically as a linear and inevitable process. Assimilation, instead, should be viewed as one possible outcome of interethnic relations. Moreover, the possibility that as a process it might be slowed, stopped, and even reversed needs to be considered. In other words, she sought to free assimilation theory from the teleological framework imposed by Park's early formulation and reinforced by modernization theory.

Perhaps the theorist most responsible for the renewal of interest in assimilation is Herbert Gans, who throughout his career has maintained that the empirical evidence clearly supports the notion that assimilation – at least for European-origin groups – is taking place. In an influential essay on "symbolic ethnicity," Gans challenged ethnic persistence and ethnic revival theories by contending that one could discern among America's white ethnics a decline in the level of intensity, consequentiality, and saliency of ethnicity over time. More specifically, he argued that for the third generation and beyond, ethnicity became a less and less important component of individual identity. Combined with the decline of ethnic institutions, the result is a situation in which ethnicity amounts to little more than nostalgia for the past – real or imagined. Symbolic ethnicity, he contends, is available to people who want to intermittently feel ethnic, without being forced to act ethnically (Gans 1979).

Related to the hegemonic rise of the cultural pluralist paradigm was a growing interest in the social construction of ethnicity, or to use the term of Werner Sollors, the "invention of ethnicity" (1989; see also the influential essay by Conzen et al. 1990). Gans (1992a) views the constructionist or invention focus as a salutary corrective to the tendency of earlier versions of "straight-line" assimilation to emphasize structure at the expense of agency. But he also thinks that this perspective has swung too far in the direction of agency, and that what is needed is a renewed attention to structural contexts. In terms of assimilation theory, what this means for Gans is that there is a need for a modified, or what he prefers to call a "bumpy-line approach," which accounts for both invention and context. By way of illustration, Gans (1992a: 50) writes:

If Jews invent the "Chanukah-bush," they do so not to be ethnically innova-tive but to discourage their children from demanding the Christmas trees and other aspects of Christianity they see among their non-Jewish friends. And if middle-class Caribbean immigrants press their children to hold on to their West Indian dialects and accents, they do so not just to preserve a language but to make sure that whites will not mistake their children for, and treat them as, poor American blacks.

In his examples, Gans refers to an older European-origin immigrant group and a post-1965 immigrant group. Regarding the former, recent research has sup-ported his claim that assimilation is indeed occurring. Perhaps the most influ-ential work in this area is that of Richard Alba, whose *Ethnic Identity* (1990) offered compelling evidence for the decline in ethnic identities and loyalties among the descendants of European immigrants. Alba points to the erosion of ethnic institutions and neighborhoods, the declining role of ethnic culture, the progressive increase in intermarriage, evidence of social assimilation, and the precipitous decline in prejudice and discrimination as clear indicators of as-similation. At the same time, he suggests that the privatization of ethnic iden-tity allows for the possibility that what Thomas Archdeacon (1990) has characterized as a low-level "ethnic hum" might persist for many generations.

Another oft-cited work from this period is Mary Waters' *Ethnic Options* (1990), which, as the title implies, is located on the agency side of the equa-tion. She is interested in examining the varied ways in which people pick and choose from their ethnic heritages in constructing their identities. De-spite this fact, her accounts of the plasticity of ethnic identities among the third generation and beyond serve to reinforce Gans' understanding of sym-bolic ethnicity. The ethnic options available to her subjects are circumscribed by the fact that they have gone a considerable way down the road to assimi-lation. The work of Alba and Waters is representative of a body of scholar-ship that has provided compelling evidence to refute the cultural pluralist claims of those who denied that white European ethnics were assimilating. Theoretically, this made possible a revisiting of assimilationist theory, not with the intent of restoring the earlier straight-line version of the theory, but to articulate a more complex and supple understanding of assimilation (Gans 1999: 225–47; see also Barkan 1995; Alba 1998, 1999).

At the same time that the pendulum was swinging back to make possible a reappropriation or a reconsideration of assimilation theory, research com-menced on what Alejandro Portes and Min Zhou (1993) have referred to as the "new second generation" – the ethnic children of the post-1965 immi-grants. As a consequence, the utility of assimilation theory for this different wave of immigration has been raised. Portes (1995), for example, has ques-tioned the assumption underlying much assimilation theory, which sug-gested that what it was that immigrants were assimilating into was unproblematic. In fact, he contends, as immigrants adapt, accommodate, acculturate, integrate, or assimilate, they do so in different sectors of American society, predicated on such factors as the financial, social, and cultural capital that particular immigrants bring with them to the receiving society, and the levels of discrimination they confront. These factors have a significant bearing on their social location and on their life chances. To account for this fact, Portes has introduced the idea of "segmented assimilation," by which he means the assimilation into particular subcultures of the host society. For example, Mexican youth living in poor barrio communities may assimilate into the subculture of the streets, replete with its distinctive codes of honor and proclivity for gang-related criminal conduct, while the children of "brain drain" immigrants compete to enter Ivy League colleges.

This idea of different types of assimilation points to one of the shortcomings evident in the underlying assumptions of earlier versions of assimilation theory. They were designed to comprehend the life trajectories of immigrants and their offspring. More specifically, the focus was on voluntary labor immigrants, particularly those entering either the lowest rungs of the economy or the world of the traditional industrial working class rooted in the manufacturing sector. The historic specificity that shaped the earliest versions of assimilation theory were predicated on the implicit assumption of an expanding industrial economy in which the demand for jobs in the manufacturing sector provided avenues for upward mobility, if not for the immigrants themselves, at least in intergenerational terms. But this means that other types of newcomers to America were undertheorized. For example, among the categories not represented by the ideal-typical model offered in Oscar Handlin's (1973) classic account of "the uprooted" – peasants turned into proletarians – are political refugees and the highly educated professionals who have come to constitute a "brain drain" from underdeveloped nations (Pedraza-Bailey 1990). Contemporary theorists of assimilation contend that it is important to attempt to account for the range of types of people who fall under the rubric of "the migrant" (Portes & Rumbaut 2001).

If assimilation theory has received a new lease on life, does this mean that history is likely to repeat itself? In other words, can we expect the newest immigrants and their offspring to assimilate in a parallel fashion to that of the wave of immigrants that arrived in the half century between 1880 and 1930? Gans (1992b) has raised these questions in a speculative essay on the possible futures for the post-1965 wave of immigrants that entered the country during its transition from an industrial to a postindustrial economy. He points to three ways that members of the earlier immigrant wave improved their economic positions: (1) education-driven upward mobility; (2) succession-driven upward mobility; and (3) niche improvement.

Each of these avenues leading to upward mobility is evident among contemporary immigrants, too. For example, while Jews in an earlier era were the paradigmatic example among groups using university credentials as a route to economic improvement, one can see a similar tendency today among some Asian groups. Succession-driven mobility occurs when the immigrant generation takes stable blue-collar work in order to provide the economic stability that would permit their children to obtain better jobs. Poles in the meatpacking industry in the earlier part of the twentieth century found their counterparts at the end of the century in Mexicans and southeast Asians who have entered these same occupations in large numbers during the past few decades. Finally, niche improvement is the route taken by those who establish retail businesses, often but not necessarily in the ethnic enclave. Again Jews are an important example from the past, establishing businesses in both Jewish enclaves and black ghettos. In the contemporary landscape, one can find evidence of the significance of enclave economies among a number of new immigrant groups, with Cubans constituting a particularly good case. Koreans are currently the primary example of a group that has established a significant presence as merchants in inner-city black neighborhoods.

But what are the limitations of assimilation theory – a theory that from its earliest conceptualizations until the present has tended to be rooted in the American experience? Even within the United States, questions can be raised about the theory's ability to account for all ethnic groups (Kivisto 1995: 66–70). Designed to comprehend the modes of incorporation of newcomers to a nation, one obvious shortcoming is that its formulators did not appear to have in mind indigenous peoples who, rather than being voluntary immigrants are the victims of colonial conquest. Thus, what does assimilation theory have to say about Native Americans? Moreover, while the ancestors of contemporary African Americans were migrants, they were involuntary, not voluntary migrants. To what extent does this fact reduce the applicability of assimilation theory for this group?

Outside of the United States further questions arise. One might suggest that for other immigrant-receiving advanced industrial nations – both historical settler states and those nations that were not prime immigrant destinations a century ago – assimilation should be a useful theoretical model. While this might be the case when considering recent immigrants, what about those nationality groups with long histories as part of the nation, but with territorial claims and demands for greater autonomy or independence? Is assimilation a useful concept when examining the Scots and Welsh in Britain or the Basques and Catalans in Spain?

Multiculturalism: assimilation as civic incorporation

If we abandon the notion that assimilation ought to be equated with or that it ultimately necessitates amalgamation, I believe that assimilation can provide a useful analytical tool for making sense of the ethnic dynamics of all contemporary advanced industrial nations. Of central importance in assessing the potential for assimilation is the role played by the state. The power wielded by the state and the power exhibited by hegemonic groups in shaping state policies will have a major impact on whether minority groups are accorded the opportunity to become incorporated into a society or will – aided by ideologies of "otherness" – be excluded from full inclusion (Touraine 1997; Walzer 1997). Assimilation as civic incorporation cannot occur without a climate of tolerance, wherein prejudice and discrimination are officially rejected, and the state plays an important role in creating and preserving this climate (Parekh 2000a: 196–238). However, reducing levels of prejudice and discrimination are not ends in themselves, but rather should be seen as prerequisites to civic incorporation. Whether or not these prerequisites are met depends on the outcome of political struggles that are shaped by differentials in power.

Note that by placing the emphasis on civic assimilation, and not on Gordon's "keystone" – structural assimilation – we can begin to envision something that earlier assimilationist theorists, particularly those under the spell of the evolutionary modernization theory, could not: namely, that civic incorporation might provide a sufficient basis for the forging of a common culture and thus societal cohesion, while assuming, permitting, and perhaps even encouraging ethnic diversity to persist over the long haul.

An interesting theoretical convergence can be seen emerging at the present time. Multicultural theorists (see e.g. Taylor 1992; Kymlicka 1995; Appadurai 1996; Parekh 2000a) have increasingly located their discussions of ethnic group affiliations in terms of notions of citizenship in pluralist democracies. This effort to consider citizenship as an overarching mode of identity and basis for societal solidarity is similar to the way Parsons addressed the issue from the perspective of his structural-functionalist version of modernization theory. Despite this parallel focus, to my knowledge no prominent multicultural theorists have invoked the legacy of Parsons. This silence is not entirely surprising given what Bryan Turner (2000: 15) has referred to as "the problem of fashion and discontinuity in social theory." However, I suspect that this problem does not tell the whole story.

Rather, there is an important difference between these contemporary theorists and Parsons which points to the salutary impact of multicultural theory in examining the significance of citizenship in the contemporary world. Parsons approached civic incorporation from the perspective of structure, and as such tended to overstate what he considered to be inherent tendencies in modern democratic states towards greater inclusiveness. By contrast, multicultural theory focuses on agency – state action, ethnic collective action, and the acts of individuals – and as such opens up the prospect of considerably more varied potential outcomes (Bulmer and Rees 1996; Joppke 1999; Glenn 2000; Soysal 2000).

It is important to point out that the idea of multiculturalism means different things to different theorists. Like assimilation and cultural pluralism before it, multiculturalism frequently involves an unspoken mixing of what is and what ought to be. In other words, the term is employed both as an analytic concept and as a normative precept. Herein we will attempt to disengage the analytic use of the term from its normative aspects. Perhaps a useful starting point is to observe the distinction that political theorist Bhikhu Parekh (2000a: 7) has made: "The term 'multicultural' refers to the fact of cultural diversity, the term 'multiculturalism' to a normative response to that fact." With this distinction in mind, I would suggest that at bedrock multiculturalism speaks to the quest on the part of ethnic groups to maintain a distinctive identity, engaging in what the Canadian political philosopher Charles Taylor (1992) has referred to as the "politics of recognition." Multiculturalism, thus, is about finding a way to preserve discrete ethnic identities, while at the same time finding in citizenship a countervailing identity that unites the disparate groups within a polity. Parekh (2000a: 219) has succinctly described this project:

> Like any other society, a multicultural society needs a broadly shared culture to sustain it. Since it involves several cultures, the shared culture can only grow out of their interaction and should both respect and nurture their diversity and unite them around a common way of life. For those accustomed to thinking of culture as a more or less homogeneous and coherent whole, the idea of a multiculturally constituted culture might appear incoherent or bizarre. In fact, such a culture is a fairly common phenomenon in every culturally diverse society.

What are the impediments to the promotion of a politics of recognition and simultaneously the inclusion of ethnics in the societal mainstream as citizens? Obviously, the major impediment comes when the hegemonic group in a society, for a variety of reasons, is prepared to engage in discrimination and promote a politics of exclusion. However, this is not the whole story. As Taylor's (1992) work reveals, there is no guarantee that those pressing for recognition are necessarily prepared to either encourage a pluralist notion of citizenship or to recognize similar desires for recognition on the part of other ethnic communities. Take Québec, which is Taylor's primary referent, as a case in point. While the Francophone community in the province demands policies designed to ensure the preservation of their culture, they have exhibited little support for similar demands on the part of the province's indigenous Indian population or the new immigrants from Asia and the Caribbean. This raises a critical question that we will address in the concluding chapter, namely how do liberal democracies promote multiculturalism in situations where one or more ethnic groups engage in practices that are illiberal, intolerant, or work against the interests of individuals?

Some critics have suggested that multiculturalism suffers from a tendency to essentialize ethnic group identity in practice – treating ethnicity as an immutable given – while in theory arguing that it is a construct subject to change. Part of this debate impacts the right and the ability of individuals to define their own identities. To what extent can and should individuals be able to exit a group? To what extent should they be able to define themselves in ways they see fit to, regardless of how ethnic groups leaders choose to define ethnic identity? Mixed-race people afford a useful example of the issues involved. Should the state be the ultimate arbiter in determining whether a person should be defined as black, white, mulatto, or whatever? Or should particular ethnic groups have this power? Or, finally, should this ability reside with the individuals themselves (see examples of these debates in Davis 2000 and Nagel 2000).

This particular issue has been addressed instructively in David Hollinger's (1995) discussion of a "postethnic America" – a discussion that can be extrapolated to include the other nations under consideration herein. Hollinger distinguishes two competing perspectives on multiculturalism. The first he terms "pluralism," by which he means multiculturalism that is primarily, or even solely, concerned with maintaining distinctive group boundaries. The second, which is the one he clearly prefers, he calls "cosmopolitanism." Such a perspective sees a value in maintaining ethnic diversity, but at the same time contends that individuals ought to be in a position to pick and choose from those multiple cultures. In other words, this would be an optional ethnicity that, going beyond what Mary Waters (1990) had in mind, not only selectively decides which things from one's own background to embrace and which to reject, but also includes the possibility of reaching out to other cultures. Richard Alba (1999: 9) nicely summarizes Hollinger's position when he writes that, "both multiculturalism and assimilationism approach each other in Hollinger's cosmopolitan, who appreciates the value of cultural diversity but is sufficiently liberated from any particularistic loyalty to take advantage of the offerings of the multicultural palette."

Transnationalism, citizenship, and globalization

The discussion above, going back to Parsons, assumed that the nation-state was the appropriate conceptual unit of analysis for making sense of processes of inclusion and exclusion. This assumption has recently been challenged by a reconsideration of the migratory process itself, and by the realization that many immigrants today manage to live at some level in two worlds at once, their homeland and their immigrant destination. As a consequence, the call has been made for a social science that is "unbound" from the nation-state (Basch, Glick Schiller, & Szanton Blanc 1994), one that recognizes the existence of "transnational social fields" (Portes et al. 1999) or "transnational social spaces" (Faist 2000). Thomas Faist (2000: 207–8) describes these social spaces when he writes:

> Transnational communities characterize situations in which international movers and dense and strong social and symbolic ties connect stayers over time and across space to patterns of networks and circuits in two countries. . . . Such communities without propinquity do not necessarily require individual persons living in two worlds simultaneously or between cultures in a total "global village" of de-territorialized space. What is required, however, is that communities without propinquity link through exchange, reciprocity, and solidarity to achieve a high degree of social cohesion and a common repertoire of symbolic and collective representations.

Alejandro Portes and colleagues (1999: 217) have attempted to describe the distinctiveness of this phenomenon in the following way:

> While back and forth movements by immigrants have always existed, they have not acquired until recently the critical mass and complexity necessary to speak of an emergent social field. This field is composed of a growing number of persons who live dual lives: speaking two languages, having homes in two countries, and making a living through continuous regular contact across national borders.

Transnational communities – to the extent that they exist – should be seen as the products of globalization (Robertson 1992, Bauman 1998, Kivisto 2001). It is useful to distinguish three, obviously interconnected, but nonetheless distinct, aspects of globalization: the economic, political, and cultural.

Economic transnationalism is generally seen in relationship to the emergence of global corporations, centered in the metropole, but active in the periphery in their ceaseless quest for cheap labor. We see it in the rise of what Leslie Sklair (2001) has termed the "transnational capitalist class." In this regard, working-class labor migrants can be seen, in effect, as the counterpart to transnational capitalists (Portes et al. 1999: 227). But economic transnationalism does not only involve the border-crossing strategies of a global working class. It also involves small entrepreneurs, who are linked to enclave economies and to the homeland (Light & Gold 2000: 11–15). Examples include Cuban entrepreneurs in Miami, Dominican businesspersons in New York City and Bengali merchants in London's Brick Lane. Such enclaves can serve to reinforce ethnic persistence and to retard assimilation. A more pervasive phenomenon is the ethnic niche, which Roger Waldinger (2001: 18) depicts as the result of the "network-based

nature of migration" that "clusters immigrants into specific economic activities" that involve various "occupational and industrial specializations." The result is that ethnics work disproportionately with coethnics. Like the enclave
economy, the ethnic niche can serve to preserve ethnic attachments. The economic impact of ethnic niches varies. Some groups that have been heavily involved in ethnic niches (Jews are a case in point) have done better than average,
while others (Latinos for example) have done worse.

The political aspects of these processes of change have been the focus of
the work of Yasemin Soysal (1994, 2000), who prefers to speak about this
in terms of what she calls "transnationalization." Ewa Morawska (1999: 20)
contends that there is a certain impreciseness and confusion in the way this
concept is conceived. Nonetheless, there are two interconnected elements
associated with it that can be clearly articulated. First, transnationalization
means that migrants increasingly attempt to define their identities in terms
of both their point of origin and their destination. They are prepared to participate in social, political, and cultural life in both the host society and the
sending state. Acting on this intention is aided by the fact that about half the
nations of the world today permit dual citizenship or nationality – and pressure is being placed on other states to follow suit (Faist 1999: 26). Second, it
means that the idea of the rights of individuals is no longer solely wedded to
particular nation-states. Rather, rights are increasingly being shaped by international organizations such as the United Nations and the International
Labor Organization, by regional transnational organizations such as the
European Community, by intergovernmental organizations such as the Organization for Economic Cooperation and Development and the World Health
Organization, and finally by nongovernmental organizations such as the
International Committee of the Red Cross and the World Council of Churches
(Soysal 1994; Joppke 1998; Delanty 2000).

It is too early to determine where we are headed in terms of
reconceptualizations of citizenship. The United States, for example, does not
recognize dual citizenship, and there is little chance that the current political
climate of the country will change that in the near future. On the other hand,
dual citizenship is increasingly tolerated insofar as in recent years the government has not taken action to prosecute individuals holding dual citizenships. It would be a serious mistake to believe that the increasing demand on
the part of immigrants for what Aihwa Ong (1999) calls "flexible citizenship" and the expanded role of transnational political entities spell the demise of the nation-state or its end as a powerful arbiter in defining the
parameters of citizenship. At the same time, it would also be a mistake to
ignore these novel phenomena, for they are in fact changing the rules of the
game (Jacobson 1996; Spinner-Halev 1999).

As noted above, transnationalism is also about culture. According to Thomas Faist (2000: 210–11; 1998: 217), transnationalism needs to be distin-

guished from globalization. Though similar in many respects, the former has a somewhat more delimited character. Faist notes that whereas the latter is decentered, the former is located in the particular "transnational social spaces" linking two or more nation-states that anchor the identities and interests of migrants. Without discounting the fact that earlier migrants also frequently took an active interest in their homeland – and in some cases this persisted for generations – theorists of transnationalism assume that contemporary migrations are in some sense different from earlier ones. At least in part, this difference between past and present is a reflection of the relative ease of travel today compared to the past and a consequence of improved communications technologies (Basch et al. 1994; Glick Schiller et al. 1996; Portes 1996; Faist 2000).

Transnationalism is conceived by Faist as a conceptual alternative and a supplement both to assimilation and to cultural (or ethnic) pluralism, while sharing an affinity with multiculturalism. Borrowing from the work of Frederik Barth (1969), he contends that assimilation and cultural pluralism share a view of culture as container. In the case of assimilation, what is involved is the pouring out of the content in the container, while cultural pluralism entails retention of that content. In contrast, transnationalism and multiculturalism introduce the element of choice – individual and collective choice – and as such anticipate a future characterized by increasing evidence of transcultural syncretism or hybridization. Metaphorically, assimilation can be associated with the image of "the uprooted," and cultural pluralism with "the transplanted" (Park & Miller 1921; Handlin 1973; Bodnar 1985; Kivisto 1990). Faist proposes as an appropriate transnational metaphorical alternative the idea of "translated people." "Migrants," he writes (1998: 239), "are continually engaged in translating languages, culture, norms, and social and symbolic ties. Trans-lated people are situated in diverse contexts."

One might note, further, that the political and the cultural have their own axial characters. Political boundaries need not necessarily be the same as cultural boundaries. Such is the argument advanced, in a somewhat provisional way, by Orlando Patterson (2000: 465–80). Contending that a global culture shaped principally by American popular culture has arisen, Patterson is at pains to challenge the simplistic view that this is nothing more than the working of American cultural imperialism. Far from it: what he sees is what Faist sees, which is a genuine syncretism occurring.

Patterson identifies four different regional cosmoses that established new forms of cultural boundaries: the West Atlantic, the Tex-Mex, the Southern Californian, and the Pacific Rim cosmos of the Northwest. His most sustained discussion is devoted to the popular music of the West Atlantic. He describes the mutual influences and the give-and-take quality of popular music: in his account, American rhythm-and-blues was introduced into Jamaica, influencing the rise of reggae, which was in turn not only embraced in the United

States, but also served as an important source of inspiration for rap music. Patterson's thesis concerns the diffusion of cultures, not of peoples, and thus is primarily about what Appadurai (1996) refers to as "mediascapes" rather than "ethnoscapes." Nevertheless, it calls attention to the role of culture in shaping the transnational identities that are the focus of concern in the writings of figures such as Soysal, Faist, and Portes.

And here, in effect, we return if not full circle, at least back to the claims made by Parsons about the centrality of citizenship for making possible a distinctive kind of assimilation, which permits the persistence of discrete ethnic groups. The difference between his perspective and that of transnational theorists is that they see the need to expand our analytic framework from the nation-state to include transnational social fields or spaces. In Parsonian language, the societal community has been expanded beyond conventionally understood political borders. Transnational theorists, in contrast to Parsons, no longer want to treat incorporation as an inevitable process involving a series of progressive stages. In resisting such an approach, Soysal (2000: 13) has argued that, "Rather than treating national and transnational as stages in progress, we need to incorporate them into our theoretical frameworks as variables, and treat them as concurrent levels within which the current practices of citizenship and identity should be understood."

In parallel fashion, as we turn to nations without states, we can look at the relationship between existing nation-states struggling to forge multicultural frameworks and concrete policies consonant with the demands of their nationalist minorities for a politics of recognition, and the desire of states to preserve their existing geopolitical integrity (See 1986). While there are obvious differences between immigrants and nationalist minorities, their futures also share much in common. These minorities, particularly in western Europe, not only raise questions about the long-term viability of existing state boundaries, but also about the prospects of forging new, transnational ideas of citizenship. This is apparent in the idea of creating a multicultural European citizenship linking the regions of Europe to Europe as a whole, and in so doing, limiting the salience of citizenship to particular existing states. Again, the issue revolves around the possibility of constructing new modes of civic assimilation. And again, it is impossible to determine what the future holds in store.

Postmodern Modesty

Soysal's above-noted proposal is no doubt a reflection of an appreciation of the predictive failure of earlier modernization theorists. Second, it is also a reflection of an awareness of the sheer complexity of the ethnic phenomenon in the contemporary world. Third, it is a consequence of a theoretical shift wherein those seeking to grant greater importance to agency have ques-tioned the structuralist bias of modernization theory and Marxism. In focusing on social actors and the choices they make, contingency comes to the fore in conceptual models. In trimming the theoretical sails of earlier structuralist process theories, of which Parsons' work is the exemplar, recent theoretical discussions associated with the revival of a tempered assimilation theory and transnationalism are consonant with postmodern suspicions about grand narratives. The consequence of this theoretical modesty is that the conceptual apparatuses we employ at the moment are essentially descriptive typologies – ideal-typical templates upon which we can measure empirical cases.

In the four substantive chapters that follow, we shall enter into a series of case studies in order to identify and examine the most salient aspects of ethnicity in those particular parts of the globe. In so doing, we shall employ the concepts discussed in this chapter – assimilation, cultural pluralism, multiculturalism, and transnationalism – in this typographic way. However, the sociological study of ethnicity calls for efforts to generalize and to identify patterns of social change. To that end, these chapters will be used to inform the concluding chapter, wherein we return to the theoretical discussions entered into in this chapter. The purpose of that chapter will be to revisit the theoretical framework developed here in order to assess its utility in coming to terms with ethnicity in a postmodern and global idiom.

The United States as a Melting Pot: Myth and Reality

The ethnic dynamics of the advanced industrial nations have been transformed during the past half-century, the result being that they are more diverse or multicultural than they were in the past, creating a situation in which cultural differences, particularistic identities, and nationalist aspirations have become more, rather than less, pronounced over time. Some of these changes are the consequence of the global diaspora of peoples from economically less-developed nations, while others are a consequence of historically embedded differences within these nations.

This chapter is the first of four chapters devoted to six case studies. Here we explore the dynamics of ethnic relations in the United States, the largest of the historic settler nations that – because it successfully cast off its colonial status in the American Revolution – has appropriately been called the "first new nation" (Lipset 1963). The first part of the chapter provides a historical overview in order to place into context contemporary developments. In so doing, it seeks to make sense of the major social forces that shape ethnicity and ethnic relations, and reciprocally the ways ethnic groups shaped their own lives and sense of what it meant to be a member of American society. The second part of the chapter turns to the present. First, it locates contemporary ethnicity in relation to the economic transformations that have arisen in what Richard Sennett (1998) has referred to as the "new capitalism." Secondly, it looks at the role played by the evolution of the nation's liberal democratic political system. Finally, it examines the cultural dimensions of these developments, both in terms of the impact of national cultures on the particularistic cultures of various ethnic groups and the reciprocal impact of these particularistic cultures on the larger national culture itself.

The United States: A Nation of Immigrants

Historian Oscar Handlin (1973) once claimed that he set out to write the history of American immigration and discovered it was the history of America. While this was an overstatement insofar as indigenous peoples – American Indians and Mexicans in the southwest – were not immigrants and Africans, though migrants, were not voluntary immigrants, nonetheless there is considerable truth to his claim. Indeed, the vast majority of the 281,000,000 residents of the nation either migrated themselves or, more often, are the offspring of earlier immigrants. They originated from a vast array of countries, with the largest numbers originating from various locales in Europe, Latin America, and Asia.

Each of the successive waves of immigration that has shaped American history has had its own distinctive ethnic character. Thus, immigrants from western Europe characterized the first major wave – from about 1820 up to the Civil War. The second wave, extending from around 1880 until the imposition of immigration restrictions in 1924, was not only considerably larger than the first, but its composition differed insofar as large numbers originated from eastern and southern Europe. The third wave, which commenced after the passage of the Immigration and Nationality Act of 1965, differed yet again as the main contributing nations to this surge of immigration were Latin American and Asian.

Immigrants were key to the evolving understanding of what it meant to be an American. National identity was forged within the reality that as a settler nation with an ever-changing ethnic composition, an overarching American identity had to be in some way reconciled with a multitude of particular ethnic identities. Historian John Higham (1999: 40) has described the situation in comparative terms in the following way:

> The truly distinctive feature of immigration to the United States is its extra-ordinary and continuing diversification from the early eighteenth century to the present. Other immigrant-receiving countries have tended to draw from a few favored ethnic backgrounds. . . . In contrast, the United States has continually attracted new groups and has thereby avoided a fixed division between an immigrant people and an older native population. As the country became more accessible to less familiar immigrant types, by fits and starts it made room for them.

Higham goes on to identify a number of factors that served to mitigate potential conflicts between and among ethnic groups. These include the fact that because the nation was rich in resources and land, it offered opportunities to newcomers and in the process blunted ethnic competition. The vast frontier of the nineteenth century contributed to this situation, and served as an impetus to geographic mobility that prevented particular ethnic groups from associating corporate ethnic life with particular social spaces. This meant that the United States would not be burdened with the intractable ethnic conflicts that are rooted in competing territorial claims. While these factors are important, for our purposes the third factor he discusses – political access – is critical. Higham (1999: 41) observes that:

> The United States presented itself to the world as a universal nation, a home for all peoples. . . . This American self-image was enormously magnetic. It implied that nationality was not exclusive, that citizenship would be widely available, and that class and ethnic boundaries would be soft and permeable. The invitation to newcomers (at first to white males only) to participate in political life on equal terms with other citizens gave outsiders some leverage in using the power of suffrage and the protection of courts. It encouraged white ethnic groups to organize, to make their weight felt, and so to use a system of liberty under law.

As Higham notes, the inclusiveness of the new republic has its limits. In connecting these ideals to reality, as we shall see in the following sections, newcomers were not always welcome and were forced to confront considerable ethnocentric animus. Moreover, for those not considered to be white, the reality of their experience was the antithesis of the universal nation ideal. A dialectical tension existed between the ideal of inclusion and actual demands for exclusion. Nowhere was this better seen than in the way democracy was initially conceived. Bernard Bailyn (1967: 60) has pointed out that though a "contagion of liberty" swept the new republic, at the same time fears were expressed about the presumed dangers that would result if political power were granted to "weak or ignorant" people. Thus, although the nation was conceived as a democracy, who was and who was not eligible for citizenship became a crucial concern. Citizenship, and how it was granted or denied, became a major means of incorporating some groups into not only the American political system, but also into social life in general, while at the same time excluding others. In most of the nation's history of incorporation and exclusion, race served as the most powerful determinant shaping policies regarding citizenship.

Thus, for the millions of European immigrants who entered the US during the nineteenth and early twentieth centuries, the "invention of the white race" and their progressive inclusion within the parameters of this racial designation proved crucial to their ability to become full-fledged Americans (Allen 1994; see also Roediger 1991). This is seen vividly in the case of the Irish. They were the first among the voluntary immigrants to confront intense nativist hostility, giving rise to such anti-Irish organizations as the Know-Nothings (Higham 1970). Viewed as a social problem, they were accused of being inclined to alcoholism and criminal activity. Their burgeoning numbers in major cities combined with their inclination to be involved in political activities fueled anxiety about their potential impact on American democracy. In this regard, critics contended that their Catholicism was inherently authoritarian and thus antithetical to democracy. Moreover, the Irish were often depicted in the popular imagination in racial terms. Cartoonist Thomas Nash, for example, portrayed them as racially similar to Africans, and it was not uncommon for them to be referred to as "white niggers." This term reflects their racially ambiguous status in the nineteenth century. Not surprisingly, part of the strategy designed by the Irish to promote their inclusion and to combat prejudice directed against them was to become unambiguously white. In so doing, the Irish sought to distance themselves from outsider groups by embracing the white supremacist oppression and exclusion of American Indians and African Americans. They acquiesced to the claim that the dominant culture was to be construed in terms of a core that was white, Anglo-Saxon in origin, and Protestant in religion, or in other words WASP.

WASP hegemony, European immigrants, and the melting pot

Throughout the nineteenth century and past the middle of the twentieth, the melting-pot metaphor was the most influential and enduring characterization of ethnic relations in the US. Yet, as Philip Gleason (1964) has pointed out, this symbol of fusion has also led to considerable confusion. During the formative decades of the new republic, French immigrant J. Hector St. John de Crèvecoeur (1904 [1782]: 39) wrote about the American experience as involving newcomers from various nations being "melded into a new race of men." Though such ideas gained common currency in the nineteenth century, it was not until the Jewish playwright Israel Zangwill's play, *The Melting Pot*, was staged in 1908 that the metaphor received its most explicit and popular articulation. Here again one encounters the idea that the American, though the composite product of individuals from various national origins, is someone qualitatively distinct from those particular origins. Thus, the American is the product of the fusion of diverse peoples with distinctive cultural perspectives. The confusion Gleason refers to involves three points. First, it is not clear whether the melting pot is intended as a description of what is an inevitable process of incorporation or as a prescription of what ought to be achieved in promoting a unified national identity. Second, it is not clear whether the idea refers only to cultural fusion or to biological fusion (that is, intermarriage) as well. Finally, it is not entirely clear whether the immigrant alone is transformed by the melting pot, or whether their presence also transforms the host society.

What was clear was that the melting pot served to justify the Americanization campaigns particularly characteristic of the early decades of the twentieth century. These campaigns were intended to eradicate all vestiges of the new arrivals' cultural heritages, while simultaneously instilling in them what were considered to be appropriate American attitudes, beliefs, and behaviors. Nowhere was this position more vividly evident than in the activities of industrialist Henry Ford's "Sociology Department," which ran training schools in his automobile plants for immigrant workers. The purpose of the schools was to teach the English language and to study in preparation for citizenship. Workers enrolled in the program took pledges that they would only speak English, and they proclaimed themselves intent on becoming "100 percent" American – rather than remaining a hyphenated American. In practical terms, this perspective required a willingness and ability on the part of immigrants to accept and to emulate the hegemonic WASP culture.

An ongoing issue confronting the political representatives of the dominant culture was to determine whether in fact particular groups had the requisite capacity and desire to become American in the WASP sense of the term. In other words, they had to determine which groups were capable of fusing or blending into the fabric of American society and which were "unmeltable." The two primary criteria employed in making these determinations were race and religion. The result was that the subsequent social history of immigrants of European origin diverged considerably from that of all others. But this is not to suggest that Europeans should be seen as a homogeneous whole. Indeed, within the composite European population, various groups experienced considerable levels of prejudice and discrimination during their early years in the US, while others managed rather quickly to gain acceptance (Jaret 1999).

While religion was a crucial variable, with the arrival of waves of Catholics and Jews between 1880 and 1924 being seen by nativists as a serious threat to the "righteous empire" created by Protestants, the saliency of race was also a key factor. As noted above about the Irish, southern and eastern Europeans also tended to be described in racial terms: the Nordic peoples of western Europe were contrasted to a variety of presumed racial inferiors, including Mediterraneans, Slavs, and Jews. Racialist thought was used by those urging immigrant restriction legislation. Their fears were articulated by Madison Grant in his diatribe, *The Passing of the Great Race* (1916: 92), when he wrote that as a consequence of the arrival of these newcomers, "Our jails, insane asylums, and almshouses are filled with this human flotsam and the whole tone of American life, social moral, and political, has been lowered and vulgarized by them."

The divide between acceptable and unacceptable Europeans emerged as the consequence of the particular character of national identity that took form during the period between the American Revolution and the Civil War. During the nineteenth century, the new nation set out with an expansionist mission to control much of the continent from the Atlantic to the Pacific, finding in the doctrine of Manifest Destiny an ideological justification for a policy of conquest. The United States was resource rich but population poor, while economic development required both resources and an expanding population. This was the case during the earlier agrarian era, but population growth became even more crucial as the nation began to industrialize in the nineteenth century. Thus, in order to attract an adequate labor supply, the nation established liberal immigration policies and continued the practices begun during the colonial era of investing heavily in the Atlantic slave trade.

Despite its general openness to newcomers, during this early phase of nation-building, the voluntary immigrants came overwhelmingly from western Europe, with the British constituting the dominant group. Over a million immigrants had already arrived by the time of the first census in 1790, with fully 89 percent of this population originating from England and Scotland. At slightly under 6 percent, the Germans were the second largest group. Among the other groups represented during the early years of the republic were the Irish, Dutch, French, and Scandinavians. The sheer size of the British population, combined with the legacy of colonial rule, stamped the British heritage on the political, cultural, and social fabric of the emerging nation. The economic domination of the British coalesced with political domination. British laws, institutions, and political sensibilities were transplanted to America. To provide but one example of what this meant, British hegemony was such that the language question never managed to rise to the level of genuine political debate during the nineteenth century, and as a result no law was passed that mandated English as the official language of the nation. It was simply assumed to be (Kivisto 1995: 117–24).

Between 1790 and 1820, the level of immigration was relatively modest, with an estimated 250,000 people arriving from western Europe during these three decades. The number picked up dramatically thereafter, with sizeable immigrant streams coming from not only Britain, but also Germany and Ireland. Though there were considerable differences among the British, as a whole they not surprisingly adapted quickly to the new environment, blending into the host society so rapidly that they became, as Charlotte Erickson (1972) has characterized them, "invisible immigrants." These new arrivals settled in the urban centers of the northeast and became the key component in the move into the frontier, first in the middle west and later onward to the Pacific coast.

The Germans, too, played a major role in the settlement of the middle west. With sufficient social and individual capital to be economically successful, the German population – diverse in terms of religious affiliation and political persuasion – established a vibrant ethnic community while exhibiting a willingness to develop social relationships outside of the confines of German America. By the latter part of the nineteenth century, the Germans were well positioned in the hierarchy of ethnic groups in America. In this regard, their experience parallels that of most other western European groups. The Irish were the exception. As noted above, this was in no small part due to the fact that they were Catholic in a chiefly Protestant nation (Jones 1960: 147–57). Moreover, the idea that they were racially distinct from the British further served to place them in a disadvantageous location in the ethnic hierarchy.

All of this changed dramatically after 1880, during which time the industrialization of the economy intensified and the demand for unskilled laborers in the manufacturing sector grew. Although immigrants continued to arrive from western Europe, their numbers were not sufficient to meet demand. The slack was taken up by immigrants from other parts of Europe. Indeed, between 1890 and 1930, the number of immigrants from eastern and southern Europe exceeded those from western Europe. The largest groups to arrive during this major immigration were Italians, Jews (from various countries in Europe, but particularly from Poland and Russia), and Poles. However, immigrants came from a wide range of countries, including Albanians, Byelorussians, Bulgarians, Croatians, Czechs, Estonians, Finns, Greeks, Hungarians, Macedonians, Montenegrins, Portuguese, Romanians, Russians, Serbians, Slovaks, Slovenes, Spaniards, and Ukrainians. Taken as a whole, as table 2 indicates, the foreign born reached a level of 14.8 percent of the total population during this period.

These "strangers in the land" (Higham 1970) were culturally, religiously, and linguistically diverse, but what was most significant to native-born Americans were their differences *vis-à-vis* those who had arrived prior to the Civil War. These were the people Madison Grant accused of constituting a cultural threat and a social problem. They confronted in varying degrees prejudice, discrimination, and social marginalization. In many instances, efforts to gain an economic foothold that allowed for upward

Table 2   US foriegn-born population, 1890–2000

Year	Number (in millions)	Percent
2000	28.4	10.4
1990	19.8	7.9
1970	9.6	4.7
1950	10.3	6.9
1930	14.2	11.6
1910	13.5	14.7
1890	9.2	14.8

Source: US Census Bureau 2001.

social mobility proved to be difficult. In response to their presence, an increasingly powerful movement to limit or altogether ban further mass immigration took root. It managed to influence immigration legislation from the 1890s forward, during which time a series of measures were taken to make admission to the US more difficult and to raise the barrier for those seeking to become citizens. These efforts to limit immigration culminated in an initial quota law in 1921 and a more stringent one passed in 1924, known as the National Origins Act. Although immigration was not altogether prohibited, the result was that with the passage of this law, the migratory movement from Europe on a grand scale came to a halt. Economic and political factors served to reinforce this situation, as the Depression of the 1930s followed by the Second World War proved to be disincentives to would-be immigrants.

Southern and eastern Europeans occupied an interstitial and ambiguous place in American society. Nowhere was this better reflected than in the social distance studies noted in chapter 1 that were conducted by Emory Bogardus (1933). In these studies of comparative levels of social acceptance of various groups, whereas western Europeans were the most readily accepted and non-Europeans (including blacks, Asians, Turks, and others) were the least readily accepted, these groups found themselves somewhere in the middle. Not surprisingly, the ethnic communities that they created expended considerable time and energy attempting to convince the larger society – and perhaps themselves – that they were in fact fully capable of being assimilated into American society (Øverland 2000). Part of these campaigns entailed efforts to convince the host society that they were indeed white. Over time, as the members of these groups adjusted to their new homeland and became acclimated to it, immigrants and their offspring relied less and less on their ethnic communities to sustain them. Rather, they began to look to the institutions of the larger society and began to involve themselves in their activities. This occurred more quickly for some groups and at a slower pace for others, depending in no small part on the variations in the levels of prejudice and discrimination that confronted particular groups. What all of these groups shared in common was easy access to full citizenship rights, which served as a major vehicle for becoming American on terms where they had a voice in defining precisely what that meant.

Coercive pluralism and the politics of exclusion

Until the second half of the twentieth century, the situation was quite different for all non-Europeans, whether they were indigenous peoples who were the victims of colonial conquest, those involuntary migrants imported into the nation as slaves, or immigrants from other shores. These groups confronted situations that reflect what Lawrence Fuchs (1990: 80–6) has described as various forms of "coercive pluralism."

Predatory pluralism

For the approximately 150 to 200 tribes that became known collectively as Indians, the form was one that Fuchs characterized as "predatory." By this he meant that these original occupants of the land were defined as outsiders that, insofar as they stood in the way of European settlement, were to be pushed aside. The consequences of contact with Europeans proved devastating for the American Indian population, which declined precipitously from the arrival of Europeans, when reliable estimates put the population at between 2,000,000 and 5,000,000, to slightly more than 250,000 by 1890 (Thornton 1987). This dramatic decline was the combined result of military campaigns, famine, and the spread of various communicable diseases introduced by Europeans for which the indigenous peoples had far less resistance.

Conflict over territorial claims intensified with the passage of time as the demand for land on the part of European settlers grew. Farmers, land speculators, and entrepreneurs increasingly sought to acquire land occupied by various tribes, and were largely successful in these efforts, the nineteenth century being a period of systematic and wide-scale displacement. Not surprisingly, it was also a period during which open conflict and warfare escalated, with the most violent pitting the US government against two formidable tribal confederations: the Iroquois in the northeast and the Creek in the southeast. The defeat of Indians made possible the process of forced relocations of numerous tribes in the eastern part of the nation to less desirable and unfamiliar lands to the west.

The federal government recognized a legal basis for American Indian claims to land ownership, and as a result entered into treaties that represented the legal basis for acquiring tribal lands. In so doing, the government's relationship to Indian tribes bore a resemblance to its relationship to foreign powers, though it refused to recognize tribes as independent nations. These treaties were unequal exchanges in which Indians confronted enormous pressure to sign, and both the government and white settlers frequently violated their terms. The status of American Indians was uncertain insofar as they were neither citizens nor aliens. From about the middle of the nineteenth century until the 1930s, the establishment of the reservation system shaped Indian relations with the US government (Cornell 1988: 12). Reservations were total institutions constructed as a means of achieving political containment and control, ensuring the physical and social separation of the indigenous population from the nation-state's societal core. In this system, tribes entered into a dependency relationship with agents of the federal government.

Some policy-makers sought to end the ambiguous status of American Indians by urging a cessation of governmental relations with tribal organizations. The idea underlying this perspective was that Indians ought to be viewed as individuals like members of other groups, and not in corporate terms. The Indian Allotment Act of 1887 (also known as the Dawes Act) was an attempt to put an end to collectively held land, replacing it instead with land owned by individual Indian property owners. This was seen as a necessary prerequisite for the granting of citizenship rights (Cornell 1988: 56–8). It was not until 1924 that all American Indians became citizens. Subsequently, the federal government has zigzagged between liberal and conservative policies. Thus, the liberalism of the New Deal era led to the passage of the Indian Reorganization Act (1934), which sought to enhance the role of tribal organizations in political and economic matters. In contrast, the conservative Eisenhower administration's "termination" approach was designed to sever governmental ties with tribes and to abolish the reservation system. Termination failed and thus the unique relationship of American Indians to the federal government remains.

Caste pluralism

In contrast to Native Americans, Fuchs (1990: 87–109) describes the system that African Americans confronted as "caste pluralism." Forcibly brought into the country in the Atlantic slave trade, they occupied a particularly oppressive location in the national economy. In an otherwise class-based economy, which permitted individual mobility, Africans in America were relegated to a subordinate position based on race-specific ascriptive criteria. This meant that not only would they not be able to experience individual or intergenerational integration into the larger society, but also all facets of their everyday lives were severely circumscribed. Slavery was only one form of caste pluralism. Although caste pluralism defined the period up to the Civil War, the elimination of slavery did not signal the end of caste pluralism.

Slavery has been succinctly defined by Orlando Patterson (1982: 334) as "human parasitism." The reason that slavery took root throughout the New World was economic. Race prejudice served as an ideological justification for slavery, but did not produce it. In short, the planter class in the southern states concluded that it was economically advantageous to use slave labor rather than indentured servants or wage laborers. Though slavery was practiced in the northern states as well, it was most closely associated with the southern plantation system. Like the reservation, the plantation system is also an instance of a total institution (Genovese 1969). The peculiarity of the plantation was that it operated internally as a total institution while being part of an international economic system, insofar as the Industrial Revolution in England would not have been possible without the availability of cotton provided by southern plantations (Hobsbawm 1969).

Ralph Ellison in his unfinished novel, *Juneteenth*, has poignantly described the impact of slavery on Africans caught up in its web. He does so in a passage where a revivalist preacher chants variations on the following theme of the deprivations endured by African Americans: "Eyeless, tongueless, drumless, danceless, songless, hornless, soundless, sightless, wrongless, rightless, motherless, fatherless, brotherless, sisterless, powerless" (Ellison 1999: 124). This lack of power did not mean that slaves accepted slavery. On the contrary, the prevalence of slave revolts, runaways, and the considerable evidence of less dangerous forms of resistance indicate that slaves on the whole refused to grant legitimacy to this "peculiar institution" (Stampp 1956; Blassingame 1972). However, in the end slaves were sufficiently powerless to be capable of freeing themselves. Instead, slavery ended as a result of conflicts among whites, pitting pro- and anti-slavery forces. As the nineteenth century progressed, the abolitionist movement's challenge to the slavocracy intensified. Throughout the northern states, slavery was progressively abolished. In 1807, federal law prohibited the further importation of slaves, though the illicit trade would continue until the eve of the Civil War. In the end, slavery was abolished, not simply by a moral campaign that challenged its legitimacy, but by a complex of social, political, and economic factors.

In the immediate aftermath of the Civil War, there were grounds for optimism on the part of recently freed blacks. The legal abolition of slavery ratified as the Thirteenth Amendment to the Constitution was followed shortly thereafter by additional constitutional measures that held forth the promise of bringing African Americans into the mainstream. The Fourteenth Amendment granted the rights of citizenship, and black suffrage was granted in the Fifteenth Amendment. These three post-Civil War Amendments formed the legal basis for a redefinition of the place of Africans in the United States. In the brief postwar period of reconstruction, blacks sought to take advantage of these changes by asserting their newfound independence in both the political and economic arenas.

However, in a combination of legal and extralegal moves, whites managed to reinstitute a new structure of white supremacy. Legal initiatives transpired at the state and local levels, as new laws were passed with two major goals in mind. The first was to prevent blacks from voting through such means as poll taxes and literacy tests, and from otherwise becoming citizens in anything but a formal sense. In other words, it led to the political disenfranchisement of African Americans. The second was to mandate racial segregation in all facets of public life, a segregation that was underpinned by the assumption that it meant racial subordination (Foner 1988). Thus, the segregation of blacks and whites in such public facilities as schools, parks, and public transportation characterized this new racial formation.

The net result was the establishment of a new era of white domination and racial segregation that became known as Jim Crow (Woodward 1974). The linchpin that accorded the legitimacy of the federal government to Jim Crow was the 1896 Supreme Court case, *Plessy v. Ferguson*, which established the basis for the "separate but equal doctrine" that was to define race relations past the first half of the twentieth century. This legal basis for racial segregation and subordination was backed up by the perpetual threat of violence and terror, seen most vividly in the activities of groups such as the Ku Klux Klan and in the pervasiveness of lynching. This system shaped race relations for the better part of a century. Leon Litwack (1998: 149) described the era of Jim Crow from the perspective of blacks: "No matter how hard they labored, no matter how they conducted themselves, no matter how fervently they prayed, the chances of making it were less than encouraging; the basic rules and controls were in place."

Sojourner pluralism

The third type of coercive pluralism Fuchs (1990: 110–27) defined was "sojourner pluralism," which characterized the situation of two particular groups in the antebellum period – Mexicans and the Chinese – and later was applicable to other Latino and Asian groups. As the term suggests, these groups were perceived as temporary residents of the country, labor migrants who would for a limited period of time take advantage of economic opportunities. The clear expectation was that they would eventually return to their respective homelands.

Because they were labor migrants, European-origin ethnics often viewed these groups as competitive threats in the labor market, and thus they were early victims of working-class racism (Roediger 1991). This was a crucial issue, as in an immigrant-receiving country with a need for labor there was a countervailing need to reconcile it with the fears of nativists opposed to the presence of the racial Other. The case of the Chinese is particularly illustrative in this regard insofar as the first attempt to prohibit specific groups from immigrating was directly solely at them.

The major pull factor that brought the Chinese to the US was the quest for gold. These were indeed sojourners, or "birds of passage," hoping to get rich on "Gold Mountain" in order to return home where they would live well. Over 90 percent of the immigrants were males, leading over time to the characterization of the Chinese in America as a "bachelor society." In this context, an ethnic community emerged from the mid-nineteenth century, dominated by business elites within the community that managed to create organizations that served to enhance their position. The institutional structure of the community included three transplanted types of organizations: clan associations, speech or territorial associations, and criminal bands known as secret societies. While the first two types were involved in various forms of mutual aid, employment, and commerce, the activities of the secret societies centered around gambling, drugs, and prostitution. The dependence of immigrants on Chinese elites within the community and the isolation of Chinatowns from the larger society that was a consequence of the intense racism of the host society meant that Chinese enclaves operated, in Ronald Takaki's (1989: 230) term, as "ethnic islands."

Though relatively small in numbers, Chinese immigrants had been targeted by a virulent nativist campaign from the time they first arrived around the middle of the nineteenth century. As noted above, organized labor played a particularly significant role in a push for the economic exclusion of the Chinese and in a quest to prevent new immigrants from entering the country. However, anti-Chinese animus was widespread throughout American society and was often exploited by politicians (Lyman 1974; Gyory 1998). Efforts aimed at economic exclusion included a variety of laws that specifically targeted the Chinese, including California's "Foreign Miners Tax," to which only the Chinese were subject, and San Francisco's "Laundry Ordinance," which imposed taxes on laundries that did not use horses, which in practice meant Chinese laundries (Hsu 2000: 59). The Chinese were banned from work in some industries, such as commercial fishing. They were also the victims of mob violence in numerous locales. They were expelled from some communities, including Seattle and Tacoma. They fell victim to hangings and burnings in Los Angeles in 1871, and murderous attacks in the gold mines along the Idaho–Oregon border in 1885 and the coal mines of Rock Springs, Wyoming, in 1887 (Lyman 1974: 60–1; Hsu 2000: 59).

Paralleling these efforts aimed at economic exclusion were those aimed at immigration restriction. Though anti-immigration agitation was initially centered in California, it became a national cause. After efforts to ban further immigration at the state level became impractical and legally suspect, a national Chinese exclusion act was passed in 1882. It prohibited the further entry of Chinese immigrants for ten years. Certain exceptions were made, such as those for students and merchants. The Geary Act passed ten years later imposed even harsher burdens on the Chinese, a situation that would remain in effect until the national legislation of 1924 that effectively halted mass migration across the board. Actually, migration did not entirely cease, for not only were some legal immigrants permitted entry, but moreover illegals also found their way into the country (Hsu 2000: 71–87).

Immigration restriction was linked to another form of political restriction, which entailed denying citizenship rights to the Chinese in America. Stanford M. Lyman (1997: 167) points to the impact this denial had on the status of the Chinese:

What proved most effective for marginalizing the Chinese in America were statutes and judicial rulings that excluded them from participation in the body politic. It is true, of course, that, as Jonathan D. Spence has recently observed, "The restrictive immigration laws levied against the Chinese – and at no other foreign nationals at the time – form a melancholy theme in late-nineteenth century American history." Even more tragic, however, was their formal exclusion from the benefits, rights, and opportunities of US civil society that, at least in the casuistry of law and the rhetoric of public policy, were then accorded to all other newcomer Americans, and, in theory but not practice, to the recently emancipated African Americans.

The Chinese were not accorded the rights of citizenship until 1943, this change occurring during the Second World War, when the Chinese Kuomintang nationalists became allies of the US against Japan (Lyman 1997: 184). Although the Chinese case is unique in many respects, their situation paralleled that of other peoples of color who, being considered neither white nor of African ancestry, confronted a legal system intent on preventing them from being deemed eligible for citizenship. Thus, a wide array of groups faced similar barriers to civic inclusion, including the Japanese, Burmese, Koreans, Hawaiians, Armenians, Syrians, Arabs, East Indians, Puerto Ricans, Filipinos, American Indians, and mixed-bloods (Lyman 1997: 128–59).

While hostility to non-Europeans in general was intense, a growing anti-immigration movement did not limit its campaign solely to these particular immigrant groups. Rather, claiming that the nation was experiencing *The Passing of the Great Race* (1916), as the title of Madison Grant's book put it, it sought to make the United States a haven for western and northern Europeans. It pressed Congress for restrictive legislation, and the Congress obliged in a series of legislative changes that ultimately put an end to wide-scale immigration. In 1891, 1903, 1907, and 1917 more stringent limitations were imposed on the nation's open door policy (Higham 1970). The 1906 Basic Naturalization Act mandated knowledge of English as a prerequisite for becoming a citizen. As noted earlier, in 1921 an initial quota law was passed, setting limits to the number of immigrants from particular countries. This was followed by the National Origins Act of 1924, which limited the number of immigrants from outside the Western Hemisphere to 153,700 per year. Nations were allotted quotas based on the percentages of their populations making up the US population in 1920. The net result was to ensure that 82 percent of new arrivals would be from western and northern Europe. As figure 1 illustrates, the consequence of this act, which took effect in 1929, was that for the next four decades mass immigration ceased and the existing ethnic hierarchy was reinforced.

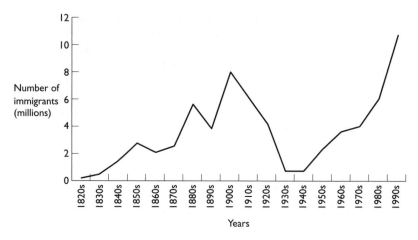

Figure 1   US immigration levels by decade
Source: US Census Bureau 2001.

The Emergence of a New Racial Formation

It is within this general historical context that a new racial formation emerged in the 1960s (Omi & Winant 1994). Three central elements of this racial formation can be identified: (1) the progressive assimilation of European ethnics that became more and more evident from the Second World War on; (2) the success of the black civil rights movement in bringing an end to the Jim Crow era and establishing laws to combat discrimination; and (3) the resumption of mass immigration that occurred after the passage of the Immigration and Nationality Act of 1965 (also known as the Hart–Cellar Act), which, because it had eliminated the racist character of the 1924 Act, had resulted in a dramatic increase in the size of the Latino and Asian populations during the last three decades of the twentieth century.

The assimilation of European ethnics

Turning to the first of these elements, for the vast majority of European-origin Americans, the immigration hiatus between the 1920s and 1960s severed the homeland ties of the third- and fourth-generation ethnic offspring of immigrants, which meant that they became increasingly unfamiliar with their homeland cultures, a key to the fact that they were progressively Americanized. Levels of prejudice and discrimination declined, as a redrawing of the racial boundaries resulted in the expansion of groups who were considered to be white. In this new dispensation, the racial category white became a synonym for European-origin. After mid-century one could still hear group-specific ethnic slurs (e.g., kike, guinea, hunkie), but such usage was on the decline.

These developments took place during the two prosperous decades following the Second World War. During this time the class structure was transformed as a consequence of the growth of large bureaucratic corporations and the parallel growth of government bureaucracies due to the expansion of the welfare state and the military during the Cold War. The net result was the dramatic growth of the "white collar" worker, the new middle class that C. Wright Mills (1951) pointed to as the primary vehicle for upward mobility for European-origin ethnics. The result was a reconfiguration of the connection between class and ethnicity. Prior to this period, the newer immigrant groups from southern and eastern Europe represented the backbone of the unskilled working class. Now their children were able to rise into the ranks of the middle class, aided by such programs as the GI Bill. The result was a growing gulf between those ethnics who went to college, entered the middle class, and moved out of ethnic neighborhoods in cities to new suburban housing developments, and those who did not pursue higher educations and tended to remain both in the blue-collar workforce and in the city. What this implied was that for blue-collar workers ethnic and class identities were mutually reinforcing, while for their white-collar counterparts the connection showed considerable evidence of unraveling.

Moreover, contrary to the claims for an ethnic revival among European-origin ethnics, the salience of ethnic identities for these groups actually declined. Even a spokesperson for the cultural transmission thesis such as Andrew Greeley could offer only a highly qualified analysis of the continuing significance of ethnicity. He argued that by the 1970s ethnicity did matter, but only "to some extent some dimensions of the ethnic culture do indeed survive and enable us to predict some aspects of the behavior of the children, grandchildren, and great grandchildren of immigrants" (Greeley 1974: 319). What some commentators saw as an ethnic revival was in fact to a large extent a backlash against what were perceived to be gains made by blacks and other people of color in the immediate aftermath of the civil rights movement. This backlash was associated with a questioning of the American dream arising because of a belief that racial minorities were the beneficiaries of government-sponsored programs at the expense of white working-class ethnics. What was at stake for these working-class ethnics was, not a returning to their roots, but finding common cause with other European ethnics against the perceived threat posed by non-European ethnics (Rieder 1985).

The differences among European ethnics eroded in part because the religious factor proved over time to be less and less divisive. When John Kennedy ran for President, anti-Catholic voices expressed a fear that the Vatican would run the White House, but his election could be seen as a tangible indication of the extent to which this kind of thinking no longer reflected the opinions of the Protestant majority. This is a revealing example of the thesis advanced by Will Herberg in *Protestant-Catholic-Jew* (1955), where he pointed to the ascendance of a new ecumenical sensibility in which these three Judeo-Christian groups would be seen as discrete bodies located under the umbrella of American civil religion. This pointed to both cultural and civic assimilation, wherein groups were united as citizens while simultaneously allowing for separate corporate identities – and thus did not necessarily imply structural assimilation.

However, by mid-century, a major structural transformation was underway that would redefine ethnic identity for European-origin groups. A precipitous decline in the number and influence of distinctively ethnic institutions occurred, accompanied by an exodus from ethnic neighborhoods, often to the ethnically heterogeneous suburbs. Mother-tongue language loyalty exhibited rapid declines, along with the erosion of many cultural values and traditions. It is not surprising that the pace of change varied across groups as well as within groups. Among the particularly relevant factors influencing the impact of assimilation were group size, degree of residential concentration, the length of time in the US, religion, homeland concerns, and the level of educational attainment and economic upward mobility.

Added to these factors was the impact of intermarriage. In the 1940s, sociologist Ruby Jo Reeves Kennedy (1944) argued that she could detect the existence of a "triple melting pot" wherein European ethnics were marrying outside of ethnic group boundaries at an increased rate, but within the religious boundaries of Protestantism, Catholicism, and Judaism. Whether or not she accurately captured that historical moment, in the ensuing decades the boundaries between specific European groups has clearly eroded as rates of intermarriage have soared. And during this time it is clear that religious boundaries increasingly did not serve as a replacement for ethnic boundaries. By the last quarter of the twentieth century, one could fairly speak about pervasive marital assimilation among European groups.

These changes could be seen for all European-origin groups (obviously excluding such religio-ethnic sectarian outliers as the Amish, Hutterites, and Hasidic Jews). The rate of change varied among groups, but it is clear that the group that remained the least maritally assimilated for the longest time was Jews. This is not surprising, given the fact that, as John Higham (1970) has argued, Jews have historically confronted far higher levels of hostility than other European groups. Moreover, the Jewish community had a particular interest in preserving a distinctive corporate identity, lest their religious heritage be absorbed into the Christian mainstream.

After mid-century, a significant majority of American Jews sought to promote civic and cultural assimilation, and to challenge anti-Semitism while simultaneously warding off structural and marital assimilation. This proved to
be a delicate balancing act, and as early as the 1950s, Herbert Gans (1956)
wrote about a phenomenon he called "symbolic Judaism." What he was pointing to was the extent to which middle-class Jews were abandoning distinctly
Jewish cultural practices, values, and behaviors in an effort to fit into the mainstream. They wanted, he suggested, to feel Jewish, on at least some occasions,
without being prepared to act Jewish in the normal routines of their lives.

The good news was that by the last quarter of the century, the levels of anti-
Semitism had fallen dramatically, and Jews were being afforded expanded opportunities in all facets of American social life. However, one of the unintended
consequences of the new tolerance and inclusiveness was the rise in intermarriage. While the rate of Jewish intermarriage in 1950 was less than 4 percent,
by 1990, 32 percent had married non-Jews. Moreover, for marriages taking
place after 1985, the figure had risen to 52 percent (Kosmin et al. 1991: 13–
14). In other words, despite the lingering persistence of anti-Semitism, by the
end of the twentieth century Jews were clearly following the intermarriage
trends of other European Americans. Thus, despite the presence of ultra-Or-
thodox Jews and the arrival of newcomers from the former Soviet Union, Israel, and elsewhere in the Middle East and north Africa, the situation of the
vast majority of Jews increasingly parallels that of other European ethnics.

In the face of the pervasive gradual decline of the salience of ethnicity for
all European-origin groups, there is also considerable evidence for ethnic
persistence. However, that persistence has taken a new form. One influential way of viewing that form is Gans' (1979) theory of symbolic ethnicity
that I discussed in chapter 1 (which is in effect an extrapolation from his
earlier, more particular concept of symbolic Judaism). Rather than relying
on community or culture, the third generation and beyond uses symbols,
primarily out of a sense of nostalgia for the traditions of the immigrant generation. According to Gans (1979: 203–4):

> most people look for easy and intermittent ways of expressing their identity,
> for ways that do not conflict with other ways of life. As a result, they refrain
> from ethnic behavior that requires an arduous or time-consuming commit-
> ment, either to a culture that must be practiced constantly or to organizations
> that demand active membership. Second, because people's concern is with iden-
> tity, rather than with cultural practices or group relationships, they are free to
> look for ways of expressing that identity which suit them best, thus opening up
> the possibility of voluntary, diverse, or individualistic ethnicity.

This individualistic ethnicity opens up a variety of, to use Mary Waters'
(1990) term, "ethnic options." According to Waters, ethnicity remains mean-

ingful insofar as it is related to the desire for a sense of community. However, ethnicity has a decidedly voluntaristic cast as people selectively determine which features of the ethnic tradition to valorize, while ignoring or abandoning others. Furthermore, Waters (1990: 112–13; 134) points to the existence of considerable cultural syncretism among European-origin groups as well as a remarkable convergence regarding what are defined as being the most important traditional values of their respective ethnic group. Regardless of group, ethnics all agreed that *their* group placed a premium on family, education, hard work, religiosity, and patriotism. As the presumed commonalities have become more significant than the differences, the idea of a shared pan-ethnic identity among European Americans has emerged.

This development has been aided by widespread intermarriage. The complex pattern of intermarriage among European-origin ethnics has produced a population with multiple ancestries, and in the process has led to a reduction in the salience of ethnic identities based on particular nations of origin. Instead, as Richard Alba (1990: 293) contends, "The transformation of ethnicity among whites does not portend the elimination of ethnicity but instead the formation of a new ethnic group: one based on ancestry from anywhere on the European continent." This situation ought to be construed as a form of assimilation, but not the melting-pot version. While I agree with Alba, something significant is missing in the way he frames the transformation, which is by referencing the white race as a nonproblematic given. In fact, the assimilation of these ethnics has necessitated a redrawing of the racial boundaries so that groups once considered nonwhite have become white. The boundaries of inclusion have changed. In everyday language, it is far less likely that people self-identify as European American and far more likely that they refer to themselves as white. Michael Omi (2001: 253) has made this point when he writes that, "In the 'twilight of ethnicity,' White racial identity may increase in salience."

This transformation speaks to the fact that the flip side of changing the boundaries of inclusion is a reformulation of the boundaries of exclusion (Lipsitz 1998; Allen 1994; Roediger 1991). In viewing Europeans taken as a whole as "we," non-Europeans are thereby viewed as "they." In this regard, the nostalgia that fuels symbolic ethnicity looks less benign, for the celebration of one's heritage can serve as the basis for criticizing or denigrating other ethnic groups. For example, to argue that their culture places a premium on family ties is to implicitly criticize groups such as African Americans because of the prevalence of single-parent households in that group. Similarly, the conviction that hard work is an important value among European ethnics can be used as a way of blaming those groups who suffer from persistently high levels of unemployment for their economic problems. Waters (1990: 147) suggests that "symbolic ethnicity persists because of its 'fit' with racist beliefs." Thus, in the ethnoracial pentagon (Hollinger 1995) that

has emerged during the post-civil rights era, non-Europeans in the new ethnic dispensation continue to be relegated to various locations of subordination and exclusion based on differing perceptions of these groups by the
hegemonic group (Winant 1994, 1999).

The new African American dilemma

Swedish economist Gunnar Myrdal's *An American Dilemma*, a monumental
study sponsored by the Carnegie Corporation and published in 1944, was
primarily devoted to chronicling the political, economic, and cultural forces
that had shaped the black experience in the US. In addition, it advanced a
thesis that – though appreciating the complexity of American race relations
– offered a remarkably simple prognosis concerning the future. The dilemma
noted in the title of the book had to do with the conflict between the national
ideals of freedom and equality for all and the reality of a legacy of black oppression and exclusion. Myrdal was convinced that in the end the dilemma
would be resolved by the realization of these key American values. He was
an advocate of assimilation who based his assessment of the future on the
assumption that the nation had a unified cultural system with commonly
shared core values. The race problem was located in the white mind, which,
as long as it maintained prejudicial views that were translated into discrimination, would ensure that the dilemma would persist. Thus, the solution to
the race problem would occur when whites rooted out their own racism and
treated blacks in accordance with the demands of the key cultural values
associated with freedom and equality. Quite remarkable was Myrdal's lack
of emphasis on ethnic competition and the potential role to be played by a
social movement of the oppressed, the latter being a curious lacuna insofar
as the book appeared just as the modern civil rights movement got underway.

The civil rights movement blossomed during the 1950s, at a time of heightened Cold War tensions and during a period of unprecedented economic prosperity. The former was significant because in the propaganda battles waged
by the US and the Soviet Union, instances of virulent racist violence, such as
the brutal murder of Emmett Till, played into the hands of the nation's enemies. The latter was important because at a time when there was a growing demand for workers and unemployment levels were very low, competition
for jobs declined, leading to a reduction in interracial conflict.

In this climate, the modern civil rights movement developed. It built itself
in part on long-established organizations such as the NAACP and the Urban
League, but also on newer organizations such as the Congress for Racial
Equality (CORE), the Southern Christian Leadership Conference (SCLC), and
the Student Nonviolent Coordinating Committee (SNCC). These newer organizations shared a strategic focus on nonviolent protest – including a will-

ingness to engage in civil disobedience – while the older organizations were more inclined to seek redress for injustice and inequality through the courts and the legislative process (Morris 1984). Thus, it was the Legal Defense Fund of the NAACP that fought a long battle in the courts to end school segregation. The newer organizations, meanwhile, were responsible for taking democracy into the streets.

The early period of the movement focused on challenges to the southern Jim Crow system. Thus, in 1953 a boycott of the municipal bus system in Baton Rouge, Louisiana, challenged the "back of the bus" requirement. Two years later a similar effort in Montgomery, Alabama, catapulted Rosa Parks into the national spotlight and served to launch the career of Dr. Martin Luther King, Jr. The movement combined protest tactics with court challenges. In various cities similar nonviolent actions were undertaken, including the sit-ins at the segregated lunch counter at Greensboro, North Carolina's, Woolworth store, and the CORE-sponsored Freedom Rides intended to affect a federal ban on segregated interstate buses. Related to these challenges to segregation were efforts aimed at political empowerment. These included voter registration drives in several southern states, capped by the 1964 Freedom Summer, the massive voter registration project in Mississippi. The number of movement initiatives grew slowly during the early 1950s and increased substantially thereafter. A dramatic escalation of activities occurred in the first half of the 1960s, culminating in a massive March on Washington in 1963. This phase of the movement effectively ended by the later part of the decade (McAdam 1982; Morris 1984).

Throughout this period, white responses varied considerably. On the one hand, black protest met with stiff resistance. Political elites in the south sought to preserve the Jim Crow system. Two particularly relevant challenges were those of Arkansas Governor Orval Faubus, who attempted to stop the integration of Little Rock's Central High School, and Alabama's Governor George Wallace, who similarly sought to prevent blacks from being admitted to the University of Alabama. Citizens Councils were founded in many communities to provide a base for white resistance, while terrorist groups such as the Ku Klux Klan experienced a revival. When the movement directed its energies to combating the *de facto* segregation in nonsouthern states, it met with intense resistance to integration (Gerstle 1995). On the other hand, many whites began to react negatively to incidents of violence against unarmed, nonviolent protesters. The unleashing of police dogs on demonstrators, the indiscriminate beatings, and similar acts of violence reached the attention of audiences via the mass media, and in particular television, which broadcast these events to a national audience. As the leadership of the civil rights movement well understood, it was essential that they make their case for dramatic change to this "conscience constituency."

The tumultuous events of the 1950s and 1960s produced a watershed in the history of blacks in the United States. The collective mobilization of the modern civil rights movement resulted in the demise of Jim Crow and the dawn of a new epoch in race relations. The judicial and legislative impacts were far reaching. The landmark 1954 Supreme Court decision *Brown v. Board of Education of Topeka* revisited the "separate but equal" doctrine of the 1886 *Plessy v. Ferguson* decision by introducing social-scientific evidence that revealed that segregation and racial inequality went hand in hand. Thus, the court ruling paved the way for promoting the integration of public schools. In the following decade, the US Congress passed three pieces of legislation that sought to remedy a three-century legacy of discrimination: the Civil Rights Act of 1964, which forbade discrimination in employment and education; the Voting Rights Act of 1965, which ensured blacks the right to political participation in the south; and the Housing Act of 1968, which prohibited racial discrimination in renting or selling housing. At the same time, President Lyndon Johnson declared a "War on Poverty," that though explicitly articulated in class-specific terms, had a disproportionate impact on blacks, who were over-represented in the ranks of the poor.

At the zenith of the civil rights movement, a more militant period emerged that suggested a legitimation crisis and a sense that more radical changes were needed to overcome the racial oppression of blacks. It took the form of Black Power, which was ideologically influenced by the Black Nationalism of Marcus Garvey and in some quarters by socialism. Black nationalists sought to achieve power and economic development without the promotion of racial integration. Part of the reason for this antipathy towards integration was the suspicion that whites may proclaim a desire to integrate, but had no real intention of actually doing so. This suspicion about the good faith of whites could be seen among the members of the Nation of Islam, who argued for racial purity and self-determination, but like Garvey tended to espouse a version of Black Capitalism.

On the other hand, influenced by Third World liberation struggles, the Black Panthers also advanced the idea of self-determination, but were also advocates of socialist internationalism. In so doing, they sought to link Black Nationalism to class struggle (Bush 1999). It should be noted that similar manifestations of militancy occurred among Native Americans in the Red Power Movement and among Mexicans in Chicano politics in general and the Brown Berets in particular. The Panthers became the victims of intense political repression and by the early 1970s the organization was moribund. While most of the disenfranchised in the black community did not join these or other militant organizations, their anger at the perceived slowness of racial progress was expressed by a wave of urban riots that swept the nation, commencing with the Harlem/Bedford-Stuyvesant riot of 1964 and the Watts riot of 1965 and extending into the early 1970s, resulting in hundreds of deaths, thousands of injured, and millions of dollars in property damage.

Joseph T. Rhea (1996) has argued that what has become known as "identity politics" has its roots in the civil rights movement, but ought to be seen as in some respects distinct from it. This is an example of Taylor's (1992) politics of recognition. Rhea has described this manifestation of identity politics as the "Racial Pride Movement." For blacks, Rhea contrasts two divergent efforts to wrestle with the legacy of the past and present aspirations. On the one hand, there is the anti-assimilationist identity politics of the Black Power movement in the 1960s and Afrocentrist thought since the 1980s. On the other hand, there is the inclusionist goal evident in the movement to establish a national holiday in honor of Martin Luther King, Jr. Both instances were manifestations of efforts within the African American community to challenge the lingering badges of inferiority that a long legacy of racist thought had perpetuated in the minds of not only the dominant white race, but within the oppressed black race as well.

To what extent did the civil rights movement achieve its goals, and where did it fail? How different were American race relations in the aftermath of the movement compared to the preceding period? Though answers to these questions produce a wide range of responses from scholars in the field, on the basis of many measures, one would have to conclude that genuine improvements have occurred, while at the same time it is clear that glaring and persistent problems and inequalities remain. Turning first to the matter of prejudice – or what Gordon would refer to as "attitude receptional assimilation" – improvement is evident. The post-civil rights era has been characterized by a significant decline in older forms of racist thought. A substantial majority of white Americans endorse racial equality and integration in principle (Jaynes & Williams 1989; Sniderman & Carmines 1997). However cautiously one needs to view public opinion surveys, using these as indicators of white attitudes towards blacks leads to the conclusion that the nation has undergone substantial gains over the past half century. At the same time, there is a more troubling side to contemporary white attitudes. Lawrence Bobo (2001: 294) summarizes the situation in the following way:

> If one compared the racial attitudes prevalent in the 1940s with those commonly observed today, it is easy to be optimistic. A nation once comfortable as a deliberately segregationist and racially discriminatory society has not only abandoned that view, but now overtly, positively endorses the goals of racial integration and equal treatment. There is no sign whatsoever of retreat from this ideal, despite events that many thought would call it into question. The magnitude, steadiness, and breadth of this change should be lost on no one. The death of Jim Crow racism has left us in an uncomfortable place, however: a state of laissez-faire racism. We have high ideals, but cannot agree on the depth of the remaining problem – we are open to integration, but in very limited terms and only in specific areas.

Bobo's analysis, in other words, argues that although the second half of the twentieth century witnessed a decline in racial prejudice and a general endorsement of the principle of fair play, this did not necessarily translate into policies designed to redress the legacy of segregation. This is particularly evident in the two most controversial policies to emerge out of the civil rights era: school busing to achieve integration and affirmative action. Busing was a policy for facilitating the desegregation of public schools, a plan of action that arose as a response to the *Brown v. Board of Education* ruling that school systems must move to desegregate "with all deliberate speed." In the period between 1964 and 1973, the percentage of blacks in the south attending schools with whites rose from 2 percent to 46 percent. While the initial phase of desegregation focused on the *de jure* segregation in the Jim Crow south, it also came to include a concern for the *de facto* segregation characteristic elsewhere in the nation.

Intense white opposition to school integration arose and led to the phenomenon know as "white flight." This took two forms, and was felt most intensely in urban public schools: (1) moving from urban to suburban school districts; and (2) enrolling students in parochial schools, or especially in the south, in newly created "Christian academies." Although the relationship between white flight and busing is complicated, by the 1980s many urban school systems were made up of only a minority of white students. For example, the white student population was only 4 percent in Washington DC, 8 percent in Atlanta, and 12 percent in Detroit. Even within schools a form of "resegregation within desegregated schools" often occurred as special academic programs effectively created what amounted to two schools within one, and each was racially quite distinct (Jaynes & Williams 1989: 76–83).

While busing became less controversial over time, affirmative action has continued throughout its career to generate intense controversy. Affirmative action is not concerned with racial integration *per se*, but rather with improving the socioeconomic status of blacks (and other minority groups). The rationale behind affirmative action plans is that merely terminating discriminatory laws and policies is not enough to realize genuine racial equality. This is due to the fact that over time such historical practices have enhanced the socioeconomic location of whites at the expense of blacks. The legal basis for affirmative action derives from Title VII of the Civil Rights Act of 1964, which banned employment discrimination and established the Equal Employment Opportunity Commission (EEOC) to investigate complaints and to refer violators to the Department of Justice. The Act did not mandate preferential treatment for minorities, but instead merely said that employers who discriminate must stop or face prosecution.

As John David Skrentny (1996) has pointed out, among the "ironies of affirmative action" is the fact that the policies to emerge within a decade were not the intentions of those responsible for the passage of the Act. In fact, the original purpose of the legislation appears to be to combat persistent patterns of ongoing discrimination. When the focus turned to the matter of the under-representation of blacks and other minorities in various occupations, a shift from what Carol Swain (2001: 321) has termed "soft" programs to stronger, preferential-treatment plans commenced. Among the key actors to promote this shift were both the liberal Lyndon Johnson and the conservative Richard Nixon. The idea of measuring success by the implementation of quotas appealed to government bureaucrats and also was embraced by corporate leaders. Affirmative action expanded to include a wide array of programs, including employment area concerns, such as those related to private-sector hiring and government contracting, but also involving the educational arena, where programs were implemented dealing with admission policies and scholarship and grant allocations.

Affirmative action became something of a lighting rod for conflict. Not only did conservatives oppose it, but so did many liberals, leading Stephen Steinberg (2000) to contend that the "capitulation" of liberals on this issue is an indication of the degree to which a racial backlash has sought to undo the advances brought about by the civil rights movement. The major complaint of opponents reflected the importance attached to individualism in American culture. It contended that preferential programs amounted to a form of "reverse discrimination" (Glazer 1975). It was on this basis that a number of court challenges to affirmative action were initiated. The most highly publicized early case was *Allan Bakke v. Regents of the University of California* (1978), wherein the plaintiff complained that he had been unfairly denied admission to medical school because 16 of the 100 slots were targeted for "disadvantaged persons," which in practice meant racial minorities. In this case, the Supreme Court ruled that the set-asides were unacceptable and demanded that Bakke be admitted. While he was, the Court also made clear that affirmative action in principle was not unconstitutional.

However, in recent years, with a considerably more conservative Supreme Court, recent judicial rulings have called the constitutional issue into question. This is seen perhaps most vividly in another university admission case, that of *Hopwood v. Texas* (1995). In this case, the white female litigant claimed that she had been denied admission to the University of Texas Law School as a result of the existence of the institution's affirmative action program, which relied on numerical goals in its quest to increase the numbers for underrepresented groups. The Court struck down the program as unconstitutional, concluding that, "The law school may not use race as a factor in deciding which applicants to admit" (quoted in Skrentny 2000: 282). In addition to such rulings, affirmative action came under assault in other ways, most vividly in California, where the electorate passed Proposition 209, which prohibited state-sponsored affirmative action programs.

The specific arguments over affirmative action must be located within a general assessment of the socioeconomic and educational situation of African Americans. In drawing conclusions, it is important to note that while at some level generalizations about the black community as a whole are valid, it is also crucial to realize that the community is increasingly divided between those who appear to be making it and those who are not. This distinction forms the basis of William Julius Wilson's (1978) "declining significance of race thesis." He argues that the current race relations regime is different from its two predecessors – the antebellum era when a caste system prevailed, and the Jim Crow era where class acquired significance for blacks that it did not have earlier, but nonetheless where race continued to play a more powerful role in shaping life chances. Today, he contends, class is coming to play a more consequential role than race in shaping the life chances of African Americans. Wilson (1978: 151) depicts a split within the black community along class lines, describing this bifurcation in the following way:

> On the one hand, poorly trained and educationally limited blacks of the inner city, including that growing number of black teenagers and young adults, see their job prospects increasingly restricted to the low-wage sector, their unemployment rates soaring to record levels, their labor-force participation rates declining, their move out of poverty slowing, and their welfare roles increasing. On the other hand, talented and educated blacks are experiencing unprecedented job opportunities in the growing government and corporate sectors, opportunities that are at least comparable to those of whites with equivalent qualifications.

Blacks have witnessed a significant expansion in educational and employment opportunities and the black middle class has grown considerably in recent decades. As recently as 1960, the black middle class constituted only 13.4 percent of the black population, compared to 44.1 percent for whites. By 1981, the figure for blacks had risen to 37.8 percent, while that for whites had risen to 54.3 percent (Landry 1987: 68, 291). Not only had it grown, but the contemporary black middle class is no longer confined to the black ghetto. Levels of home ownership and suburban living among this segment of the black population have risen. Due to opportunities afforded this class sector of the black community, according to Reynolds Farley (1999: 123), "the 1980s were the first years in which there were unambiguous decreases in black–white residential segregation." Blacks have entered the political arena, and are now one of the key constituencies in the Democratic Party. In terms of racial pride, blacks in professional sports and the entertainment industry have assumed roles of genuine prominence. One need only think of the impact of Michael Jordan and Bill Cosby to get some sense of the changes that have occurred in the collective conscience. These and similar changes have led some neoconservative thinkers to proclaim that we have reached the "end of racism" (D'Souza 1995).

However, such a conclusion overlooks a great deal. In the first place, white resistance to black improvement has been far more persistent throughout the post-civil rights period than this view appreciates (Feagin & Vera 1995). Moreover, while the black middle class has grown, it has not achieved parity with the white middle class and serious gaps in income remain. Perhaps more significantly, as Melvin L. Oliver and Thomas M. Shapiro (1995) have pointed out, if one looks at wealth and not income, the disparities between the black and white middle classes is stark. Blacks, they discovered, own only 15 cents for every dollar of wealth possessed by whites.

Moreover, despite the changes in levels of prejudice noted above, discrimination remains a serious problem. While this may have a greater negative impact on poor blacks, even middle-class blacks continue to be victimized by subtle and not-so-subtle forms of discrimination in everyday life, including avoidance, poor service, verbal epithets, harassment, and threats (Feagin 1991). For example, research by the Urban Institute has discovered that housing and employment discrimination is far more common than the public at large thinks is the case (Fix & Struyk 1993). While the black middle class has moved from central cities to the suburbs at an expanded rate, this has not necessarily meant that they have moved from segregated to integrated neighborhoods. Indeed, the collar suburbs of many large cities today have become black communities as whites have headed to outer ring suburbs. The case of the Chicago suburb of Matteson, Illinois, is illustrative. In 1980 the community was 84 percent white. Fifteen years later, it was only 47 percent white (Terry 1996: A6). This white flight is not a response to avoiding poverty and its attendant problems, as has been argued to explain earlier white flight from cities. Blacks arriving in Matteson were members of the middle class. Thus, the movement of whites out of the community is a reflection of Bobo's (2001: 294) claim that there are severe limits to the willingness of whites to integrate. In short, the gains of the black middle class are decidedly mixed. The black middle class is pointed to as the success story of the post-civil rights era for good reason. Yet, it is also clear that they not only confront newer forms of institutional discrimination, but are not immune from the older forms as well.

For the other sector of the black community, those whom William Julius Wilson (1987) has referred to as the "truly disadvantaged," the world not only continues to be segregated, but in some cases there is evidence of even greater levels of segregation than in the past, leading some researchers to refer to this as "hypersegregation" (Massey & Denton 1993). Inner-city blacks in such neighborhoods attend segregated schools, worship in segregated churches, shop in segregated stores, and so forth. The exodus of the black middle class from inner cities for new neighborhoods has left behind only the poorest of the poor in communities increasingly disconnected to the larger urban economy and bereft of the institutional social supports that once helped ghetto dwellers to survive in a hostile world. These are communities hard hit by deindustrialization, where residents are forced to cope with the consequences of what happens to neighborhoods "when work disappears" (Wilson 1996). In other words, for this segment of the African American community, life is more rather than less difficult than in the past.

Social problems – including the explosion of drug use, high crime levels, endemic violence, the pervasiveness of gangs, the problems associated with teen pregnancy, and low academic achievement – have taken a huge toll (Anderson 1990). To appreciate the depth of the problems one need only realize that the leading cause of death among young black males is murder, usually at the hands of another young black male. Add to this the fact that blacks have been particularly hard hit by the AIDs epidemic. As a consequence of all of these problems, a segment of poor blacks engulfed in a pervasive anomie has concluded that it continues to be victimized by the "scar of race" and will never realize the American Dream (Sniderman & Piazza 1993). Cornel West (1993: 15–31) has concluded that the most appropriate term for describing the worldview of this sector of black America is "nihilism."

The lives of blacks at the lower end of the socioeconomic ladder have been complicated by deindustrialization and by the arrival of new immigrants since the 1960s. The decline in the number of manufacturing jobs has prevented many blacks from the kind of upward mobility available to unskilled workers in the past. New immigrants have posed a new challenge insofar as they compete with blacks for unskilled jobs (Bean & Bell-Rose 1999: 24), and as their numbers grow, also become a new political constituency that can dilute the impact of blacks.

In the aftermath of the conservative administrations of Ronald Reagan and his successor George Bush, levels of class-based social inequality became considerably more pronounced. The neoliberalism of the Clinton years did little to remedy this trend. For the haves, the past two decades have been very good, while for the have-nots life has grown more difficult. Moreover, the number of people in the ranks of the have-nots has grown as levels of poverty have increased, particularly in the inner cities of major metropolitan areas. What this suggests is that class and race converge insofar as the majority of the residents of the nation's inner cities are racial minorities – largely black or Latino.

Wilson (1999: 64) attributes many of the economic problems confronting lower income blacks to transformations brought about by the new global economy. He continues to argue for the prominence of class-related factors in contributing to this situation, and in seeking solutions to it. Thus, he makes a case for the creation of a multiracial coalition of workers and for progressive legislative initiatives such as full-employment legislation and other universal entitlement programs rather than race-specific ones. In so doing, he is urging policies akin to those of the social democracies of western Europe.

However, at the same time, he argues that insofar as racial discrimination and segregation continue to contribute to the problems confronting blacks, there is a need for a renewal of commitment to race-specific affirmative action – or as he renames it, "affirmative opportunity." While sympathetic to the argument on behalf of a class-specific version of affirmative action, he argues that because race cannot be reduced to class, color-blind policies cannot in and of themselves solve the problems, and therefore race-based policies are also necessary (Wilson 1999: 95–116).

American Indians in the aftermath of the Red Power movement

Part of Lyndon Johnson's Great Society expansion of the welfare state entailed an effort to revive aspects of the New Deal's Indian Reorganization Act. In addition, it sought to address the endemic poverty and attendant social problems that characterized reservation life. The significance of these efforts was that Indians were given more power than they had previously had in controlling their communities. Antipoverty, educational, and cultural programs were funded through the Office of Economic Opportunity, and thus often circumvented the much-criticized Bureau of Indian Affairs and many traditional tribal leaders perceived to be pawns of the BIA. The result was the outbreak of considerable internal conflict, linked to the birth of the Red Power movement (Nagel 1996). Unsatisfied with what they viewed as the paternalism of the federal government, militants demanded greater efforts aimed at self-determination. The Red Power movement began at the local level with such confrontational tactics as "fish-ins" and hunting out of season. Defying state laws was intended to highlight the fact that the states had violated treaty rights, which guaranteed American Indians special fishing and hunting privileges.

The movement was catapulted into the national spotlight with three dramatic episodes in political theater: the 1969 occupation of Alcatraz in San Francisco Bay; the 1972 Trail of Broken Treaties March that culminated in the occupation of the BIA headquarters in Washington DC; and the 1973 takeover of Wounded Knee, the site of an 1890 massacre of 150 unarmed Sioux Indians. This movement played a singularly important role in encouraging ethnic renewal. It aimed to resist the melting pot and to stimulate instead a renewed vitality of American Indian culture and society (Cornell 1988: 187–201; Nagel 1996). Although the militancy of the era waned over time, considerable conflict persists. Recent examples include the ongoing court battles over hunting and fishing rights and land-related treaty disputes. One of the consequences of the assertiveness of American Indians is an anti-Indian backlash on the part of whites.

Today life on reservations continues to be colored by deeply rooted poverty. Housing is considerably worse than that of most Americans, while unemployment and underemployment rates are exceedingly high (Snipp 1989: 96–126, 259). Linked to poverty are a variety of health and social problems. American Indians may be the least healthy ethnic group in the US. Their infant mortality rate is higher than the national average, and their life expectancy is 10 years shorter than that of most Americans. The community suffers from both extremely high suicide and homicide rates. Alcoholism is a serious problem, with the alcohol-related death rate registering at five times that of all other racial groups. Linked to this problem is fetal alcohol syndrome, which takes a major toll within the Indian community.

During the Reagan years, James Watt, the Secretary of the Department of Interior (in which the BIA is located) and extreme right-wing politician, contended that reservations were socialist and speculated about reviving the idea of termination. While this did not happen, nonetheless during the past two decades little serious effort has been undertaken by the federal government to improve the quality of life for American Indians while also helping in efforts aimed at cultural preservation. Meanwhile, the efforts of reservation leaders have met with only limited success. At present, economic development plans tend to revolve around establishing gambling casinos on reservation land (permissible because they are not bound by state laws regarding gambling) or using such lands for the disposal of hazardous wastes. Not surprisingly, both of these endeavors are controversial within the community and have contributed to significant internal conflict.

Given the economic and social problems on reservations, increasing numbers of people have left them for cities. Though the movement began in the 1950s, it has increased during the past two decades. Sizeable enclaves exist in such cities as Los Angeles, Chicago, Denver, San Francisco, Phoenix, and Minneapolis–St. Paul. Urban Indians are far more likely to intermarry – and indeed they have a high intermarriage rate. Moreover, though urban poverty exists, so do opportunities for economic improvement. Cities have been crucibles for both an emerging pan-Indian identity and for assimilation. For urban Indians, ethnic identity becomes more a matter of choice than is the case for counterparts on reservations. As a result, it appears that the future of the more upwardly mobile urban American Indians will likely be quite different from that of reservation dwellers.

The new immigrants

Between 1924 and 1965, immigration did not cease, but it ebbed considerably. Between 1931 and 1960, the total number of immigrants (which includes refugees during the Second World War and Displaced Persons in the war's immediate aftermath) was approximately 4,000,000. In other words, the total during this three-decade period was less than half the 8,800,000 immigrants that arrived in the single decade between 1901 and 1910. As figure 1 indicates, it also stands in stark contrast to the levels reached in each of the decades from 1970 to century's end.

The resumption of mass immigration after 1965 was made possible by changes in US immigration laws. In the 1954 Immigration and Naturalization Act (McCarran–Walter Act), although the national-origins system was preserved, Asians and other groups excluded entirely by the 1924 Act were allowed to enter in small numbers. However, it was only with an amendment to the Immigration and Naturalization Act in 1965 ending the national-origins system that the way was paved for the current wave of immigration, which has been dominated by groups from Latin America, Asia, and the Caribbean. Each decade since its passage has witnessed a rise in immigration levels. The figure for legal immigration between 1971 and 1980 was 4,500,000. That figure rose in the next decade to 7,300,000. By 1997, the figure was 6,900,000 (US Census Bureau 1999: 10). According to Roger Waldinger and Jennifer Lee (2001: 32), "the intake during the century's last decade exceeded that in the first decade by 500,000."

The demographic impact of this new wave of immigration can be seen by considering the following facts. In terms of the sheer number of newcomers, the United States is at present the leading immigrant-receiving nation in the world. As a percentage of the total population, the foreign-born comprise 9.3 percent of the total population, a level the country has not seen since the early decades of twentieth century. However, this figure is lower than those registered at the dawn of the twentieth century because the overall population of the nation in the year 2000 was three times larger than it was a century earlier. Historically, European-origin whites made up a very large percentage of the overall population. In 1950, for example, the figure was 87 percent. While it is too early to speak, as some forecasters have, about the dawn of the "majority minority," it is certainly the case that racial minorities will constitute a larger part of the overall mix than at any other time.

In addition to the different points of origin of today's immigrants compared to those from the previous period of mass immigration, there are a number of other features that make this wave distinctive. In the first place, it is characterized by far lower levels of return migration. There are also far more undocumented or illegal immigrants, refugees and asylum seekers, and nonimmigrants who might become immigrants (such as tourists, foreign students, and temporary workers) than in the past (Zhou 2001: 204). Because the 1965 immigration law encouraged professionals to migrate, the number of middle-class or potentially middle-class immigrants is larger today compared to earlier periods (Kivisto 1993: 94). Finally, the origins of the new immigrants have had implications for the American religious landscape. On the one hand, given the fact that Latino groups are heavily Roman Catholic, their presence has resulted in the growth of that religious community. On the other hand, due to the presence of Asians and Middle Easterners, three major world religions, Islam, Buddhism, and Hinduism, are now making their presence felt (Warner & Wittner 1998).

The browning of the US

As figure 2 indicates, Latinos are by far the largest of the new immigrant pan-ethnic groups. Constituting 12.5 percent of the population today, depending on how one factors mixed-race people into the picture, the 2000 Census reports that the Latino population is either slightly larger or slightly smaller than the African American. What is clear is that they will soon replace African Americans as the largest racial minority if they have not already done so. Already in a number of cities, including some of the nation's largest, such as Los Angeles, Houston, and Phoenix, Latinos outnumber blacks. Mexicans are the largest of the Latino groups – with over 3,500,000 arriving between 1981 and 2000 – followed by Puerto Ricans and Cubans. Puerto Ricans, it should be noted, are not strictly speaking immigrants given the territorial status of the island. Since the political conflict between the US and Cuban governments makes the free flow of immigrants impossible, the Cuban population is not growing like other Latino groups. In addition to these groups, smaller numbers have arrived from various points in Central America, South America, and the Caribbean. Given the fact that Mexicans have a long history in the US, the Mexican American is by far the largest Latino group, and it is also by far the largest component of the new immigrants. Indeed, 66 percent of Latinos currently in the US are Mexican, compared to only 9 percent for Puerto Ricans, the second largest group (US Census Bureau 2001: 1).

The three largest Latino groups share many things in common besides a language, but they also exhibit important differences (Bean & Tienda 1987). The Mexican community is not only the largest, but because of its long history in the US, contains an extremely diverse population. It includes people who were in regions of what later became the United States long before the arrival of Anglos to the area, and also includes illegal immigrants who crossed the border today in search of work. Due to the permeability of the border, Mexicans frequently head for *El Norte* when political or economic conditions become difficult. They fled to the US in the aftermath of the Mexican Revolution in 1910. Between 1942 and 1964 they were encouraged to work in US agricultural fields as contract laborers prohibited from seeking citizenship under the terms of the "bracero program." Finally, since 1965 they have immigrated in increasingly large numbers (Gutierrez 1995).

A well-established ethnic community has existed for many decades and out of it have arisen political demands for an end to discrimination and a

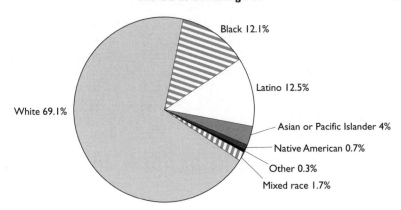

Figure 2 Ethnic groups in the US, 2000
Source: US Census Bureau 2001.

greater voice in social and political life. The Chicano politics of the 1960s promoted ethnic pride and entailed an assertive demand for improvements in economic and educational opportunities and greater political power in regions where Mexicans were highly concentrated (Gutierrez 1995; Rhea 1996). Mexicans were, for example, the most important ethnic group involved in the multi-ethnic coalition that made up the United Farm Workers movement. Given the prominent role they have played historically as agricultural workers, their role in this unionization campaign is not surprising. The militancy of the period ended by the mid-1970s, with mixed results in achieving their goals.

The poverty rate among Mexican Americans has risen since the mid-1980s. Today the group has a higher poverty rate than African Americans, and a higher than average unemployment rate (Blank 2001: 32). Economist George Borjas (2000: 15–49), a critic of current immigration policies, contends that this is the case in no small part because of the fact that there has been a decline in the human capital of more recent immigrants (with educational attainment levels being of particular importance for his argument). While not all scholars of the new wave of immigrants concur with this claim or concur with his position on immigration control, it is the case that the sheer number of recently arrived unskilled and comparatively poorly educated Mexicans who have not yet had time to gain a real foothold in the US economy can help account for this recent rise in poverty. Connected to this, Mexicans Americans have a high school dropout rate. Moreover, as with other disadvantaged groups, barrio residents confront a range of social problems, including the particularly destructive impact of gangs and drugs (Moore & Pinderhughes 1993).

On the other hand, the Mexican American middle class has grown – chiefly composed of third-generation ethnics and beyond. Thus, in a trend that parallels that of African Americans, this community too is increasingly bifurcated between a middle class moving into the mainstream and their poorer counterparts left behind in inner-city barrios. The middle class is likely to reside in suburbs and thus is spatially separated from the poor (Alba et al. 1999: 451). They are more likely to find careers in white-collar professions and to own their own businesses. In contrast, more recent arrivals are typically located in the bottom tier of the dual labor market, working in the garment industry, in service industries such as hotels and restaurants, and as agricultural laborers. In the Midwest, they constitute a key component of the workforce in the meat-packing industry, and as that industry has increasingly located operations in rural communities, their presence has transformed heretofore ethnically homogeneous communities in the agricultural heartland (Stull et al. 1992).

Given their geographic concentration in southwestern border states, Mexicans have become increasingly important politically. Both major parties have courted their vote (in the 2000 Presidential elections, both George W. Bush and Al Gore addressed Latino audiences in Spanish), although at the moment their allegiance remains firmly located in the Democratic Party. Efforts to mobilize Mexican American voters have produced notable successes at the ballot box as several thousand Mexican ethnics have been elected to various federal, state, and local offices. At the same time, they remain underrepresented given their size in the overall population.

Turning to Puerto Ricans and Cubans offers a study in contrasts. Neither group has as long a history in the US as Mexicans have had. Although Puerto Ricans have been citizens of the US since 1917, large-scale movement from the island to the mainland did not begin until after the Second World War. Perhaps more than any other group, Puerto Ricans exhibit considerable "circular migration," moving back and forth depending on where better economic opportunities present themselves at any particular moment (Fitzpatrick 1987). In the Cuban case, the exodus only really commenced with the installation of the revolutionary government of Fidel Castro in 1959 and with the decisions that led to it becoming a client state of the Soviet Union. Cubans entered the US in several distinct waves, in part of a cat-and-mouse game of international relations between the two nations: the "Golden Exiles" in the early 1960s, the "Freedom Flight" immigrants who arrived between 1965 and 1973, and the "Marielitos" in 1980 (Pedraza 1992). These represented distinctive immigrant waves characterized by considerably different levels of capital – financial, human, and social. Thus, the first wave consisted of the better off in Cuba who were hostile to communism, and thus were hailed as welcome refugees. In stark contrast, the Marielitos consisted of social undesirables, including convicts, that the Cuban regime was glad to rid itself of, and which posed serious problems and resistance to their presence in the US.

Puerto Ricans are the poorest of the Latino groups, experiencing high levels of unemployment, underemployment, and welfare dependency. In New York City, many have found work in low-paying blue-collar jobs, especially in the service sector. Given their limited resources and relative lack of economic success, their ethnic community is more fragile and less institutionally complete than either the Mexican or Cuban (Fitzpatrick 1987). In contrast, the Cubans are the most economically successful Latino group, due largely to the fact that the earliest people to emigrate from Cuba came from the upper and middle classes and brought both financial resources and educational credentials that gave them a distinct advantage.

Cubans in Miami have created an ethnic enclave economy that has provided opportunities for entrepreneurial success. At the same, it has benefited Cuban workers, especially those with limited English-language abilities. The community has been quite cohesive and has been able to exert considerable political clout, especially in south Florida, where Cubans have aligned themselves – unlike other Latino groups – with the Republican Party. This was evident in the soap-opera drama that developed around Elián González. The older generation remains rooted in the ethnic community, still fighting an ideological war with the Castro regime. Younger Cuban Americans, by contrast, are moving out of the community at a growing rate. Among the American-born generations, English is generally the language of choice, they are less likely than the older generation to claim to have encountered discrimination, and they have a comparatively high level of educational attainment (Portes & Schauffler 1996; Rumbaut 1996).

While Latino groups share much in common, this brief overview also points to significant differences among groups, and thus to the difficulties involved in efforts to get particular nationality groups to begin to perceive themselves in more pan-ethnic terms. However, they do share one thing in common that makes them unique compared to earlier immigrants and to other contemporary immigrants: their overall size as a percentage of the immigrant population and their close proximity to their homelands. These two factors contribute to a situation that facilitates the development of transnational social spaces and the emergence of a regional cultural cosmos steeped in Latino culture.

Asians: strangers from a different shore

The Asian presence in the US has also grown dramatically during the past three decades. Collectively, Asian Americans are sometimes referred to as a "model minority" (Takaki 1989) because they have higher per capita incomes and educational attainment levels and lower levels of poverty than other ethnic groups. Indeed, in many ways they appear at least on the surface to be doing better than whites. At the same time, they confront a variety of exclusionary policies and practices that prevent their full incorporation into the mainstream (Tuan 1998).

The largest Asian immigrant groups include Filipinos, Chinese, Koreans, Vietnamese, and groups from the Indian subcontinent. Of these groups, only the Chinese had a significant presence before 1965 (along with the Japanese, who have in recent decades not been major contributors to the new immigration). Due to the combination of an earlier presence and substantial migration since 1970, the Chinese American community has grown dramatically. Not only have the old historic Chinatowns in major centers such as New York City, San Francisco, and Los Angeles experienced dramatic growth, but in addition new middle-class enclaves have arisen in places such as Monterey Park, California, which Timothy Fong (1994) has referred to as "the first suburban Chinatown." Thus, at present the Chinese constitute a diverse group, including on the one hand middle-class Chinese whose ancestors have been in the US for several generations, and on the other hand recent arrivals who do not speak English and who therefore are highly dependent on the powerful business interests that control Chinatowns. Thus, their circumstances bear a resemblance to those of Mexican Americans. Poorer new arrivals live in crowded Chinatowns, work long hours for low wages (often in Chinese-owned establishments), and confront a range of economic and social problems that make adjustment difficult. On the other hand, much of the middle class has chosen to live in the suburbs, where they no longer live in isolation from the larger society (Fong 1994).

In contrast to the Chinese, both the Filipino and Korean populations are overwhelmingly the result of the post-1965 immigration. Although people from a wide spectrum of Philippine society have emigrated to the US, a significant number are college-educated professionals, with a particularly large number having been trained in the health professions, including doctors, nurses, and pharmacists. As a result, despite the fact that it is typical to experience a sustained period of occupational precariousness as they adjust to the new society, many appear to be gaining an economic foothold. Women play a prominent role here insofar as most nurses are women, and it is estimated that over 50,000 Filipina nurses work in the US, representing over half of the total foreign-trained nurses (Fong 2000: 25). In part because Filipinos are divided along regional and dialect lines, and due to internal conflicts over homeland politics, a powerful and coherent ethnic community has not evolved. This has accentuated the gulf between the first and second generations. The American-born generation that is currently coming of age tends to be quite acculturated and exhibits far less interest in the politics and culture of the homeland than is the case with their parents (Tizon 1999).

   Korean immigrants differ from the vast majority of the Korean population
in two respects. First, they are overwhelmingly Christian in a nation where
the vast majority of people are Buddhist. Second, a substantial number are
educated white-collar professionals. These cultural and economic factors
contribute in part to the fact that despite the relatively short time they have
been in the US, Koreans are, comparatively speaking, doing quite well. They
have an especially high level of self-employment. Many own small family-
run businesses, such as grocery stores, fruit stands, flower shops, repair shops,
liquor stores, and clothing stores. Though a partial explanation for this entrepreneurial activity, scholars are divided over the extent to which recent
arrivals have managed to get into business by relying on *Kye*, which are revolving credit associations within the Korean community (Min 1996: 102;
Light & Gold 2000: 114, 255). Many Korean businesses are located in inner-city black neighborhoods, and as a consequence considerable tension
has developed between blacks and Koreans. In the 1992 Los Angeles riot,
Korean stores were targeted by rioters, resulting in the destruction of more
than 1,000 Korean-owned businesses at a price tag of over $300,000,000
(Min 1996; Abelmann & Lie 1995). Korean Americans place a premium on
education as a means for their children to become economically successful.
Thus, it is quite clear that they do not wish that their offspring continue in
family-owned businesses, but instead want them to enter the world of the
professional classes.
   Collectively, although Asian Americans are a distinct numerical minority, their presence has become more consequential in recent decades, especially on the west coast and in major urban settlements elsewhere such as
New York City and Chicago. Thus, the Korean shopkeepers noted above,
Chinese workers in the garment industry, and many Asian students in colleges and universities are perceived by some members of other groups as a
competitive threat. On the other hand, Asian Americans have been held up
as a model of success. Without downplaying their genuine achievements,
two points are in order. First, as Deborah Woo (1999) has made clear, it is
important to disaggregate data on Asians, since some groups do far better
than others, and some within particular groups do far better than others
within the same group. As an example of the former, one need only point to
the Vietnamese (and other southeast Asians) to find groups that lag behind
the others economically and suffer from relatively high levels of poverty.
Regarding the former, the Chinese community is divided between those making it and those left in impoverished circumstances in Chinatowns, which
are beset with a variety of social problems, including those associated with
gangs and drugs. Second, the term "model minority" is often used to make
invidious comparisons between the Asian success story and the failures and
presumed personal shortcomings of blacks, Latinos, and American Indians.
The message amounts to a form of blaming the victim, suggesting that if

only these groups could emulate the work ethic and family values of the model minority, they too would be successful (Takaki 1989: 474–84).

Immigrant futures

What are the implications of the presence of the new immigrants taken as a whole for America? Reciprocally, what kinds of futures can the new arrivals expect for themselves and their children? Will the heirs of the new immigrants follow paths of inclusion that parallel the paths of earlier waves of immigrants? These are difficult questions to answer for two reasons. In the first place, the sheer diversity of the new immigrant groups makes generalizations difficult. Cultural differences, class differences, variations in the possession of cultural and social capital, the presence or lack of a preexisting ethnic community, and so forth make for marked differences among the newcomers. Second, since the second generation is only now coming of age, social scientists must be circumspect in drawing comparisons between the immigrants of today and those of yesterday (Portes & Zhou 1993; Perlman & Waldinger 1999; Portes & Rumbaut 2001). Third, there is a need to consider the shifting character of the nation's racialized ethnicity.

The economy is considerably different today from the past. While immigrants in the early twentieth century entered a capitalist economy characterized by a burgeoning manufacturing sector, today's advanced capitalist economy has substantially restricted the role of manufacturing. Instead, the two areas where major job creation has occurred are in the service sector and in the technology sector. The demand for unskilled labor is high in both sectors, while the latter also exhibits a high demand for skilled labor. Thus, present economic conditions provide opportunities at both the lowest and the higher tiers of the economy. Low-paying jobs are available to the majority of immigrants, especially if American workers do not want them, while for a more elite sector of immigrants, who arrive with high levels of human capital, rapid entrée into the middle class is possible.

The impact of recent immigrant is uneven. Around three-quarters of all new immigrants have settled in six states: California, New York, Texas, Florida, Illinois, and New Jersey. The distinctiveness of California should not be underestimated, as it has become home to over a third of all new immigrants (Tienda 1999: 132). It's not surprising that in this state the battle over whether or not to keep the doors open is most intense. Thus, political controversies over Proposition 187, bilingual education, and affirmative action in the state's public universities reflect the divisiveness resulting from current levels of immigration. It is also here that the new racial faultlines are most evident. The 1992 Los Angeles race riot has been described as the nation's "first multiethnic riot." As with the Watts riot in

1965, blacks were pitted against whites; however, unlike that earlier riot, Latinos and Asians were also involved (Sears 1994). Of particular importance was the conflict between blacks and Koreans, the latter often finding their businesses being targeted for attack (Abelmann & Lie 1995; Min 1996).

Drawing larger conclusions about the future of the salience of ethnicity and the nature of interethnic relations must be done circumspectly. However, what does appear to be the case is that the new immigrants have recast the nation's racialized ethnic landscape. Whereas in the past, the racial divide was defined in terms of whites and nonwhites, Peter Rose (1997) has suggested that in the future the racial faultline might be between blacks and nonblacks. One reason for this is that while the nation as a whole benefits from the presence of the new immigrants, blacks do not (Bean & Bell-Rose 1999; Borjas 2000). In fact, especially for unskilled workers, the competition for jobs has intensified and blacks have been the net losers while the immigrants are the net winners. Although Latinos have at the moment replaced blacks as the nation's poorest group, this is in no small part due to the fact that there are so many young new arrivals just getting a foothold in the economy. What this means in terms of a recasting of racial identities is uncertain. Will Asians – the so-called "model minority" – become white the way the Irish, southern Europeans, and eastern Europeans did? What about Latinos, who in terms of indices of economic and educational success are closer to blacks than whites or Asians? What are the chances that they will become white? If both pan-ethnic groups do become white, what does this mean for the two groups with the longest legacies of exclusion, blacks and American Indians?

Are the new immigrants following the trajectories of inclusion of earlier immigrants? Are they assimilating? In terms of such indices as home ownership, citizenship, learning English, intermarriage, and acculturation of values, it appears that the experience of today's immigrants and their children is in many respects comparable to that of earlier generations of immigrants (*Economist* 2000a: 13). Nonetheless, there are also salient differences reflecting a new historical moment. Richard Alba (1998: 18–24) has suggested that post-1965 immigrants may be exhibiting a new path to inclusion distinct from the older notion of assimilation. One such difference can be seen in what Alejandro Portes and Min Zhou (1993) refer to as "segmented assimilation." As I noted in chapter 1, in this scenario some immigrants become acculturated into mainstream values and behaviors, while others become acculturated into the adversarial culture of impoverished groups. This bifurcation results from what they describe as an "hourglass economy" in which those entering its bottom tiers find themselves confronting a bottleneck preventing upward mobility. Thus, the future is one of considerable complexity and uncertainty.

Toward a Transnational America?

What has been the impact of the new racial formation – the new racial pentagon – on what it means to be an American and on the continued efficacy of
the melting-pot image? For one thing, the melting pot as an ideal has been
rejected by many, and in its place has arisen the vision of the US as a
multicultural nation. This vision, harking back to Horace Kallen's (1924)
earlier cultural pluralist vision, valorizes the preservation of ethnic group
identities. However, despite the fear of some critics of multiculturalism that
it will lead to the "disuniting of America" (Schlesinger 1992), there is abundant evidence to suggest that assimilation is occurring. Nathan Glazer (1997:
119) describes assimilation today in the following way: "The word may be
dead, the concept may be disreputable, but the reality continues to flourish."
At the same time, however, he proclaims, "we are all multiculturalists now."

It is clear that many European-origin ethnics, despite the abundant evidence of assimilation, nonetheless are intent on preserving vestiges of their
ethnic identities long into the future. For them, assimilation is not perceived
to entail the deracination of ethnic identity, but instead allows for the possibility that one can be fully American while maintaining a distinctive ethnic
identity. Similarly, many new immigrants reject the old melting-pot ideal of
the 100-percent American. But more than that, they also reject the idea of
the hyphenated American. Instead, they are opting to be "ampersand Americans" (*Economist* 2000: 13). In other words, they are embracing
transnational identities in which they seek to become an American while
also preserving the homeland identity: American and Mexican, American
and Chinese, and so forth. Some are interested in the possibility of obtaining
dual citizenships. Many more remain actively involved in their homelands,
often by maintaining the ties of kinship and friendship, but also by remaining involved politically, economically, and culturally in the larger homeland
society (Levitt 2001). For Mexicans and other Latinos, transnationalism is
aided by geographic proximity that makes frequent trips home feasible. For
other groups, those within the groups with sufficient social and human capital
are able to become global villagers by taking advantage of communication
technologies and the relative ease of travel in order to forge transnational
identities (Portes 1996). Whether in the long run – when the third and beyond generations come of age – this will prove to be a permanent and distinctive feature of the new immigration, or a transition along the road to an
incorporation much like that encountered by earlier waves of immigrants,
remains an open question.

Voluntary ethnics and their offspring have choices about, as Glazer (1997:
120) puts it, "how they will define their place in American society." This, he
goes on to observe, makes the case of African Americans (and, I would also

add, American Indians) unique. These two groups, simply, have less latitude in terms of choice-making as the politics of exclusion continues to impact their lives to a greater extent than it does for other groups. To the extent that they live lives separate from the larger society – be it in a hypersegregated ghetto or on an isolated reservation – they inhabit a multicultural world whether they want to or not.

In this general context, what might be emerging is what Randolph Bourne (1977), writing at around the same time as Horace Kallen, called "transnational America." By this he meant an America open to the influence of distinctive ethnic identities. Whereas Kallen's pluralism and some versions of multiculturalism tend to treat ethnic identities and the core national culture as fixed and distinct, Bourne had a more dynamic view in mind, one that expected that ethnic groups would change as a result of their encounter with the larger American society. It also assumed, however, that American society would be transformed in positive ways by this encounter insofar as the core culture was subject to a constant process of reinvention. In a society that is today more open to diversity than it was during Bourne's lifetime, it might well be that a transnational America is in the making. However, it is certain that such a development will meet resistance and the outcome cannot be predicted.

As the next chapter – which turns to two other major settler nations, Canada and Australia – will show, this is not a phenomenon unique to the US. Indeed, these two nations have also become multicultural in recent decades and have begun to rethink what it means to be, respectively, Canadian and Australian. However, quite unlike the US, the national governments in both countries have played active roles in defining and advancing the cause of inclusion and multiculturalism.

CHAPTER THREE

Canada and Australia: Ethnic Mosaics and State-sponsored Multiculturalism

Along with the United States, Canada and Australia are the two other significant advanced industrial nations whose histories have been shaped by wide-scale immigration. This chapter, in conjunction with the preceding one, affords the basis for a comparative portrait of these three nations. At the outset it is worth noting two features that Canada and Australia share in common, but that serve to differentiate them from the US. First there is the matter of historical trajectories. While the birth of all three nations was the result of British colonial expansion, and thus all share the imprint of English customs, culture, laws, and language, only the US severed its political linkage with Britain. Both Canada and Australia remain part of the British Commonwealth to this day. Though for all intents and purposes they are today independent nations, the titular head of state in each country is Queen Elizabeth II. Though her role is symbolic, and the prime minister of each nation is responsible for domestic and foreign policy, nonetheless this role serves to highlight the continuing ties that bind these two settler states to Britain.

Second, Canada and Australia also share a demographic identity that distinguishes them from the United States. The population of Canada in 2000 was 31,000,000, while that for Australia was 19,000,000. These figures stand in sharp contrast to the 281,000,000 people in the US. Since each of these nations is around the same geographic size, with Canada being the largest and Australia the smallest, this means that these two countries are very thinly populated. The population density of the US is 69 persons per square mile, while the comparable figures for Canada and Australia are 7 and 6 respectively. Moreover, their populations are not evenly distributed across their landmasses. Rather, the overwhelming majority of Canadians lives along the nation's southern border with the

US, while Australians are heavily concentrated along their country's eastern coast.

In the context of these historical and geographic realities, the governments of Canada and Australia have in the past few decades been the international pioneers in forging state-sponsored multicultural policies. Indeed, whereas the terms assimilation and cultural pluralism were first used to describe the particularities of the US, the term multiculturalism originally gained currency in these two countries. At the moment, in contrast to the US and the nations of western Europe that will be discussed in the following two chapters, these two nations are unique insofar as they have implemented explicit multicultural policies that speak to an emerging national self-identity that is not only cognizant of the presence of considerable ethnic diversity, but also views that diversity as positive. How this came about in each of these nations will be the focus of attention in this chapter.

Canada: The Vertical Mosaic Revisited

Like the United States, Canada is a paradigmatic settler state with a similarly diverse population. Like the United States, European colonizers gained control of what would become the nation by subjugating native peoples and consigning them to social, economic, and political marginality. Like the United States, Canada's comparatively open immigration laws are a reflection of the fact that this resource-rich land needed immigration to meet labor demands, particularly as the nation shifted first from an agrarian to an industrial economy and more recently as it has become an advanced industrial society. Like the United States, immigrants have encountered differing levels of nativist hostility based on varied ethnocentric responses to particular groups. And, finally, as a consequence of prejudice and discrimination, again like the United States, some groups have managed to be incorporated into the mainstream more readily than others (Lipset 1990: 172–92).

However, Canada is not simply a mirror image of the United States. One salient difference that frames all other differences involves the respective roles of British and French ethnics in Canadian history. Due to a legacy of tension and overt conflict between the Anglophone and Francophone communities, nothing comparable to the melting-pot ideal emerged in the nation's collective conscience. Instead, Canadians were from the beginning more likely to view themselves as a mosaic, and thus in pluralist or more recently multicultural terms. John Porter's influential *The Vertical Mosaic* (1965) used this metaphor in an analysis of class structure and power. In one chapter, he analyzed the connection between ethnicity and social class, and in so doing, located ethnic groups in terms of the social class hierarchy.

While Canada today confronts many of the same issues as the United States regarding current high levels of immigration, it confronts another situation quite foreign to their southern neighbor: the Québecois separatist movement that, if successful, will result in the break-up of Canada (Jacobs 1980). Thus, it confronts not only the issues related to an immigrant-receiving nation, but also those associated with a mobilized ethnic nationalism. In the following pages, a brief historical background will contextualize contemporary ethnic relations, focusing on those factors and events that shape the framework defining the possibilities and problems confronting a nation officially committed to a policy promoting multiculturalism.

Charter groups and indigenous peoples in the early phase of nation-building

The history of Canadian colonization entails a vying for control of the territory by the French and British. The former could lay claim to being the founding group insofar as the French explorer Jacques Cartier claimed the land around the St. Lawrence River for the King of France in 1534. The French established the first settlements in the early seventeenth century, but British incursions later in the century led to a situation where not only did both nations claim vast expanses of land, but some areas, such as what was known as Rupert's Land (which included land surrounding Hudson's Bay and extending into today's prairie provinces) were simultaneously claimed by both nations. At the conclusion of four wars that began in 1689 and ended in 1815, the British finally managed to gain control of this vast territorial expanse from the French. In 1755, for example, the British attempted to force French settlers in Acadia (now Nova Scotia, New Brunswick, and Prince Edward Island) to sign an oath of allegiance to the British king. When they refused, they were pushed off the land, with around 4,000 undertaking an exodus to what is now the state of Louisiana, where they became known as Cajuns. The most decisive turning point occurred in 1763, four years after winning a crucial battle for Quebec City, with the signing of the Treaty of Paris.

The British eventually outnumbered the French in Canada as a whole, and this population disparity was further accentuated at the time of the American Revolution, when approximately 40,000 American colonists who remained loyal to the crown moved to Canada. Thus, although they were one of the founding or "charter" groups instrumental in the formative period of nation-building, the French would end up a minority, located in a politically and economically subordinate position *vis-à-vis* the English. However, they remained a majority of the population in Quebec. But British merchants began to settle in urban centers in Quebec and soon became even in the Francophone heartland the dominant economic force, wielding considerable power over the largely rural French community. The conflict between the English and French was not only economic and political. It was also cultural, revolving around differences in language and religion (Lower 1977; McClellan 1977).

As perhaps an indication of things to come, the Quebec Act was passed in 1774, granting linguistic and religious rights to the French majority. Rather than seeking to blend the French into the British mainstream, this law established the basis for a non-assimilative and asymmetric policy of inclusion of the French into Canadian society – one that officially recognized difference and at the same time the hegemonic status of British Canada. Thus, the French language and Roman Catholicism became the two most potent symbols defining the Francophone community and differentiating it from the Anglophone community. The law did one more thing. It allowed for the use of French civil law within the Francophone community and permitted within limits the expansion of territory. The intention of such a policy was to promote French loyalty to British rule. However, the law, in conjunction with the Constitution Act of 1792 that divided the nation into Upper and Lower Canada, had an unintended consequence insofar as by allowing the French a degree of control over their own internal affairs, the Francophone community was able to experience what it might be like to be an independent state. In short, from the events that transpired at this early date, the germ of a separatist movement would grow into a serious challenge to a unified Canada by the twentieth century (Thomson 1995).

The relative autonomy of the Francophone community needs to be seen in context. During the first two-thirds of the nineteenth century, a unified nation-state had not yet emerged. Instead, during this period the provinces exhibited a considerable degree of self-government. However, concerns about the possibility that the United States might seek to expand northward prompted the British government to push for a confederation in order to create a politically united front against such a possibility. Despite resistance to confederation by some provinces, this new political arrangement became a reality in 1867, when the British Parliament passed the British North America Act. This Act formally established four provinces as constituting the Dominion of Canada, which was modeled after the British parliamentary system, with the British monarch serving as the head of state. To reinforce the connection to Britain, the national flag's design was that of a modified Union Jack, which from the French perspective was seen as a potent symbol of their subservient role in the new nation. From this point forward, the status of the French in Canada became one in which they represented a minority of the population of the nation as a whole, and thus had little hope of expanding their power outside of Quebec and of effectively countering a British-dominated federal government. Dale Thomson (1995: 73) summarizes the situation by noting that "These factors discouraged many French Canadians from identifying with Canada as a whole."

Not only was British political domination complete, but a British financial and business elite also dominated the emerging capitalist industrial economy. This British economic dominance continued to be the case even in Quebec, despite the fact that the French continued to comprise a substantial majority of that province's population. The response of the Francophone community was to turn inward in order to protect their culture from the pressures of assimilation. In this regard, the Catholic church wielded enormous power. It controlled the educational system, and through this control it aggressively sought to preserve traditional religious and cultural values. These efforts were directed at an overwhelmingly rural population living in largely segregated communities (Porter 1965: 91–6). The result was that the French population remained highly traditionalistic in terms of culture and was not well prepared for a world that would soon become increasingly industrial and urban.

Over time the original symbiotic relationship that had existed during the early phase of European settlement between native peoples and European settlers, which had been chiefly based on the fur trade, increasingly gave way to conflict, a situation that intensified with the westward expansion. Despite King George III's Proclamation of 1763 that guaranteed certain rights to the indigenous population, by the middle of the nineteenth century European settlers' quest for land for farming and for the development of cities meant that the Indian peoples were forced off of ancestral lands, and parallel to what occurred in the United States, experienced forced relocations, economic marginalization, and political oppression. To put the Canadian case into comparative perspective, historian Robin Winks (1988: 23) has argued that the Australian colonizers had the worst record in terms of their treatment of native peoples, while the New Zealand colonizers the best record. Within this framework, Canada was, according to Winks, closer to the New Zealand end of the spectrum (the US, meanwhile, was closer to the Australian end).

This process intensified after confederation in 1867. Some tribes were annihilated, while the rest were caught up in a reserve system in which the federal government forced Indians off their tribal lands and onto the counterpart of the reservation system in the US, where they became wards of the state. Until the second half of the twentieth century, the First Nations people remained effectively powerless and without political voice (Frideres 1996: 19).

The emergence of the "third force"

At the time of confederation, the population of Canada was divided almost entirely between the indigenous peoples and the two charter groups. While a small stream of Chinese immigrants arrived around this time, confined particularly to British Columbia, and small numbers of other Europeans also began to enter the country, mass immigration did not commence until late in the nineteenth century. As the nation began to industrialize, the need for labor became acute, and though immigrants from Britain continued to enter the country, their numbers were not sufficient to meet economic demand. Thus, from the late 1890s until the early 1920s, the Canadian government, under the direction of Minister of the Interior Clifford Sifton, actively promoted and structured immigration (Hawkins 1989: 4–21).

The Immigration Act of 1910 and its 1919 amended version established the basis for a "white Canada." The clear preference was for settlers from western Europe, with eastern Europeans seen as less desirable, but nonetheless potential future Canadians. On the other hand, people of color from other parts of the globe, and in particular Asia, were not welcome. As in the United States, nativists soon singled out the Chinese as a group to be barred from entry; in Canada the first anti-Chinese bill was passed in 1885, which not only put a brake on immigration, but also denied Chinese already in Canada the right to vote. Subsequent laws passed in 1900, 1903, and 1923 were designed to either make Chinese entry difficult or impossible. The restrictive character of Canadian immigration policies was intended to prevent not only the Chinese, but other Asians, including East Indians, from settling in large numbers (Hawkins 1989).

Two and a half million immigrants arrived in Canada prior to the First World War. Although Britain and the United States contributed by far the largest number of immigrants, thereby expanding the size of the Anglophone community, about 500,000 other Europeans arrived in significant numbers during this period, including Germans, Scandinavians, Dutch, Poles, Ukrainians, Italians, and Jews (Hawkins 1989: 15–16; for case studies, see for example Harney 1978; Swyripa 1978; and Karni 1981). Anti-immigration sentiments were directed towards groups from eastern and southern Europe. Nevertheless, unlike their Asian counterparts, these groups were not prevented from entering the country or from becoming citizens.

As a consequence, as they accommodated to Canadian society, and as levels of discrimination and prejudice directed against them declined, they complicated the political conflict between the Anglophone and Francophone communities by constituting a collective "third force." During the Depression and the Second World War, immigration levels were low, but in the immediate aftermath of the war, large-scale immigration once again resumed. Many of the newcomers were Displaced Persons (DPs) who left their war-ravaged nations in eastern Europe, particularly as communist regimes took over their homelands. However, larger numbers of the new arrivals were more traditional labor immigrants. Among the largest groups to arrive during this period were Italians, Greeks, Poles, and Portuguese – thereby enlarging the size of the third force *vis-à-vis* the two charter groups (Elliott 1983; Hiller 1991).

Canadian identity and the reconfiguration of the vertical mosaic

It is within this historical context that contemporary ethnic relations have developed (Helmes-Hayes & Curtis 1998). By the middle of the twentieth century the nation was affluent, and it has developed a welfare state to protect the least advantaged citizens. However, during this time, the nation proved incapable of forging a singular sense of what it means to be Canadian. The Constitution of 1867 was content to define Canadian identity in terms of the distinct identities of the two charter groups, without managing to articulate a more overarching vision of Canadian identity that merged or incorporated these two particularistic identities. According to Gilles Bourque and Jules Duchastel (1999: 185):

> Throughout the period up to the Second World War, the state had a liberal form, and Canadian identity was more or less bifurcated along "simple" ethnic lines: Anglo-Saxon/Protestant extraction and French Canadian/Catholic extraction. A proper Canadian identity began to emerge only during the 1940s with the rise of the welfare state. The introduction of social policies that transformed state interventions in Canada contributed to the formation of a broader *national* Canadian identity based upon common membership and social citizenship. This new civic nationality was linked to a universalistic system of redistribution via the social security system adapted after the Second World War. However, this purely Canadian identity made very poor use of the concept of nation; rather, it focused on the idea of a *community of citizens*, with each citizen entitled to the same services through shared national institutions.

Another feature of the problematic nature of Canadian identity revolved around the nation's relationship with the United States. The economic dominance of the much larger nation to the south combined with its impact on Canadian culture – especially popular culture – led many to express anxiety about Canada becoming little more than the fifty-first state. This anxiety served to define Canadian identity as that which was other than American, but such a reactive and negative understanding was not complemented by a more positive appreciation of a unified Canadian identity (Lipset 1990: 42–56).

Within this context, the decade of the 1960s signaled the beginning of a new era in Canadian ethnic relations, predicated on three interrelated developments: (1) the emergence of a potent separatist movement in Québec; (2) changes in immigration laws that paved the way for a new wave of immigration from Asia and the West Indies; and (3) a resurgent group consciousness on the part of aboriginal peoples. In combination, these developments have resulted in a reconfigured vertical mosaic that constitutes the social structure within which multiculturalism as ideal and as social policy arose.

Québecois nationalism and the potential break-up of Canada

In the three decades prior to the birth of an organized separatist movement in the form of the Parti Québecois, the Francophone community was, as Everett Hughes (1943) characterized it, "in transition," shifting from being a predominantly rural to becoming an urban community. At the turn of the century, 60 percent of the population lived in rural areas. That figure had fallen to 37 percent by 1931 (Legendre 1980). In response to these changes, which were seen by some in the Francophone community as a threat to their way of life, including a threat to the hegemony of the Catholic church, a new political party, the Union Nationale, was founded. Its goal was to preserve a traditionalistic French Canadian world resting on the twin pillars of Catholicism and the French language. In 1936, under the leadership of Maurice Duplessis, it gained control of the provincial government and would maintain control for much of the next two decades (Quinn 1979: 70–6). However, the party's attempts to ward off modernization and the economic power of national and international corporations within the province proved to be unsuccessful.

Urbanization – with Montréal serving as the major recipient of new arrivals – continued apace, and this also meant the advance of industrialization. As the French entered industrial work, they confronted not only British-owned enterprises, but also work situations in which British managers ran plants and British workers dominated as skilled workers. Thus, the French occupied the lowest tiers of the occupational hierarchy. Porter contended that the church-run educational system combined with its transmission of values antithetical to the capitalist spirit put the Francophone population at a distinct disadvantage in adapting to industrialization. While true, his contention that "it is difficult to accept the theory of British exploitation" fails to appreciate the impact that discrimination played in keeping the French a decidedly second-class charter group (Porter 1965: 93).

Gradually a Francophone middle class emerged. In this regard, the role of the church and its related agencies was crucial because they came to increasingly rely on an educated professional class from the laity to run its expanded investments in real estate, business, and industry (Guindon 1960). At the same time, the traditionalistic worldview of the Catholic church began to lose influence among many in this more upwardly mobile sector of the community. An equally important development for contemporary nationalism was the entry of the middle class into provincial politics, both as bureaucratic officials and as politicians. By the 1960s these trends had led to the beginning of a new political assertiveness and a new form of nationalism. As Michael Ignatieff (1993: 154) has pointed out, earlier manifestations of nationalism, such as that of the Union Nationale, had reflected "a revolt against modernity, a defense of the backwardness of economically beleaguered or declining classes and regions from the flames of individualism, capitalism, Judaism, and so on." In contrast, the new nationalistic articulation was one in which nationalism meant "being a progressive, being modern, being a French North American."

The gestation period became known as the "Quiet Revolution," and was characterized by demands to end economic and social discrimination, and to increase provincial (and thus French) power *vis-à-vis* that of the federal government. Led by the Liberal Party, the Quiet Revolution was more about advancing the civil rights of the Francophone community than in promoting a separatist agenda. However, a key aspect of the demands emerging out of the Quiet Revolution focused on the promotion of respect for the French cultural heritage. As the Catholic church lost some of its power and as language retention became a growing topic of concern, the preservation and enhancement of culture could not be separated from demands for economic advancement and political empowerment (Evans 1995; Guentzel 1999).

Regarding this point, a central issue in Taylor's (1992) "politics of recognition" is the matter of language, and it served as the first important issue pitting the national government against the French population of Québec. Whereas in the past, English served as the official language of government and business, and English-speaking Canadians did not feel compelled to learn French, demands for the establishment of a bilingual Canada were intended to recast the status of the French-language community. Despite Anglophone resistance, in 1963 the Royal Commission on Bilingualism and Biculturalism recommended that the nation become officially bilingual, a recommendation that was actively promoted in the late 1960s by the government of Liberal Party Prime Minister Pierre Trudeau (who was from Québec). Bourque and Duchastel (1999: 186) describe the passage of the Official Language Act in 1970 as the "federal government's answer to Québec's demands for recognition" and as "the first step toward the particularization of identity in Canada."

This latter development was not the primary objective of the law, for the federal government was committed to attempting to forge out of its ethnic diversity a unified and coherent sense of what it meant to be Canadian that could be shared by all. Thus, at around the same time, the federal government also sought in symbolic terms to recast the stature of the two charter groups by replacing the flag that reflected the nation's ties to Britain with a new, neutral flag featuring a red maple leaf as the symbol of the new Canada. By distancing itself from explicit reference to Britain in this symbol of national identity, there was a concerted attempt to find new common ground, particularly between the two charter groups (Smith 1991; Evans 1996).

These and similar initiatives were intended to placate French political aspirations. They were also a reflection of the realization that the federal government was forced to respond to an increasingly powerful nationalist movement in Québec. The number of French Canadians in Québec who sought independence rather than incorporation into the mainstream of Canadian society grew. As map 2 illustrates, if Québec becomes independent, the Maritime Provinces would be geographically separated from the rest of Canada. A separatist political party, the Parti Québecois, headed by René Levesque, was established in 1968, challenging the policies of the incumbent Liberal Party through legitimate political channels. The Parti Québecois operated with the assumption that if the majority of Québec's voters decided to secede from Canada, the federal government would be forced to permit the province to do so (Corbett 1980).

At the same time, more militant separatists affiliated with the Front de Liberation du Québec (FLQ) emerged. They sought to depict Québec as an internal colony and their struggle for independence as parallel to independence campaigns in the Third World. They rejected the legitimacy of the national government and engaged in a campaign of terrorism that forced the hand of Trudeau, who invoked the War Measures Act to quell the militant insurgency.

During the next two decades, French nationalists upped the ante over the language issue. Contending that the preservation of the French language was essential to the survival of a distinctly Francophone cultural identity, they moved past the demands for creating a bilingual Canada to attempts aimed at securing French language preeminence in Québec (Jackson 1977; Levine 1990). Though constituting a substantial majority of the province's population, the French community was concerned about two demographic trends. The first involved the steep drop in the French birthrate, which had been exceptionally high up to the 1960s, but ended up being the lowest in Canada. Second, new immigrants who were neither English nor French began to enter Québec – particularly Montréal – at an increasing rate. The fear of separatists was that the combined impact of these trends would be to dilute the political clout currently possessed by the Francophone community.

In 1974 a provincial government controlled by the Liberal Party abandoned the idea of bilingualism at the federal level by declaring French to be the official language of Québec. This shift was greeted with an uproar of protest from the Anglophone community. English business elites threatened to move their operations to Ontario, and when the government refused to back down, a significant exodus of firms did in fact occur. A section of the new law pertained to the language of instruction to be used in educational institutions. While the English were permitted to send their children to English-

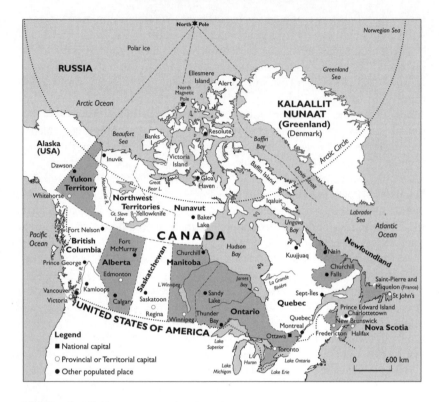

Map 2   Canadian provinces and territories
Source: Canadian government.

language schools, new immigrants were not given the right to choose
whether to send their children to English or French schools. Most immigrants
preferred English schools because they felt that given the dominance of English in the rest of Canada and in the United States, it was in their children's
best interest to learn English. Thus, they resented the requirement that their
children attend French-language schools (Fontaine 1995).

   Despite the intense opposition from these two quarters, Québecois nationalists showed little interest in compromise. In fact, in 1976 the Parti Québecois
won control of the province for the first time. In the following year they passed
an even more far-reaching legislative act – Bill 101 – that mandated French
not only as the language of government, but also the official language of
commerce and industry. Not surprisingly, this law exacerbated the conflict
with non-French groups and resulted in a costly exodus from the province of
individuals and businesses. From the perspective of French nationalists, this

change in official languages was necessary if English hegemony in Québec's economy was ever to be overcome.

Part of the problem faced by the Francophone community in terms of the language issue is that it represents a very small linguistic minority in North America. This is significant insofar as American popular culture has a profound impact on Canada, and this means that a fortress-mentality approach to language preservation is doomed. As an indication of the problems posed by the American culture industry, Michael Macmillan (1990: 122) reports that in the half decade after the passage of Bill 101, 38 percent fewer French-language music albums were produced – due to the comparatively small size of the market combined with the demand for English-language music within the Francophone community itself.

Perhaps sensing the depth of the problem, the success of French nationalists over the language issue did not manage to curtail their desire to break from Canada rather than remain a part of the confederation. Instead, it appears to have fueled the independence struggle. In 1980 the Parti Québecois called for a referendum on the future of Québec. Aware that many in the Francophone community sympathetic to the nationalist cause were divided between those seeking outright independence and those who preferred greater provincial autonomy within the existing confederation, the referendum was vaguely worded in order to encourage both blocs to support "a new partnership" conceived in terms of "sovereignty-association." Despite this effort to maximize support for the referendum, it failed by a 60/40 margin (Evans 1996).

In the aftermath of the defeat, the federal government began to seek a means to diffuse Québecois separatism. The initial effort culminated in 1987 in the Meech Lake Accord, which was an attempt to keep Québec in the confederation while also addressing the concerns of French nationalism. It did so by declaring Québec to be a "distinct society" and by increasing the autonomy of provincial governments. Quickly endorsed by Québec's leadership, the accord failed to receive the necessary support of all 10 provinces due to a growing backlash in the rest of Canada against Québecois nationalism. In 1992 another attempt, the Charlottetown Agreement, was undertaken in an effort to grant Québec the distinct society status nationalists demanded. It failed in a national referendum when 60 percent of the electorate nationwide rejected the plan.

This failure revived the fortunes of the Parti Québecois, which returned to power and resumed the separatist vision. The party's leader, Jacques Parizeau, ran on a platform that promised a quick referendum on independence. The party was elected in 1994, and in the following year a new referendum was proposed, again worded in ways intended to appeal to hard and soft nationalists alike. Voters were asked if they would support the idea of the sovereignty of Québec within the framework of a "new economic and political partnership" with Canada. Once again, the referendum was rejected, but this time in an exceptionally close vote. In the end, a scant 50.6 percent voted against the proposal. This included overwhelming majorities among the Anglophone community and the new immigrants. In the aftermath of defeat, the latter were blamed by many nationalists for the defeat, and with this sentiment came a call for immigration restriction (Bourque & Duchastel 1999). At the beginning of the twenty-first century, the separatist movement has lost ground compared to its position in the preceding two decades. The Liberal Party governs the province at the moment of this writing. The English minority in the province has been joined by other ethnic groups – ranging from Greeks, Portuguese, and Italians to more recent arrivals from various points in Asia and the Caribbean.

One of the ironies of the separatist campaign is that it comes at a time when the socioeconomic status of French Canadians has improved dramatically, leading some researchers to conclude that, in terms of the two charter groups, the vertical mosaic as conceived in the 1960s by John Porter no longer existed (Lian & Matthews 1998). In other words, the separatist movement henceforth would not be shaped by economic disadvantage or political exclusion. Instead, it would be increasingly exclusively a matter of cultural or identity politics linked to the new economic interests of the Francophone middle- class (Rousseau 1999). And, as the two following sections reveal, it serves to frame the ethnic formation as it involves the third force, including both the new immigrants and aboriginal peoples. Thus, the new vertical mosaic increasingly distinguishes between European-origin immigrants (charter groups and third force) and more visible minorities, including aboriginal peoples as well as more recent immigrants from Asia, the Middle East, the Caribbean, and Latin America.

New immigrants, race, and the reconstitution of the third force

During the 1950s, a concerted effort to open Canada's doors to new immigrants commenced. The motive behind this shift was the conviction that the nation's population needed to grow if it was to expand economically and compete successfully in the world market. In other words, the impetus for a liberalization of immigration policies derived from the dictates of a capitalist economy. In the words of the Conservative Prime Minister John Diefenbaker, the choice was to "populate or perish" (Hakwins 1989: 38). In response to this dire prediction, immigration laws were revised to encourage mass immigration. The result was a dramatic increase in immigration levels during the last four decades of the twentieth century. Indeed, the volume of immigrants entering the country makes it one of the world's major receiving countries. Though the number of immigrants entering the US during this period exceeded that entering Canada, with a population one-tenth the size of the

US, immigration has had a more profound demographic impact on Canada. By the 1990s, there were 8.8 immigrants per 1,000 in Canada, compared to only 2.5 per 1,000 in the US (Fleras & Elliott 1996).

The Immigration Act of 1910 articulated a clear preference for English and French immigrants and had an explicit anti-Asian bias. As noted above, in the immediate post-Second World War decades, the former part of this legislation was relaxed as Canada relied heavily on Displaced Persons from eastern Europe (Lipset 1990: 185–6). This included waves of arrivals coming in the immediate aftermath of the war, especially from Poland and the Ukraine. Later groups included Hungarians fleeing the failed uprising against Soviet domination in 1956, and Czech refugees who fled their nation's failed attempts to reform communism in 1968. In addition, many arrivals came from southern Europe. Immigration policy during these years has been described as a "tap on, tap off" approach in which policies were shaped by short-term labor market conditions and not by the longer-term concern with population building (Ongley & Pearson 1995).

A watershed in Canadian immigration policy occurred in 1962, when the government put an end to the "white Canada" policies of the past. Racial discrimination in immigration law effectively ended that year. The impetus behind this change was in part due to a desire to improve Canada's reputation *vis-à-vis* nonwhite Commonwealth countries as well as within the United Nations, and in part because the economy needed workers. Five years later, a points system of preference went into effect that was to be applied to all immigrants regardless of place of origin. The result, as indicated in figure 3, was a substantial shift in the countries of origin. Prior to 1962, over three-quarters of all immigrants came from either the United States or Europe. Three decades later, although Europeans continued to come, around three-quarters of all newcomers arrived from Asia, the Caribbean, and Central America (Richmond 1969; Richmond 1994; Kelley & Trebilcock 1998). Among nonwhites, at around 50 percent Asians comprise by far the largest number of immigrants. The largest groups making up the Asian population include the Chinese, Indian, Pakistani, Filipino, Vietnamese, and Sri Lankan (Israel 1987; Liu & Norcliffe 1996). The smaller number of black immigrants came overwhelmingly from the Caribbean, especially from Jamaica, Trinidad and Tobago, and Haiti. The numbers from such Central American countries as Guatemala and El Salvador are even smaller.

The nonwhite newcomers settled overwhelmingly in cities, and in particular in the country's three largest cities, Toronto, Montréal, and Vancouver. Indeed, Toronto alone has become home to a third of all new immigrants (Marger 1994: 481–2). However, other cities have also witnessed significant in-migration, including Edmonton, Calgary, Winnipeg, and Ottawa. The new arrivals have within the course of three decades changed the character of multicultural Canada (Samuel 1990).

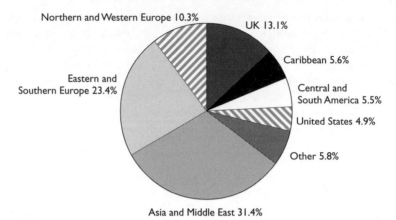

Figure 3 Birthplace of immigrants in Canada, 1996 (total immigrant population 4,971,070)
Source: Statistics Canada, 1996 Census.

Many of the most recent immigrants have entered the lowest tiers of the economy, finding employment in unskilled industrial work and in the service sector. In this regard, the segmented labor market is increasingly defined along racial lines. Others, particularly in large communities such as the Chinese, have found work in enclave economies. Yet another segment represents brain drain professionals and entrepreneurs. Though this group constitutes a minority of the nonwhite immigrant population, it is a comparatively larger segment than in the United States or Britain due to the highly selective nature of immigration policy in Canada, which more explicitly than policies in those two nations, gives preference to immigrants with higher educational backgrounds and particular occupational skills (Richmond 1994: 163). Nonetheless, the earned income of most nonwhite immigrants lags behind that of the country as a whole. This has led some to conclude that in the wake of the demise of the old vertical mosaic, a new "color-coded vertical mosaic" has arisen (Geschwender & Guppy 1995: 2).

Asians and blacks tend to live in more residentially segregated neighborhoods than is the case for other ethnic groups, though the levels of segregation are typically lower than in most American cities (Breton et al. 1990; Johnson 1992; Fong 1996). In research on housing quality and cost, Eric Fong and Milena Gulia (1999) found that "southern Europeans, Asians, and Blacks live in neighborhoods with less desirable social qualities, despite paying expensive housing costs. In particular, most neighborhood qualities of Blacks are consistently seen as least desirable."

Although Canadians generally perceive their country to be tolerant and accepting, there is ample evidence that many of the new racial minorities confront discrimination in various forms (Li 1990). As in all of the western democracies, the new immigrants have to confront the organized threat of right-wing extremism and of less organized forms of racist violence (Barrett 1987). In regard to the latter, Richmond (1994: 166) points out that Francophone ethnocentrism is greater than Anglophone ethnocentrism, and not surprisingly due to the siege mentality of Francophone separatists, Québec has had more than its share of violent attacks against immigrants. While racist violence is cause for concern, the more subtle everyday manifestations of prejudice and discrimination within the mainstream of Canadian society have had a more significant negative impact on employment, housing, and other aspects of social integration than extremism has had (Ramchavan 1982). Moreover, as Rita Simon and James Lynch (1999: 459–64) point out, although the Canadian public has a somewhat more favorable attitude about the current level of immigrant than its American counterpart, the majority nonetheless would like to see fewer immigrants accepted into the country than current law allows. That being said, it's worth noting, as Seymour Martin Lipset (1990: 186) has, that Canada and the US "remain more universalistic and socially heterogeneous in their immigration patterns than other white First World countries."

Perhaps for this reason, there is reason to think that as these communities begin to acculturate and coalesce into political constituencies, these groups individually and as part of the reconfigured "third force" have the potential for becoming an important factor in redefining Canadian multiculturalism. The political mobilization of the Indian and Chinese communities in British Columbia is an example of the role these groups are beginning to play in Canadian politics. In 2000, Ujjal Dosanjh ran and won as the New Democrat candidate for premier of the province, becoming the first nonwhite provincial premier in Canadian history (Brooke 2000). One can find in other arenas of social life indications pointing to the integration of the new immigrants into the mainstream – in the media, education, business and industry. This points to the fact that the voices of inclusion in the Canadian mainstream have not been drowned out by the voices of exclusion.

Native people: life on the margins

The circumstances of Canada's First Nations peoples parallel that of American Indians. They are divided by the government into four legal categories: status Indians, who are registered with one of Canada's 605 Indian bands; nonstatus Indians; Métis, with European and aboriginal ancestry; and Inuits. Collectively, they represent 3.7 percent of Canada's total population and remain by far the most disadvantaged minority in Canada (Fleras & Elliott 1996: 193).

Three-quarters of status Indians continue to live on reserves under the provisions of the Indian Act, and thus outside of the urban industrial nexus and in a continued dependency relationship with the federal government. In all measures of well-being, it is clear that these native peoples' life chances fall far short of those of most Canadians. High rates of unemployment, poverty, school dropout, and related measures are reflections of their socioeconomic plight (Siggner 1986). Compounding these problems are various social problems, including high rates of alcoholism, infant mortality, general health problems, suicide, and violence. The fact that the average life expectancy of native peoples is 24 years less than that of the general population perhaps more than any other single fact reveals the extent to which they live on the margins of Canadian society (Grescoe 1987: 127–8).

The nonstatus Indians tend to be more urbanized than their status counterparts, and thus are not as isolated from the economic mainstream. Nonetheless, the two groups share many of the same problems. Though comparative data is often difficult to come by, it would appear that the Métis are in a somewhat better position than full-blooded natives. Nonetheless, the 192,000 strong Métis National Council has functioned as a civil rights organization seeking to advance the interests of this community, which at times has led to calls for including the Métis under the jurisdiction of the Indian Act.

Concurrent with the mobilization of Native Americans in the United States in the 1960s, a Red Power movement also developed in Canada, and one way it has manifested itself is by attempting to revisit land claims and other treaty provisions. For example, a land dispute in Québec involving Mohawks resulted in a siege that lasted for several months. Related to the matter of land is the demand for greater political empowerment. One of the key locales where these demands are being played out is in Québec. Some Indians have suggested that if Québec were to secede from Canada, they ought to have the right to leave Québec and create their own independent nation. Outside of Québec, one can at present witness aboriginal rights campaigns currently being waged by the Mi ' Kmaq and Maliseet bands in the maritime provinces over the right to engage in commercial fishing in protected areas. In Ontario, the Métis have waged a hunting rights campaign, while in British Columbia aboriginal rights have been pitted against the corporations seeking to explore the potential of offshore oil and gas fields. To date, these and other disputes are percolating, but the federal government has not attempted to formulate an overarching approach to these matters, opting instead for dealing with them in piecemeal fashion.

Competition for land has not characterized Inuit relations with the rest of Canada in the same way that it has for Indians. The small number of people living in the northern regions of the nation have found few Canadians interested in moving into their areas. But the Inuit, like Indians to the south, have demanded greater political control over their lives. After lengthy negotiations, the federal government recently entered into an agreement with Inuit leaders to create a new territory out of 135,000 square miles of the eastern sector of the Northwest Territories. Called Nunavut (the term for "our land" in the Inuit language), the new territory began as a functional political entity in 1999 (see map 2).

Multiculturalism and Canadian national identity

As this overview suggests, the ethnic mosaic of Canada is a fractured one and it serves to exacerbate the problematic nature of efforts aimed at forging an overarching Canadian national identity that will at once recognize ethnic diversity while transcending ethnic particularism (Breton 1986; Wilson 1994; Roy 1995). Canada, along with Australia, has been in the forefront of attempting to implement multiculturalism as official government policy. The Canadian government's policies no longer call for an assimilation into an Anglophone identity, but rather suggest that cultural differences can and should persist over time. To that end, unlike the United States, Canada has been prepared to promote ethnic group rights and not only individual rights.

In part, Canadian multicultural policy is a reflection of the reality of politically mobilized ethnicity in the cases of Québecois nationalism and First Nations rights advocates. However, the goal of multiculturalism is not to further balkanize Canada, but to keep it together. In other words, it is hoped that ethnic diversity can be contained within an overarching sense of a shared Canadian identity and loyalty to the nation-state (Wilson 1993; Harles 1997). Whether or not this goal is likely to be achieved remains an open question.

Australia: From Settler Country to Multicultural Nation

Since the 1970s, Australia has become a "laboratory for multiculturalism" (Smolicz 1997: 171). Over the past quarter-century, the nation has dramatically revised its national policies regarding ethnic minorities – both immigrant and indigenous peoples – and in so doing has, along with Canada, become a nation that is officially committed as a matter of national policy to the preservation and enhancement of ethnic diversity. What makes this transition all the more remarkable is that into the 1960s, Australia maintained an explicitly racist "White Australia" assimilationist stance regarding immigration and continued its long history of political oppression, economic degradation, and cultural suppression of the nation's Aborigines.

In 1996, Prime Minister John Howard's government proposed a Parliamentary Statement on Racial Tolerance that was supported by the opposition leader and passed unanimously. In the statement, the Australian Parliament's House (Department of Immigration and Multicultural Affairs 2001: 2):

- "reaffirms its commitment to the right of all Australians to enjoy equal rights and be treated with equal respect regardless of race, colour, creed, or origin;
- reaffirms its commitment to maintaining an immigration policy wholly nondiscriminatory on grounds of race, colour, creed, or origin;
- reaffirms its commitment to the process of reconciliation with Aboriginal and Torres Strait Island people, in the context of redressing their profound social and economic disadvantage;
- reaffirms its commitment to maintain Australia as a culturally diverse, tolerant, and open society, united by an overriding commitment to our nation, and its democratic institutions and values; and
- denounces racial intolerance in any form as incompatible with the kind of society we are and want to be."

A year later, the government launched the National Multicultural Advisory Council in order to formulate policy recommendations for the twenty-first century. The report, *Australian Multiculturalism for a New Century: Towards Inclusiveness*, was published in 1999. It made 32 specific recommendations designed to create an agenda that would improve and enhance existing policy. Underpinning these recommendations were four core principles: civic duty, cultural respect, social equity, and productive diversity (Department of Immigration and Multicultural Affairs 2001: 1). Cultural respect and social equity, both enshrined in the 1996 Statement on Racial Tolerance, refer to entitlements. Groups have a right to expect that they can express their cultural preferences without hindrance, but they must do so in a context of mutual or reciprocal tolerance. Social equity refers to the expectation that the government will not only protect groups from discriminatory and exploitative treatment, but will also work to ensure equality of opportunity.

Productive diversity offers a rationale for multiculturalism by contending that the nation as a whole benefits in a variety of ways – cultural, economic, and political – by having and maintaining diversity. In other words, the claim being advanced is an explicit refutation of the earlier views in Australia about the presumed advantages of maintaining a homogeneous British – or at least western European – ethnic character. Finally, civic duty involves not an entitlement, but an obligation. Specifically, all Australians are obligated "to support those basic structures and principles of Australian society which guarantee us our freedom and equality and enable diversity in our society to flourish" (Department of Immigration and Multicultural Affairs 2001: 1). This is a concrete instance of the claim made by Bikhu Parekh (2000a: 219) regarding the necessity of multicultural societies to construct an overarching notion of civic or national identity within which multiculturalism can play out.

The context within which this framework evolved is a reflection of two distinct but interrelated social realities: the evolution in the treatment of the original settlers towards the Aborigines and the growing inclusiveness that has shaped the development of immigration policies. We turn to each of these topics in the following two sections.

Terra nullius *and the Aborigines*

It is thought that the Aboriginal people of Australia arrived on the continent around 40,000 years ago from points in Asia via New Guinea. Encounters with European explorers commenced in the 1500s, with contact being made by Portuguese, Spanish, and Dutch navigators, who viewed the land that they saw as inhospitable and lacking valuable resources, and did not undertake colonization efforts. This was left to the British, who in the wake of the American Revolution were interested in finding an alternative penal colony to the one they had established in Georgia. In 1770, James Cook had surveyed the eastern coast and claimed the land – which he named New South Wales – for Great Britain. In 1776, the British government decided to use this territory for a penal colony, which opened under the governance of Arthur Phillip two years later. The government would continue to use the continent as a penal colony, gradually moving operations westward with the expansion into the interior. Over an 80-year period, it is estimated that approximately 160,000 convicts were sent to Australia (Inglis 1974; Sherington 1980).

All of this occurred without any consultation or consideration of the indigenous peoples. Estimates of the size of the Aboriginal population during the era of colonization range from 300,000 to 1,000,000 (Macintyre 1999). They were divided into perhaps as many as 500 different tribes speaking over 200 different languages or dialects. Unlike the North American experience, the British government did not enter into treaties with the Aborigines. Thus, once voluntary migrants began to enter the country in the nineteenth century, they had little difficulty taking control of Aboriginal lands; the Aborigines were displaced so that settlers could use the land for agriculture and for sheep and cattle grazing. An Australian version of Manifest Destiny, shaped by the fusion of Christian belief and scientific racism, served to justify this process. The dislocations took a tremendous toll on the Aborigines, who suffered not only from conflicts with settlers but as a result of being exposed to new diseases and to the ravages of alcoholism. The population decrease during the nineteenth century was precipitous, declining to perhaps as few as 50,000 at the dawn of the twentieth century. Not surprisingly, many assumed that Aboriginal people were destined to disappear (Broome 1982).

They did not die out. Instead, an institutional system of reserves and mission settlements was created that served both to control and marginalize the Aboriginal population. Rather than being granted citizenship, they became dependants of the state, subject to its dictates. Jan Pettman (1997: 209) describes this system in the following way: "Aboriginal people were wards of the state, administered with a mixture of neglect and control. They were required to seek state permission to move, marry, or get a job; or directed to work for pitiful rations. The camps and missions functioned as labor reserves for white stations, farms, and households." They were an underprivileged caste in a class society, deprived of the same political rights and economic and social benefits as their white counterparts. They have consistently experienced high rates of unemployment, lower income levels, lower educational levels, and significantly shorter life expectancies than the national average. Moreover, segregation in public facilities – schools, hospitals, theaters, and the like – was commonplace.

Another aspect of the exploitation of the Aboriginal community was sexual. Despite legal prohibitions against miscegenation, liaisons between white males and Aboriginal females were common during the nineteenth and early twentieth centuries – particularly in the interior where white females were often in short supply. The emergence of a societal recognition of a growing mixed-race community led the government to establish the draconian policy of seizing such children from their Aboriginal families and either placing them in orphanages or putting them up for adoption. Begun in 1910, the practice did not cease until 1970. Part of the underlying motive for such a practice was the belief that mixed-bloods might be capable of assimilation, at least at some level. Another rationale offered for the practice involved the belief that these particular children could be "saved" from a "doomed race." For the Aboriginal community, these "stolen generations" represent a particular bitter testimony to the oppression and exploitation they confronted in "white Australia" (Pettman 1997: 209).

Beginning in the 1930s, organizations within the Aboriginal community were created to combat oppression and exclusion and to campaign for social justice. The movement of Aboriginals to cities, the participation of many men in the Australian military during the Second World War, and the changing international climate after the war all served to bolster this campaign. Significant change in the status of the Aboriginal community did not begin until the 1950s, in part as a result of a growing civil rights movement that was at least in part modeled after the movement in the United States. Aborigines formed alliances with various church groups, labor unions, and student organizations. The following decade marks something of a watershed in Aboriginal–white relations. This is also, coincidentally, the decade that Australia began to rethink its immigration policies and to formulate a new, multicultural understanding of Australian national identity. More explicitly than in both of the preceding cases, the connection between policies towards indigenous peoples and immigrants was a direct one as the nation wrestled with a legacy of racism (Rickard 1996).

Efforts directed at redressing the most egregious disparities between whites and Aborigines began during this decade. For instance, in 1966 the Commonwealth Arbitration Commission declared that Aboriginal workers must be entitled to the same work conditions and wages as white union members. In a 1967 national referendum, the electorate overwhelmingly voted to grant full citizenship to Aboriginals and to establish a government agency entrusted with promoting their assimilation into the mainstream. In this regard, from the point of view of the Aborigines the referendum represented only a partial victory. While they saw citizenship as crucial if they were to be able to pursue their collective interests within legitimate political channels, they also understood that the intention of the referendum was to dismantle their culture and community. As Christine Fletcher (1998: 455) described the situation, "For Aboriginal people in Australia, the citizenship mantle represented a denial rather than a protection of rights, and at some levels, citizenship was a reminder that they were captives in their own land."

Aboriginal demands became more radical thereafter, not only seeking redress to long-standing land claims, an end to discrimination, and remedies for the social problems afflicting the community, but also demanding self-determination and the recognition of and respect for cultural differences. In other words, Aborigines were not prepared to equate citizenship with the loss of cultural identity and with the abandonment of ethnic attachments. In rejecting this equation, they became an important social force in advancing the shift from assimilation to multiculturalism as official government policy.

The Labor government of Gough Whitlam ran on a progressive platform that set in motion changes intended to redress a legacy of oppression and discrimination and to reshape in fundamental ways what it means to be Australian. Regarding the former, an antidiscrimination act was passed in 1975. Five years later the federal government established the Aboriginal Development Commission. It was operated by Aborigines, not white government bureaucrats, and was designed to promote economic development. The Commission was entrusted with managing Aboriginal-held lands and with administering a low-interest loan program for home ownership and the creation of Aboriginal-owned businesses.

In 1988, the bicentennial of the arrival of British settlers, the Parliament issued a statement acknowledging "the prior occupation of Australia by

Aborigines . . . and their subsequent dispossession" (Rickard 1996: 270). Though the statement fell short of suggesting that the Aborigines possessed the land prior to European settlement, it was a symbolic move towards reconciliation. In a more substantive way, the 1992 Mabo decision of the Queensland Supreme Court decided a land dispute in favor of an Aboriginal named Eddie Mabo. The court determined that he held legal title to land in the Murray Islands. The decision had more broad-reaching ramifications insofar as it determined that "there may be other areas of Australia where native title has not been extinguished and where Aboriginal people, maintaining their identity and customs, are entitled to enjoy their native title" (Rickard 1996: 271).

This ruling overturned the 1971 ruling of Supreme Court Judge Richard Blackburn that nullified aboriginal claims to land by recourse to the doctrine of *terra nullius*, with its domain assumption being that before European settlement nobody owned the land. Soon after the Mabo decision, the Parliament passed a Native Titles Bill to establish procedures for dealing with aboriginal land claims. Since that time a series of land claims have begun to work through the administrative system. In one 1996 case, the Supreme Court decided that the native claims of the Wik people could coexist with the pastoral titles held by white farmers (*The Economist* 2000b: 12). What this suggests is that at present there is an effort to adjudicate claims in a non-zero-sum fashion – attempting to find compromises that accommodate the claims of both parties.

On May 28, 2000, a quarter of a million people crossed the harbor bridge in Sydney as a symbolic gesture of support for the Aboriginal population, estimated today to be about 390,000. While Prime Minister Howard expressed "deep personal sorrow for those . . . fellow Australians who suffered under the practices of past generations towards indigenous people," he did not offer a formal apology. Rather, on that day an anonymous skywriter spelled it out in simple terms: "Sorry" (*The Economist* 2001: 12). While there is general consensus that additional money and programs need to be directed towards addressing the most serious problems confronting Aboriginals, there is less agreement about the call from some segments of the Aboriginal community to enter into a treaty similar to ones that New Zealand has entered into with the Maori and the Canadian government has with its First Nation people.

Australian immigration policy in the nineteenth century

During the first fifty years of the nation's history, the vast majority of people who immigrated were from Britain and Ireland (Partington 1997). Given the fact that the nation served as a penal colony well into the nineteenth century, a substantial percentage of these people cannot be seen as voluntary migrants. Up to the 1830s, convicts accounted for about 40 percent of the white residents of Australia. This percentage would steadily decline during the remainder of the century, as the nation would shift from being primarily a penal colony to becoming a free community. The number of white residents remained at under a million people until the discovery of gold in the 1850s brought about a gold rush not unlike that which occurred in California around the same time. The prospect of striking it rich attracted newcomers not only from Europe, but also from China. As with the US, the Chinese who came to make their fortunes confronted intense hostility on the part of whites, and after episodes of violence, the door to Chinese immigration was closed for over a century. As Brian Murphy (1993: 22) observes, "Opposition to the Chinese was a mixture of economic, social and racial considerations, and of course it became a political question."

Until 1901, the colonies had great discretion in developing their own immigration policies. However, whatever the differences, there was a clear preference given for European-origin immigrants. This would be part of a larger strategy for over a century to, on the one hand, encourage immigration in order to facilitate economic growth and, on the other hand, carefully define who was welcome to enter the nation and who was not. While the clear preference throughout the nation was for British immigrants, the Irish were also accepted. When the combined impact of these two sources of immigration did not meet labor needs, immigration from the US was encouraged along with that from other points in western Europe, with Germans and Scandinavians being seen as especially suitable newcomers. Southern and eastern European immigrants were not encouraged to move to Australia, but neither were they prevented from doing so. Their numbers up to the early twentieth century remained comparatively low (Murphy 1993: 24–5). This set the stage for the articulation of an explicitly racist immigration policy that would characterize Australia for the first six decades of the twentieth century.

The codification of white Australia

For the first two-thirds of the twentieth century, Australia defined itself legally and culturally as "White Australia." The Immigration Restriction Act of 1901 codified this understanding of national identity by erecting a racial divide between those deemed to be capable of assimilation into Australian society and those who were not. In making this invidious distinction between whites and nonwhites, policy-makers relied on the Social Darwinian racialist theories of the era, with their conviction that the "inferior" races would lower the quality of life and that miscegenation was a distinct threat that must be prevented at all costs. Part of the concern about racial purity was linked to geopolitical concerns that were captured by the notion of "Awakening Asia," which meant that the Australian government was wary of the emerging nations of the region, and in particular Japan, which it felt might well be a political threat (Murphy 1993: 30).

Complicating matters was the fact that some sectors of the economy relied on cheap labor from various points in the Pacific, none more than the sugar industry in Queensland, which had made use of indentured laborers for decades. The Pacific Island Labourers Act was also passed in 1901. It forbid the future importation of such workers and called for the repatriation of those already in the country within a five-year period. In the end, people of color remained in Australian, particularly the Chinese who had arrived earlier in the nineteenth century. However, the policies shaping White Australia set the terms for their presence. In addition to the fact that nonwhites were prevented from becoming citizens, there were, as Brian Murphy (1993: 35) observes,

> also legal barriers to ownership and property matters, restraints on business operations, and, of course, exclusion from certain occupations. Control over coloureds thus satisfied the two grounds on which White Australia had traditionally been based. Exclusion from certain areas of Australian life itself endorsed racial difference and white superiority. It also reduced, if it did not remove, competitive labour.

Whites who were permitted entry were expected to assimilate – which from the point of view of the Australians meant something akin to the melting pot. Preference for British immigrants remained central, as was evident with the passage of the Empire Settlement Act in 1922. While Britain continued to contribute the largest number of immigrants, the numbers tapered off during the Depression and the Second World War. The other privileged western European groups contributed fewer and fewer immigrants after the First World War. Instead, the new Europeans tended to come from southern and eastern Europe, with Italians constituting the largest group. Other nations that supplied immigrants between the wars included Greece and Yugoslavia. In addition, during the 1930s, Jewish refugees began to arrive, though in relatively small numbers. These newcomers were often viewed with suspicion, and at times racialist terms were used to describe them – raising in the process questions about their ability to assimilate. This suspicion was reinforced with the establishment of ethnic communities and institutions that addressed the prospect that the newcomers would refuse to assimilate. In these developments, the boundary between white and nonwhite was ambiguous and contested, but in the long run white and European came to be coeval terms (Hawkins 1989).

After the Second World War, the government, aware of growing needs for labor in the manufacturing sector and of the declining birth rate, initiated an ambitious immigration program. Once again, British immigrants were the most preferred, followed by immigrants from elsewhere in western Europe. Unfortunately for the authorities, few immigrants from these points of origin were interested in settling in Australia. On the other hand, Displaced Persons from eastern Europe were interested in moving to Australia and thus from 1947 to 1952 they contributed the largest number of newcomers to the nation. As refugees, these arrivals had little hope of returning home, at least in the short run, and thus they tended to view themselves as permanent residents rather than temporary sojourners (Castles & Miller 1993: 101).

Assimilation as cultural and social absorption remained the main objective of immigration policies during the postwar period. Immigrants were construed to be potential New Australians. Labor unions, employer organizations, churches, and schools all played a role in helping to transform white aliens into Australians. One novel feature of this era was the founding of the Good Neighbour Movement, which was an umbrella organization representing voluntary organizations that were committed to assisting and encouraging the newcomers to assimilate (Murphy 1993: 140–4). Many immigrants resented the combined efforts of these agents of assimilation, and took steps to protect their ethnic heritages. Thus, ethnic communities often sought to find ways to both acculturate into Australian society while simultaneously preserving ethnic identities and group life.

From the perspective of many Australians, this raised the specter of the hyphenated Australian, something that their particular ideology of assimilation did not find acceptable. Cultural homogeneity versus cultural heterogeneity, in short, became a contested matter during this period. Complicating the situation was the fact that class and ethnicity were often interwoven, as the Displaced Persons tended to be located in the working class and among the most disadvantaged sectors of white Australia. Thus, to the extent that assimilation was occurring, it took on a segmented character.

The emergence of multicultural Australia

By the late 1950s, voices within and without government circles began to question the viability and appropriateness of the assimilationist strategy. At the same time, as Australia's economy became increasingly enmeshed in the regional Asian economy, the racism of the White Australia policy proved to be problematic in dealings with trade partners such as Japan (London 1970: 179–204). Both practices crumbled during the 1960s, to be replaced by integration and by a racially inclusive orientation towards immigrants. Integration became official policy from the mid-1960s until 1972, proving to be in retrospect a stepping-stone to multiculturalism. Integration meant a recognition and appreciation of cultural pluralism. Murphy (1993: 164) contrasts assimilation to integration by noting that, "Assimilation aimed at cultural uniformity; integration envisaged a community built on diverse cultural patterns." The shift from assimilation to integration entailed an awareness that ethnic communities served a valuable function in aiding in the process of acculturation and it also suggested a more sensitive approach to the difficulties that newcomers often encountered – such as difficulties involved in English-language acquisition.

The end of White Australia commenced in 1956 with the introduction of modifications to existing law that allowed for non-European immigrants to enter the country either on humanitarian grounds or because they possessed critical occupational skills (London 1970: 25–6). The latter part of this policy would underpin subsequent challenges to the racist policies of the past as the nation shifted from considerations based on race to considerations based on occupational utility. A series of subsequent reforms further chipped away at the White Australia policy, such that by 1966 it was effectively dead.

Beginning in 1972, the Australian government embarked on a new approach to ethnic diversity. Influenced by developments in Canada, it embraced multiculturalism in place of integration. It was meant to apply to all of Australia, and in particular, it was conceived not only in terms of immigration, but also in terms of the Aboriginal community. While there is a clear similarity between integration and multiculturalism, there were significant differences as well. Part of making it possible for multiculturalism to flourish entailed combating racism. With the Whitlam administration's passage of the Race Discrimination Act in 1975, the government assumed a more proactive role in the protection of minority groups than it had in the past. Moreover, multiculturalism meant not merely tolerating the presence of difference, but viewing the core of Australian identity as embedded in the notion of diversity. This implied that Australian national identity, rather than being a fixed notion located in the past, and thus defined in the constrictive terms of Anglo-Australia, was open, fluid, and future-oriented. In concrete terms, the government committed itself to helping to preserve and enhance ethnic identities, which included supporting the preservation of non-English languages and heritages.

As with the US and Canadian cases, Australian critics of multiculturalism contended that such a policy implied the "balkanization" or the "disuniting" of the society. However, as the New Agenda of 1997 makes clear, multiculturalism is to be understood in relationship to "civic duty," which is the term used to locate cultural diversity within a framework of shared values and orientations as citizens. Multiculturalism in this sense encourages cultural pluralism, accepts structural pluralism, and necessitates civic assimilation.

During the last quarter of the twentieth century, the number of immigrants arriving from Britain and elsewhere in western Europe has declined dramatically. At the same time, the number of immigrants arriving from the former Soviet Union, the former Yugoslavia, the Baltic states, and Poland has increased. There have also been increases in new white arrivals from New Zealand and South Africa. However, complementing these immigrant groups are people of color from such places as Viet Nam, India, the Philippines, the People's Republic of China, Hong Kong, Taiwan, India, Sri Lanka, Malaysia, Indonesia, and Fiji. Added to this are asylum seekers, some entering the nation illegally, from such nations as Iran and Afghanistan. Table 3 provides an overview of the impact of these developments.

Concerned about the fact that the median age of the Australian population is increasing, signaling a growing segment of retirees in the relatively near future coupled with potential labor shortages, the government remains committed to increasing immigration at least in the near future. In 2000, Prime Minister John Howard announced increases in the number of immigration slots available by 6,000, with preference given to people with skills in occupations experiencing shortages, such as in the technology sector. Those with English-language skills will be accorded preference, as will those willing to live in less populated parts of the country (Collymore 2000).

Critics of governmental policies can be found on both ends of the political spectrum. Human rights groups and agencies concerned with refugees and asylum seekers complain that by giving such priority to skilled workers, the

Table 3   Foreign-born persons in Australia

Top 10 countries	1989	1994	1999
United Kingdom	1,225,800	1,223,500	1,227,200
New Zealand	280,200	295,900	361,600
Italy	272,500	264,100	244,600
Former Yugoslav Republic	NA	179,400	208,400
Viet Nam	103,900	150,400	175,200
China (excluding Hong Kong and Taiwan)	65,300	102,200	156,800
Greece	148,200	143,400	140,200
Germany	121,300	119,900	123,500
Philippines	64,200	93,200	116,900
India	58,400	75,600	100,700
Other	1,443,400	1,446,000	2,855,400
Total	3,773,200	4,093,000	4,482,000
Percent of population	22.4%	23.0%	23.6%

Source: Australian Department of Immigration and Multicultural Affairs, 2000.

needs of other potential immigrants are being ignored. On the other hand, overt hostility to nonwhite immigrants – such as the campaign led by Queensland politician Pauline Hanson – can be heard in some quarters, with the recurring refrain that these particular groups are not capable of assimilating into Australia. In other words, the view pursued by these right-wing groups harks back to an earlier period of Australian history.

Simon and Lynch (1999: 460) contend that "Government policies are more pro-immigrant than public opinion seems to support." That being said, however, while many Australians are critical of illegal immigrants and concerned in various ways about adjustment problems that members of some groups experience, the majority of the public rejects this politics of the rearguard and embraces in principle the idea of multiculturalism (Ho 1990; Beckett 1995). In the wake of the September 11, 2001, attack in the US, fears of terrorism were exploited by the Prime Minister, John Howard, in his reelection campaign. His pledge to get tough on illegal boat people is thought to have contributed to his victory. At the same time, the One Nation party headed by Pauline Hanson lost ground, while such mainstream voices as the Australian Chamber of Commerce have stressed the need to increase current immigration levels (*The Economist* 2001: 39). It is difficult to predict how the concept of multiculturalism will evolve over time, and likewise to know what kinds of changes will transpire to reshape the meaning of Australian identity. Suffice it to say that with the shift from assimilation to multiculturalism, the nation has embarked on a profound reconsideration of diversity and national identity.

Multi-ethnic Japan: a comparison

To appreciate the significance of the cultural and political transformation underway in Australia, a comparison with Japan, the other major advanced industrial nation in the region, can be instructive. Like Australia, Japan confronts a demographic challenge. In fact, given the nation's exceptionally low birth rate of 1.38 per woman, it is predicted that the population will decline by as much as 17 percent by 2050 (French 2000: A1). Thus, like Australia, there are good reasons for looking to immigration as a way to redress this trend. The problem is that the Japanese have historically viewed themselves as a homogeneous society that is racially distinct from and superior to outside ethnic groups (Shigematsu 1993–4).

The reality, as John Lie (2001: 138–9) has recently documented, is actually considerably more complex and the nation has historically been less homogeneous than popular opinion would suggest. Moreover, it has become more diverse in recent years. He contends that the factors that have contributed to the perpetuation of the myth of homogeneity include the fact that non-Japanese ethnic groups tend to remain socially isolated, the ideology of monoethnic Japan has allowed both the government and the public to ignore other groups (for example, the government does not collect statistics on ethnic groups), and individuals from non-Japanese groups who have been in the country for a time tend to succumb to the demand for Japanization rather than mobilizing in ethnic collectivities. That being said, Japan in fact does remain the most homogeneous of the major industrial nations. According to Lie's (2001: 4) estimates, the total non-Japanese population – indigenous minorities and immigrants combined – represents somewhere between 3.2 percent and 4.8 percent of the nation's 125,000,000 residents.

The mainstream majority population is known as the Yamato – or Japanese – people. Three of the main ethnic groups that have resided in the country for centuries, the consequence of internal colonization, include the Ainu, Okinawan, and Burakumin. The Ainu are the indigenous peoples of the northern part of contemporary Japan, and as such occupy a place in Japanese society not unlike American Indians, First Nation peoples, and Aborigines. Like their counterparts, they have suffered from marginalization and oppression and their social circumstances include serious problems associated with poverty and alcoholism. What makes their situation unique is the fact that for much of the past two centuries, the Japanese government has refused to recognize the Ainu as a distinct culture. It did so for a short time between 1950 and 1953, and again after 1987, by which time the desire to protect their culture had found expression in the activities of the Utari Kyokai (the Utari Association). Once assimilationist and passive, it became a voice for Ainu intent on preserving their culture and making demands for political empowerment and economic improvement (Lie 2001: 89–94).

Parallels between the Okinawans and Ainu can be made. The former reside in the Ryukyu island chain between Japan and Taiwan. Once residing in an independent kingdom, the Okinawans were annexed by the Meiji government in the nineteenth century, and as a consequence they came to view themselves as a colonized people. They are, however, more culturally and linguistically similar to the Yamato than are the Ainu. Despite these similarities, they have been the victims of considerable prejudice that serves to justify their location in the lower tiers of the socioeconomic ladder. Okinawans have been for most of the twentieth century an important component of the low-wage, unskilled sector of the economy. What complicates the situation for contemporary Okinawans is the fact that the US military has had a significant presence in their territory since the end of the Second World War. Thus ethnic activists not only resent long-standing Japanese demands to assimilate, but also view the American presence as that of an occupying force. Lie (2001: 101) notes that in recent decades these activists have increasingly "asserted Okinawan autonomy and difference. . . . In fact, voices for cultural and even political independence are ascendant."

The Burakumin case is somewhat more complicated than the preceding two. In the first place, the origin of this group is not entirely clear. Some contend that their ancestry is Korean while others view them, not as a distinct ethnic group, but as a group of long-standing social outcasts or "polluted people" (*eta*) who perform occupations that are essential but nevertheless considered unclean. While much about the Burakumin's history and identity is contested, it is clear that they have occupied a segregated, caste-like position within Japanese society, excluded from moving into the social and political mainstream. Because ethnicity and class location are so intertwined in this particular case, it is perhaps not surprising that from the early part of the twentieth century an organization called Suiheisha (Leveling Society) was politically leftist, influenced as much or more by socialist ideals than by notions of ethnic mobilization (Neary 1989). Since the 1960s, a number of civil rights organizations, including the Buraku Liberation League, have pushed the government to take steps to combat discrimination and in other ways work to integrate the Burakumin into the upper tiers of the labor market. While there is considerable evidence that improvements have been made during the past three decades, it is also the case that they have not reached economic parity with mainstream Japanese society and discrimination has not altogether ceased (Lie 2001: 87–9).

Added to these three ethnic minority groups are immigrant minorities, the largest of which are the between 750,000 and 1,000,000 Koreans and 200,000 Chinese. In addition, in smaller numbers immigrants from the Philippines, Thailand, Pakistan, Malaysia, Bangladesh, and Iran have sought employment opportunities in Japan during the past few decades. Together, these foreigners constitute only 1 percent of the Japanese population. Many of these immigrants perform the most unpleasant unskilled jobs that the Japanese disdain. These jobs are generally referred to as 3K (*kitsui, kitanai,* and *kiken*) – which translate into English as difficult, dirty, and dangerous (Papademetriou 1997–8: 20). While this is in many respects no different from the situation of recent immigrants in other industrial nations, what is distinctive is the fact that sexwork is one of the most important occupations for female immigrants. Thus Filipina entertainers, South Korean bar hostesses, and Thai masseuses have become central to organized prostitution, and thus they end up being enmeshed in the criminal underworld controlled by the *yakuza* (mafia).

To date, the government has done relatively little to combat discrimination or the economic and sexual exploitation of immigrants. Moreover, it has done little to address the issue of incorporation of historic ethnic minorities or of more recent immigrants into the mainstream of Japanese society. Japanese ethnocentrism remains a potent force preventing serious consideration of incorporation or of forging a society committed to multiculturalism. Lie (2001: 35) writes that, "To put it crudely, Japanese believe themselves to be more cultured and civilized than foreign workers." He might have added that this same view also shapes Yamato Japanese attitudes towards Ainu, Okinawans, and Burakumin ethnics. Not surprisingly, no serious effort to consider the possibility of pursuing a multicultural strategy has developed.

Postscript

Thus, the situation in Japan offers a stark contrast to the multicultural experiments underway in contemporary Australia and Canada. Japan harbors a racialist vision of national identity that is similar, as we shall see in chapter 5, to Germany. This type of nationalism is particularly resistant to considerations of multiculturalism. In a different way, the United States differs from Canada and Australia. In part, this is due to the American emphasis on individual rights and its aversion to considerations of group rights. In part, it is because the US has a more substantive sense of national identity, forged as a consequence of its self-creation as a nation out of the crucible of revolution. In contrast, since neither Canada nor Australia succeeded in completely severing their ties to Britain, they have both suffered from a weaker sense of national identity. It is within this context that their experiments with multicultural policies take on particular significance, and pose unique challenges. Given this fact, whatever the shortcomings of multiculturalism in theory and practice, it is clear that in both nations large sectors of the public, governmental leaders, and cultural elites are sympathetic to multiculturalism. While both nations confront outright challenges to multiculturalism from the extreme right and considerable sniping on the part of the more mainstream right wing, the most substantive political debates tend to revolve around the particular version of multiculturalism to be advanced rather than whether or not multiculturalism in general ought to be promoted.

John Bull's Island: Britain in a Postcolonial World

Until the mid-twentieth century, the nations of western Europe tended to be characterized by the emigration of their people to settler nations such as those discussed in the preceding two chapters. Between the seventeenth and nineteenth centuries, colonial migrations from various western European destinations to North America, South America, Africa, Australia, and New Zealand were substantial. Meanwhile, the sum of labor immigrants moving into western Europe during the Industrial Revolution, mainly from eastern Europe and north Africa, was considerably smaller than the number of emigrants (Carsten 1994; Sassen 1999).

Since that time, however, these nations have become major immigration-receiving sites. As a consequence, they display a heterogeneity today quite unlike earlier periods in their histories. Moreover, since many of the new immigrants are people of color, the new ethnic formations currently emerging are being shaped within a racialized crucible (Miles 1993). In this respect, western Europe is coming to parallel developments in the settler nations discussed in chapters 2 and 3 (Castles & Miller 1993; Papastergiadis 2000).

As a consequence of the new immigration, the ethnic character of every western European country except Iceland is far more heterogeneous and complex that it was four decades ago. Moreover, the pervasiveness of ethnic conflict is such that even the heretofore basically ethnically homogeneous Scandinavian countries have experienced tensions, and have been forced to confront the racism of right-wing extremists. Thus, for example in Norway, one of the bastions of liberal democracy where residents have prided themselves on their tolerance and their openness, the presence of 250,000 foreign workers from such nations as Chile, Vietnam, Bosnia, and Iraq has called this self-image into question. Overt discrimination in housing and jobs is common, and immigrants have discovered that Norwegian laws fail to protect them adequately from such treatment. Moreover, the anti-immigrant

Progress Party has emerged to crystallize a growing "European-only" sentiment (Bowcott 1999). In this regard, Norway is no different from its Scandinavian neighbors or for that matter from anywhere else in western Europe.

At the same time, these nations are also confronting profound and in many respects novel cultural and political challenges and conflicts that have arisen as a result of the renewed vitality of nationalist movements (Hobsbawm 1990; Taylor 1992; Moynihan 1993; Kymlicka 1995; Anderson 2000). In all of these cases, national minorities are able to rely on invented traditions in defining deeply felt grievances: the legends, myths, and actual historical events that are used to define mutual antipathy. Competing territorial claims are at the root of the conflict, as nationalists seek to arrive at a situation where the boundaries of nation and state should coincide. This is the case for nationalist movements harboring either secessionist or irredentist aspirations (Foster 1980; Gurr 1993; Kristeva 1993).

While not every western European country has active nationalist minorities seeking independence, greater autonomy, or a reconnection with another nation, many do. These include Britain, which confronts nationalist movements in Scotland, Wales, and Northern Ireland; France, with movements in Corsica and Brittany; the Basque, Catalan, Andalusian, and Galician nationalists in Spain; the Lega Nord in Italy; and the Walloon/Flemish spilt in Belgium (Watson 1990).

In attempting to comprehend these developments, and in particular making sense of the impact of multiculturalism on received ideas of citizenship, Canadian philosopher Will Kymlicka (1995) has suggested that it is useful to distinguish between what he refers to as "multination states" and "polyethnic states." The former refers to states containing nationality groups capable of making historically rooted territorial claims and demands for either greater regional autonomy or outright independence. National minorities represent what Montserrat Guibernau (1999) depicts as "nations without states" that are able to rely on vast reservoirs of historical capital. They are the products of what Michael Hechter (1975) calls "internal colonialism," a process linked to both industrialization and nation-building. The latter refers to states composed of voluntary immigrants who, leaving their homelands for a variety of economic, political, and/or religious reasons, opt to settle in another nation where they perceive greater opportunities for themselves. In this case, the issue of territory is moot since the newcomers cannot make claim to territory. The central issue with such groups is how and to what extent they want to assimilate and whether the host society is willing to accommodate them in the process of incorporation.

While analytically the distinction can readily be understood, when applied to actual nation-states, it is difficult to determine which characterizes any particular state. Thus, if one focuses on Catalan or Basque nationalists in Spain, it would appear that one could call it a multination state. However, if one turns to north African immigrants in the country, it would appear that it is a polyethnic state. In reality, of course, it is both. Thus, herein a modification of Kymlicka will be used whereby what are distinguished are not nation-states, but the particular ethnic groups residing within a nation's boundaries. Thus, national minorities (the group counterpart to the multination idea) will be distinguished from ethnic groups (the group counterpart to polyethnic states). This chapter will focus on the United Kingdom, one of the three largest and most powerful nations of western Europe, while the following chapter will turn to the other two: Germany and France.

Britain and the End of Empire

The end of the Second World War marked a watershed in British history. Once the world's preeminent industrial power, the devastation of the war was the final contributing factor to a process of economic decline *vis-à-vis* other industrial nations that dated to the 1890s. Though still one of the most important capitalist industrial economies, its earlier preeminence was no more. At the same time, the British Empire, which had been the largest empire during the imperialist age, was progressively dismantled. The independence movement in India can be seen as marking the beginning of the end of Britain as a colonial power. From the perspective of the metropole, its colonies were increasingly seen as too costly to maintain in both economic and political terms. Moreover, the legitimacy of the racist ideologies that had shaped imperialism and served as rationales for colonial rule were undermined by their association with the racist ideology of Nazi Germany (Füredi 1998). However, at the same time, the nation began the process of wartime recovery and rebuilding, and thus served as a spur to immigration. As it did so, it became clear that as the economy of England prospered – particularly the southeast of England – the regions of Scotland and Wales lagged behind.

Within this general context, what it meant to be British in these new circumstances was posed from two quarters, opening to question various possible futures. First, as a multination state, the United Kingdom confronted challenges that called into question its future from resurgent nationalist movements in Scotland, Wales, and Northern Ireland. Second, beginning in the 1950s immigrants from Commonwealth countries – particularly from the Caribbean and the Indian subcontinent – began to enter the country in large numbers, making it for the first time a racially mixed, polyethnic state as well. We explore each of these developments respectively in the following two sections.

The Break-up of Britain?

The British Union, according to the influential and controversial thesis of Tom Nairn, is sliding down the slippery slope leading to its ultimate dismantling. He first articulated this thesis in his book *The Break Up of Britain* (1977), and reasserted it more recently in *After Britain* (2000), in light of the initial impact of Westminster's policy of devolution. Whether it takes the form of the restrained nationalist movements of Scotland and Wales or the violent challenge to British rule posed by republicans in Northern Ireland, what has been called into question is whether or not these stateless nations will in the end remain united to a nation with an English core. In short, Nairn (1999) suggests that while it may be true that there will always be an England, it is not necessarily the case that there will always be a Britain.

The future, in other words, is one in which Scotland and Wales may well become independent states, while the irredentist aspirations of the IRA might be realized as Northern Ireland is reunited with the rest of Ireland. This section will assess the reasons that such an argument has gained plausibility during the last quarter of the twentieth century. It will also ask whether Nairn's prediction is premature and whether other possible futures might, in fact, be more likely.

England's first colonies: a historical excursus

Scotland and Wales share an island with the larger and more powerful England, and their histories must be understood within this geopolitical context (see map 3). In the Scottish case, whether or not Scotland was to be independent or a part of a union with England has been a subject of debate and conflict for almost 1,200 years, dating to the founding of the Kingdom of Scotland in 844. Between that date and 1707, when the Act of Union joined Scotland with England and Wales in the Kingdom of Great Britain, Scotland and England were pitted against each other, with Scotland typically forming alliances with England's enemy, France. Images of the rebellious William Wallace captured in the popular film *Braveheart* reflect something of the ongoing resistance over many centuries to incorporation into a political union with England (Houston & Whyte 1989; McCrone et al. 1989; Devine 1999). A similar situation was found in Wales, though union occurred earlier and more gradually, especially after the Welsh prince Henry Tudor became King Henry VII of England. The first English-Welsh Act of Union dates to 1536 (Williams 1982; Levack 1987; Jones 1994).

The history of Ireland differs from Scotland and Wales insofar as the Irish managed to partially cast off British rule early in the twentieth century. The

Map 3 The United Kingdom
Source: Gershon 1995.

partial nature of their independence struggle accounts for the particularly intractable nature of the conflict in Northern Ireland today. Like these other two nationality groups, the Irish were forced to contend with the incursions of outsiders into their lives, in this case dating back to the twelfth century when Norman barons seized vast tracts of land and swore fealty to Henry II of England. It was not until the reign of Henry VIII in the sixteenth century, however, that Ireland was fully controlled by the English crown. Subsequent monarchs sought to strengthen the ties between England and Ireland. Mary, for example, established "the plantation of Ireland," wherein extensive land grants were given to English settlers. She also vigorously sought to suppress Roman Catholicism and replace it with Protestantism. Such policies continued into the seventeenth century as more Protestant settlers acquired land in Ireland. These included both English and Scottish Protestants, the latter – chiefly Presbyterian – locating in heavy concentrations in the northern part of the island. By the beginning of the eighteenth century, Irish Catholics owned only one-seventh of the nation's land, were excluded from political power, and found their culture under assault (Foster 1988).

In this context, resistance to English rule was intense. Malcolm Anderson (2000: 28) writes in this regard, "The Irish identify the permanent establishment of an Anglo-Norman presence in Ireland in 1291 as the beginning of the long struggle by the Irish people against English rule." Periodic revolts were put down, but served as tangible manifestations of the unwillingness of the majority of the Irish population to grant legitimacy to English domination. Moreover, many Irish Protestants (like their peers in the American colonies) chafed under English rule, and demanded greater autonomy. A growing independence movement emerged, culminating in an unsuccessful revolt in 1798. The result of this rebellion was the push by Prime Minister William Pitt to pass the Act of Union, which in 1801 made Ireland officially a part of the United Kingdom of Great Britain and Ireland.

Thus, while the Irish entered into a union not unlike the ones that incorporated Scotland and Wales into the nation's core, the difference was that from virtually the moment of union, organized resistance developed. In the early 1800s, a movement for "home rule" would have established an Irish Parliament and thus accorded the Irish greater political autonomy. Protestants, as a minority, feared a Catholic-dominated legislative body and therefore opposed the movement. The British Parliament refused to grant home rule, with the result being a growing desire on the part of Irish Catholics for complete independence.

A political organization reflecting this position, Sinn Féin (in Irish, literally, "we ourselves"), was founded in 1905, along with a secretive group known as the Irish Republican Brotherhood. The British Parliament responded to this growing nationalist fervor by passing a home rule bill in 1914, though due to the First World War it was never actually implemented. The battle for independence commenced two years later, beginning with the Easter Rebellion. Over the next three decades, an independent Ireland was forged. In 1920, the British parliament passed the Government of Ireland Act, which established the Irish Free State and divided the island in two, with the six counties of the northern, Protestant-dominated regions becoming the separate political entity of Northern Ireland.

Although self-governing, the Free State remained a part of the United Kingdom. This arrangement divided the Irish people over two issues. First, some accepted it, while others held out for complete independence. The latter position was reflected in the military campaign against British rule conducted by the Irish Republican Army (IRA). Equally divisive was the matter of Northern Ireland, which became, in effect, a captive of history (MacEoin 1974). Some accepted the partition of the island, while others held out for its reunification. The first of these issues was settled in 1949, when Ireland declared itself to be a republic, and thus for the first time became a genuinely independent nation. It is in this context that the campaign of the IRA to unite Northern Ireland with the Republic of Ireland, which exploded onto the scene in the 1960s, needs to be understood (Ruane & Todd 1996).

Within this long historical perspective, represented by nearly three centuries of union, the most recent manifestations of nationalism have arisen. They need to be contextualized in terms of several significant developments in Britain which it might appear ought to have resulted in the further integration of the periphery into the center, rather than stimulating a resurgence of nationalist activism. First, Scottish, Welsh, and Irish nationalism since the Second World War have arisen at a time of dramatic changes in transportation and communications. As a result, Britain was transformed into a mass society beginning in the 1950s. At the same time, the expansion of the welfare state served to improve the socioeconomic position, the educational attainment, and the health of the working class and the poor, and to reduce some of the most pronounced differences in regional standards of living.

Linked to the above, the Labour Party, while maintaining much of the socialist rhetoric of its formative years, nonetheless came to act like a partner in power – reflecting a historical compromise between capital and labor. In other words, the adversarial edge was blunted, as the working class was increasingly defined as a partner in the capitalist economy, rather than as a class intent on overthrowing capitalism. Changes in the postwar economy resulted in the expansion of the middle class, particularly professional "black coated" workers. With the expansion of higher education via the postwar construction of the "red-brick" universities, new avenues of upward mobility were opened to working-class youth. This, too, served to take some of the edge off of the class divisions that have been such a pronounced feature of British society.

In and of themselves, these changes do not suggest that they would necessarily contribute to the emergence of nationalist activism. Indeed, they might actually suggest the opposite: namely, that the non-English regions of Britain would be further incorporated into the fabric of the nation-state. However, by the 1970s, three very active and consequential nationalist movements were underway in the regions of the United Kingdom.

Scotland, Wales, and the politics of devolution

Montserrat Guibernau (1999: 89–113) distinguishes three phases in the evolution of nationalist social movements: (1) an early period of scholarly interest in which the role of intellectuals concerned about the revival or preservation of a national culture and identity is paramount; (2) a period of patriotic agitation, in which middle-class elites factor prominently; and (3) if the first two are successful, the rise of a mass nationalist movement in which what was initially a predominantly middle-class phenomenon is transformed into a movement with broader appeal. Each stage, she contends, entails the development and refinement of a distinctive nationalist discourse, which contains in varied mixtures moral, economic, and political rationales for activism. The varieties of nationalism – ranging from the relatively tame aspiration for cultural preservation to the call for a war of national liberation against an oppressor – are reflections of the variability of nationalist discourses. In the cases of Scotland and Wales, their respective nationalist ideologies have led to a call for working through existing democratic political channels. As we shall see below, the most significant difference between the two is that the Scottish case is more overtly political, while Welsh nationalism is chiefly a cultural phenomenon.

Vindicating Scotland

Contemporary Scottish nationalism has its origin in the mid-nineteenth century with the establishment of the Association for the Vindication of Scottish Rights, an organization dedicated to enhancing the role of Scotland in British politics. The rights that the association pointed to were located in the distant past, specifically in the 1321 Declaration of Arbroath, which was seen as an early declaration of the rights of the Scots against the incursions of English monarchs (Anderson 2000: 28). However, the organization viewed itself as forward, not backward, looking. Out of it arose the first expressions of a desire to achieve greater regional autonomy. Though limited in influence, the Association served as the forerunner of further organizing efforts (Houston & Whyte 1989; Devine 1999).

The left-of-center National Party of Scotland was formed in 1928 in an effort to promote home rule, and to convince the Labour Party leadership of the popularity of the idea north of the border. Four years later a moderate right-wing nationalist party, the Scottish Party, appeared on the scene. In 1934, the two joined forces to create the Scottish National Party (Devine 1999: 325). The Depression and the Second World War stifled nationalist aspirations, and internal conflicts between leftist and rightist sectors of the SNP further weakened the movement.

Although the idea of the reestablishment of a Scottish Parliament had been floating in Scottish politics for at least a decade, the late 1960s marks a watershed for nationalism. It coincided with the discovery of oil in the North Sea in 1966. The following year the SNP won a parliamentary seat in what was seen as a safe Labour constituency. This marked the beginning of a profound shift in Scottish politics. From that point forward, the Conservative Party became an increasingly insignificant force in Scotland. Thus, Labour dominated Scottish politics, even through the long years of national rule by the Conservatives. The SNP emerged as the principle opposition party. In 1974, one-third of Scottish voters voted for the SNP. Theirs was a protest vote and a warning that Westminster could no longer afford to ignore the Scottish question. Most SNP voters wanted to press the central government to action and desired greater regional autonomy, though it was not entirely clear what they meant by autonomy or how much they demanded. Only 12 percent of voters actually embraced the idea of outright independence from Britain (Devine 1999: 577–8).

However, during this decade the issue of an independent Scotland was embraced by a growing sector within the SNP leadership, which made the case that North Sea oil made possible the economic viability of a Scottish nation. Moreover, they consistently pointed out the incongruity of a region with high unemployment and a vast natural resource at its doorstep. Others in the SNP also sought to exploit the North Sea oil issue, but in order to push for greater regional autonomy rather than outright independence.

The Labour Party felt the impact of the SNP challenge and was forced to find a way to respond to it that didn't alienate the Scottish electorate, but did manage to take the wind out of the sails of the SNP. Offering the possibility of the creation of a Scottish Assembly, Labour presented its first version of a policy that became known as "devolution," which entailed the ceding of some central-governmental powers to the region, while maintaining the political integrity of Britain. Devolution quickly proved itself to be a controversial matter within the Labour Party. Some opposed it because they were convinced that Scotland's problems could only be successfully addressed by Westminster. Others thought that devolution was a useful tactic in undermining the SNP challenge. Still others were genuinely sympathetic to the idea of home rule (McCrone 1992). A referendum on devolution was held in 1979. Although a slim majority of the Scottish electorate voted in the affirmative, the ruling Labour government argued that since this represented less than 40 percent of all eligible voters, the referendum was defeated. This decision produced a major rift between Labour and the SNP, and led to an electoral debacle for a demoralized SNP.

At the same time, this marked the beginning of the Thatcher years. Her neoconservative policies led to a dramatic and painful economic transformation of Scotland. The decline in manufacturing jobs accelerated the region's severe economic decline and societal strains, the latter seen in a rise in crime, drug abuse, and other related social problems (vividly depicted, for example, in the film *Trainspotting*). During the 1980s, the SNP moved to the political left, in no small part as a reaction to the Thatcher government. Some of the policies of the Party amounted to what Jack Brand (1990: 28) has referred to as "cost-free radicalism": calling for an end to nuclear weapons, supporting the anti-apartheid campaign of the African National Congress in South Africa, and supporting Nicaragua's Sandinista government. The call of young Turks in the party to promote the idea of a "Scottish socialist republic" paralleled the leftward swing of the Labour Party in Scotland, which had come under the influence of the Trotskyite Militant Tendency. A focus of industrial activism during the 1980s revolved around efforts to save industrial enterprises that were threatened by the Thatcher administration's aggressive promotion of deindustrialization (Devine 1999: 599–606).

The Thatcher regime was intractably hostile to the aspirations of Scottish nationalists. In the first place, it was unwilling to entertain the prospect of a weakening of a centralized state with a powerful Prime Minister because these were seen as key to economic modernization efforts and to attempts to roll back the welfare state. In addition, given the fact that the Scottish electorate had essentially abandoned the Conservative Party, Thatcher had little to lose in refusing to appease nationalist aspirations. Her firm opposition to devolution provided the impetus for the SNP to consider the possibility of entering into alliances with the Labour Party and the Liberal Democrats in keeping devolution alive in the form of the Campaign for a Scottish Assembly. In 1986, the SNP entered into an agreement with its Welsh counterpart, Plaid Cymru (in Welsh, literally, "party of Wales"), which proclaimed in part that the two nationalist parties were willing to work with other parties to further devolution, and furthermore, they agreed to refuse to work cooperatively with the Conservative Party because of its opposition to their aspirations (Brand 1990: 30).

By the late 1980s, the SNP had also changed its views on the European Economic Community, shifting from opposition to entry into the Community to support for it. Independence-minded elements in the SNP wanted to rid the party of a fortress-Scotland mentality. In other words, rather than looking inward and backward to a Scotland before British rule, the SNP promoted a view of itself as a party that looked outward and to the future. Concretely, this meant that they increasingly came to define their position as one that sought independence from Britain and membership in the European Union. This was an embrace of the idea of a Europe of the regions. An independent nation, they argued, would be fully integrated into Europe. This position served to reinforce the notion of the irrelevance of being British: Scotland's citizens in the future would be Scottish and European.

In 1995 the Scottish Constitutional Convention, in which the SNP served as a partner in a coalition that included Labour and the Liberal Democrats, along with an array of religious, labor, and civic organizations, presented a plan for the reestablishment of a Scottish Parliament. Though fearful of a repeat of 1979, the moderate "Third Way" Labour government of Tony Blair, who has campaigned on a platform supportive of devolution, decided to hold a referendum in 1997. The result was a resounding victory, as 74 percent of the electorate voted in favor of a Scottish Parliament (Guibernau 1999: 47; see also *The Economist* 1997).

The first Scottish Parliament since 1707 met at Holyrood in Edinburgh in July of 1999. It has considerable power regarding domestic issues, including agriculture, culture and sports, economic development, education, environment, fisheries and food, health, housing, justice, planning, roads, rural affairs, and social work services. The parliament does not have authority over foreign policy, defense, macroeconomic policy, social security, abortion, and broadcasting. Thus, what this act of devolution succeeded in doing was to transform Scottish politics while simultaneously preserving the unity of Britain (*The Economist* 1999).

New Labour's idea of devolution is unsympathetic to the politics of recognition. Tom Nairn pointed this out when describing the criticism leveled against the SNP by the Labour government's Chancellor of the Exchequer, Gordon Brown (himself a Scot). Nairn (2000: 99–100) writes:

> One of the features of New Labour's campaign against independence has been a consistent denigration of "identity." The Chancellor of the Exchequer, for instance, accused [the SNP] of attaching far too much importance to it, rather than to the substantial issues of social and economic policy which Holyrood ought to focus upon. What the Scots need, he argued recently, is more money spent on education and health, not the mere appearance of [in Brown's words] "the old nation state: The real battle . . . will be between those who put the politics of social justice first, and those who practice the politics of national identity above anything else."

Brown's juxtaposition of the politics of social justice and the politics of identity was intended to drive a wedge between the aspirations of many Scots for an enhanced ability to make political decisions at the local level rather than having them made by Westminster, and the desire of the leadership of the SNP and a minority of the Scottish electorate for independence.

The unanswered question for Scotland at the beginning of the twenty-first century is whether this new arrangement is the final word, or proves to be merely a step on the way to the break-up of Britain. In terms of the nationalism advanced by the SNP, does a parliament mean that sufficient autonomy has been achieved to satisfy most Scots, and thereby undermine the long-term role of the SNP in Scottish politics? Or should it be seen as a victory that will serve to stimulate nationalists to press for total political independence? At the dawn of the new century, some influential members of the SNP were predicting that independence would be achieved within the decade. Could Scotland, as one commentator (Reed 1999) put it, "turn into Tony Blair's Quebec?" While much remains uncertain, the reality at present is that although an overwhelming majority of Scots favor devolution, the SNP remains the second party of Scotland after Labour, garnering around 30 percent of the vote (Freedland 1999).

Moreover, as I write, only a quarter of Scots favor outright independence. The majority believes that they can be both Scottish and British. Some commentators have suggested that British identity was shaped by empire, and with the demise of the empire, it becomes an increasingly empty container. Perhaps this is the case, but it is also true that when Andrew Wilson, a rising star in the SNP, referred to the Union Jack as an "offensive symbol" at the party's conference in late 1999, he was met with a storm of criticism. In his subsequent apology, he acknowledged that a substantial majority of Scots retain an affinity with British identity (MacAskill & Seenan 1999). In speculating about the short-term future, I concur with Francis Mulhern's (2000: 63) assessment:

> The main political variable in the years ahead will be the general one of the pragmatic success of Blairism as a pan-British formula for economy and society. Short of an electoral crisis at that level – above all, short of a major revival of Conservative fortunes in the south – "de facto independence," or strong devolution, may prove a habitable state for the Scottish majority.

The defense of Welsh culture

Welsh nationalism parallels its Scottish counterpart in fundamental ways. Founded in 1925, Plaid Cymru (for its first two decades the party was known as the Welsh Nationalist Party), the main Welsh nationalist party, began its history in the same era as the SNP. The party grew gradually. In 1930 it had no more than 500 members, and by the end of that decade the figure had only risen to around 2,000. Like the SNP, the party was committed to working through democratic political channels, committed to ballots not bullets. From its inception, Plaid Cymru confronted appeals from within its ranks for promoting an independent Wales. Nonetheless, this was from the beginning a minority position within the organization. The majority of those attracted to the party viewed Welsh nationalism as a vehicle for greater political autonomy, but in their view this was sufficient. Also like the SNP, Plaid Cymru managed to win only a small minority of the electorate to its side during its first several decades. In fact, it was not until 1970 that they received over 10 percent of the vote.

One of the distinguishing features of Welsh nationalism is its singular focus on cultural matters, and particularly on the issue of the preservation of the Welsh language (Williams 1985; Trosset 1993). It was from its early twentieth-century conception fundamentally a moral and intellectual nationalism (Balsom 1990: 9). As such, it has a culturally conservative character. The precipitous decline in the use of the Welsh language had been a matter of concern for many Welsh since the 1930s – whether or not they spoke the language – because the potential loss of the language (and they could simply look to their Cornish neighbors to their south for an example of a people who in recent memory had experienced the loss of their language) could be seen as a sign of the end of Welsh culture.

However, many Welsh were uncomfortable about the prospect of linking cultural preservation with a campaign of separation from Britain. While intent on protecting the Welsh language and culture, most Welsh also wanted to remain involved in a wider British world. They rejected what Kenneth Morgan (1981: 258) has referred to as "an inward-looking exclusiveness." The result was that Welsh nationalism came to be characterized as a less overtly political variant than Scottish nationalism. This is not to suggest that Welsh nationalism was apolitical. Indeed, it was as the result of a nonviolent political campaign that the Welsh Language Act was passed by Parliament in 1967, which established among other things a Welsh-language television station (Guibernau 1999: 122).

As with the SNP, the late 1960s marked the beginning of a period during which Plaid Cymru's influence grew. With less than 20 percent of the Welsh population continuing to retain Welsh-language proficiency, the cultural issue was seen as reaching a crisis stage. However, this alone cannot account for the changing fortunes of the party. Like the SNP, it began to address a variety of social issues from a distinctly left-of-center position. And like the SNP, it campaigned vigorously for devolution during the 1970s. However, Welsh nationalism has failed to attract the levels of support obtained by their SNP counterparts. The defeat of the 1979 referendum by a sizeable margin was a major blow to Welsh nationalism. Indeed, its defeat even in the Welsh-speaking heartland reflected the political limitations of Plaid Cymru (Balsom 1990: 16).

Economic problems came to the fore during the Thatcher years. Wales had a higher proportion of its workforce employed in the public sector (including nationalized industries such as coal) than any other place in western Europe. With its zealous ideological commitment to privatization, the Thatcher government's policies had a profound negative impact on Wales during the 1980s. Deindustrialization on a wide scale resulted in high un-employment rates and a substantial population exodus from traditional in-dustrial communities to the London region, where the economy was doing considerably better. The bitter and protracted miners' strike of 1984–5 fueled antipathy toward the Conservative Party and disappointment with Labour's response. This provided Plaid Cymru with a window of opportunity to offer its own left-wing economic platform (Balsom 1990: 15–18).

At the same time, cultural anti-English sentiment took an overtly political form in the 1980s with arson attacks conducted by the Sons of Glendower (Meibion Glyndŵr) on holiday homes owned by English people. As the Welsh nationalist character in Jasmin Dizdar's 1999 film *Beautiful People* explains, the rationale for the campaign revolves around the claim that Welsh resi-dents are being deprived of homes, at the expense of wealthy English people who only occupy the residences for short periods of time each year. This is an instance of a situation where cultural concerns become intimately linked to economic considerations.

Despite these acts of violence, Welsh nationalism is overwhelmingly a matter of nonviolent actions conducted through established political chan-nels (Wigley 1996). In its alliance with the SNP, Plaid Cymru revived the devolution campaign in the 1990s, reversing its 1979 referendum loss with a victory in 1997. As with the Scottish Parliament, the Welsh Assembly con-vened for the first time in 1999, assuming responsibilities for such domestic matters as agriculture, culture, economic development, education and train-ing, the environment, health, transportation, social services, regional plan-ning, and tourism (Meredith 1999).

Again, as with Scotland, the unanswered question is whether the au-tonomy granted by devolution will dampen the nationalist movement or in-vigorate it. Prior to the referendum, the then president of Plaid Cymru, Dafydd Wigley, was quoted as supporting "an independent democratic Wales inside a united Europe" (quoted in Osmond 1995: 8). Given the fact that the Welsh have been less inclined than the Scots to favor outright independence from Britain, whether the nationalist party will need to modify its position in favor of advancing Welsh interests within Britain or will push the independence button remains unclear – as do the future responses of the Welsh people and the British government.

The Catalonian comparison

Catalonian nationalism in Spain is the movement in continental Europe that most resembles the Scottish and Welsh cases (Shafir 1995). Catalonia has a long and complex history of cultural distinctiveness and political autonomy from the centralist, Castilian-dominated Spanish state dating from the sixteenth century (see map 4). The roots of contemporary Catalonian nationalism are located in the nineteenth century, an important component of which was a linguistic and cultural revival known as the *renaixenca*. During the same time, another thread of nationalist ideology emerged, this one promoting a modern Catalan culture at home with the modernist trends throughout cosmopolitan Europe. Thus, entering the twentieth century there were two oppositional versions of Catalan nationalism: one rooted in Catholicism was conservative and tradition-bound; the other was modern, democratic, and secular (Edles 1999: 315–22; Guibernau 1999: 41).

In the early twentieth century Catalonia achieved a measure of autonomy. This, however, was challenged after the coup that brought Miguel Primo de Rivera to power in 1923. Autonomy was briefly revived during the early 1930s, including a provision that made Catalan the official language of the region. However, due in no small part to the role Catalan republicans played in the Spanish Civil War, the fascist dictatorship of Francisco Franco not only ended autonomy, but enacted a series of governmental policies designed to crush Catalan nationalism. The long Franco regime – from 1939 to 1975 – was a dark period for nationalists. Prohibitions were imposed on the use of the Catalan language and of nationalist symbols. Because the Catholic Church had sided with the Franco regime, the most conservative sector of the nationalist movement lost credibility, and thus during these years the secular, modernist type of nationalism acquired hegemonic status (Edles 1999: 325–7). Moreover, this particular nationalistic discourse was increas-

Map 4   Catalonia and the Basque Region in Spain
Source: Gershon 1995.

ingly fused with the language of the political left. This was especially the case after the leftist defeat in the Spanish Civil War and the embrace of Catalan nationalism by communists and socialists (Guibernau 1999: 95).

Current manifestations of Catalan nationalism arose out of this repressive climate, and must be seen in the context of Spain's subsequent transition to democracy after the death of Franco (Bonime-Blanc 1987; Diez Medrano 1995). They must also be seen in light of the fact that Catalonia is the most successful economic region in the Iberian Peninsula. Though constituting only 6 percent of the total land of Spain, it produced an estimated 19 percent of the nation's GNP. Moreover, about one-quarter of all foreign investments in Spain are made in Catalonia, and the region boasts the country's lowest unemployment rate (Gies 1994).

Though fringe nationalist elements engaged in a short-lived bombing campaign, the mainstream of the movement has opted for a moderate approach that takes advantage of and works through legitimate democratic political channels. The Catalan case is clearly one that fits Saul Newman's (1996) description: "mostly ballots, rarely bullets." In 1977, early in the democratic transition, a provisional "Generalitat" was instituted. Though this political body had little real political power, it served as a symbol of the potential for greater regional autonomy, and represented the first shift of power from Madrid to Barcelona. A new constitution went into effect the following year that contained provisions for a form of bilingualism that preserved Castilian as the official language, but elevated the status of regional languages such as Catalan (Woolard 1989). In addition, regional government was accorded greater power over issues related to culture and the delivery of government services.

Since then, Catalan nationalists have continued to push the language issue. In 1983 the Law of Linguistic Normalization made Catalan the dominant language of the region. Controversies over language in schools and government have persisted, with many contending that for Catalonians to function within a Spanish framework, Castilian needs to remain the official language of the region. On the other hand, cultural nationalists fear the erosion of the Catalan language (Gies 1994).

Jordi Pujol, head of Convergencia i Unio (Convergence and Union), became the first president of the Catalan parliament in 1980 and held that post for over two decades. This dominant nationalist party has combined a politics of recognition with a social-democratic approach to economic development and social welfare. Pujol has proven to be adept at working with other political parties and with the central government in Madrid to the benefit of Catalonian autonomy (Edwards 1999). As with the Scottish and Welsh cases, it remains to be seen if the end result of Catalonian nationalism is the establishment of a new autonomous place within Spain or if it will lead to a call for exit from Spain. At the moment, the latter prospect appears very unlikely.

This is even more likely in Catalonia given the fact that its economic dynamism has meant that many non-Catalans have migrated there for work. The response of the mainstream nationalism to these outsiders has been one of tolerance, arguing that their nationalism is of a cosmopolitan variety.

Northern Ireland: the politics of a polarized community

In stark contrast to the three cases that have just been examined, Northern Ireland represents one of the most intractable political conflicts in western Europe (Lijphart 1977). For Irish Catholic nationalists it represents the unfinished business of achieving independence from Britain that began with the 1916 Easter Uprising. For Protestant unionists it represents a life-and-death struggle against breaking the tie with the United Kingdom and being absorbed into the Republic of Ireland. For the British government, it has been a source of unrelenting frustration.

The Catholic community is a minority in Northern Ireland, though it represents the majority if one considers all of Ireland. The reverse is the case for Protestants, who constitute a 2 to 1 majority in Northern Ireland, but represent a relatively small minority in the Irish Republic (O'Brien 1972; MacEoin 1974; Darby 1976). This demographic reality underlies the reason that Ireland is divided, and poses the dilemma it has confronted since partition. If one seeks to determine the will of the majority in deciding the fate of Northern Ireland, should it be the will of the Irish people as a whole or the will of the citizens of the six counties making up Northern Ireland?

The underlying basis for Northern Ireland's political polarization rests with the divergent nationalist ideologies of the two ethnic communities. Catholic republicans define their particular nationalist vision as being both Irish and Catholic. In contrast, the unionists define their vision in terms of Britain or Ulster and the Protestant religion. The exclusivist content of both ideologies serves as a wedge preventing mutual accommodation (Boyce 1990; Murphy 1990). Since the aspirations of both communities have been posed in zero-sum terms, the tension and the potential for conflict between the two contesting ethnic communities is pronounced. As a consequence, they are in many arenas of social life isolated from each other. High levels of residential segregation are typical, particularly in cities (Darby 1976; Marger 1989), Catholics are overwhelmingly educated in parochial schools while Protestants attend state schools (Murray 1986), and the rate of intermarriage is low (Gallagher & Dunn 1991). In short, Catholics and Protestants tend to live in separate social worlds.

Although class differences are not as pronounced as in some other nations with similar ethnic divisions, and it would be a mistake to attempt to reduce the ethnic conflict to class conflict, nonetheless class differences do play a role in defining the Northern Ireland situation. Protestants are more likely to be found in professional white-collar jobs than their Catholic counterparts, while Catholics are over-represented in the ranks of the unskilled sector of the working class and among the unemployed. However, recent decades have witnessed the growth of the Catholic middle class, thus reducing the communal differences in employment status and thereby the advantages that Protestants have had in the past (Smith & Chambers 1991; Breen 2000).

The political system in Northern Ireland differs from those of both Scotland and Wales. When it was partitioned from the rest of Ireland in 1921, Northern Ireland was accorded local home rule in the form of its own prime minister and parliament (known as the Stormont parliament). In other words, devolution was a reality from this early date, even though the term was not used. Founded in 1921, the Official Unionist Party remained the sole political voice of the unionist community until the late 1960s. With its solid electoral majority, it was the controlling party for five decades. In this separate and unequal society, a variety of political responses emerged from the republican side. The main political organization of the Catholic minority was the Nationalist Party, which sought to find opportunities for compromise and was willing to play the role of the opposition party at Stormont.

More militant sectors of the Catholic community thought that this willingness to work within the system was tantamount to capitulation to the British and unionist desire to keep Northern Ireland part of the United Kingdom. A campaign of political violence orchestrated by the Irish Republican Army failed in the late 1950s and early 1960s, lending credence to the belief that most Catholics sought to find ways to improve their situation within the existing political structure. This belief appeared reasonable given the fact that the liberal government of Prime Minister Terence O'Neill promoted policies aimed at improving the economic position of Catholics and enhancing their political power, while simultaneously working to achieve cordial relations with the Republic of Ireland. In what was considered to be an act of capitulation by militant unionists, he met with Seán Lemass, the Prime Minister of the Republic of Ireland. O'Neill's efforts to find avenues for accommodation where the conflict between Catholics and Protestants would no longer be posed in zero-sum terms met with failure, as militants from both sides of the divide were invigorated to resist such efforts.

By the mid-1960s the Nationalist Party's situation cast it increasingly into a defensive posture. The Northern Ireland Civil Rights Association was founded in an effort to combat discrimination and inequality. The movement was in part inspired by the civil rights and student protest movements in the United States, and received transnational support (MacEoin 1974; Maney 2000). Though members of the middle class founded the organization, it managed to capture the disenchantment of working-class Catholics. The

NICRA disavowed violence, but increasingly looked to London and away from Stormont for direction. The result was a weakening of the principal *modus operandi* of the Nationalist Party, which by the end of the decade had fallen apart. In its place, a new party, the Social and Democratic Labour Party, was founded in 1970, committed to a position of constitutional nationalism within the existing political framework (McAllister 1977).

NICRA's tactics of nonviolent protest evoked a hostile backlash from right-wing Protestant elements. In August 1969, Protestant militants attacked civil rights marchers in Londonderry. This led to riots that resulted in attacks by the Royal Ulster Constabulary, Northern Ireland's police force, that were directed at Catholics rather than the Protestant provocateurs. The British government was forced to send troops to quell the violence, which initially was viewed positively by Catholics who believed, with good reason, that the RUC actively sympathized with the Protestant community. This was the beginning of the period known as "the troubles."

In 1970, the nonviolent political course of the Official IRA, or Sinn Féin, came under increasing criticism and led to the birth of the Provisional IRA, which became the main Catholic paramilitary organization committed to a sustained terrorist campaign against continued British rule. The immediate goal of the Provisional IRA was to force the British out of Northern Ireland. The ultimate goal was to effect the reunification of Ireland, despite the growing lack of interest on the part of Dublin for such efforts (O'Malley 1983; Ruane & Todd 1996).

At the same time, the newly formed Democratic Unionist Party (DUP) challenged the OUP. Presbyterian minister Ian Paisley, a rabidly anti-Catholic demagogue who evoked a paranoid siege mentality, headed the party (Murphy 1990: 58). The DUP emerged as the Protestant counterpart to Sinn Féin. Protestant paramilitary groups appeared on the scene, the most powerful being the Ulster Defense League (UDL). Thus, the stage was set for a three-decade period of interethnic violence in a society that became ever more polarized over time. The presence of British troops, though deemed necessary by many, served to exacerbate tensions. Catholics were particularly angered when the British Army opened fire on unarmed protesters in Londonderry in 1972, killing 13 people. Known as "Bloody Sunday," this tragic event became a powerful symbol of anti-British sentiment (O'Leary & McGarry 1993).

In the same year, the British government suspended the Northern Ireland Parliament and instituted direct rule. During the next few years, efforts to establish the basis for some form of interethnic power sharing and a restoration of home rule were met with waves of terrorist attacks by paramilitaries on both sides, neither of which was willing to engage in the politics of compromise (Lijphart 1975; Burton 1978). Both camps stepped up their terrorist campaigns. Unlike the largely isolated Protestant paramilitaries, the IRA elicited considerable support from outside of Northern Ireland, of particular importance being the financial and other support provided by Irish-Americans. The IRA evoked the image of a national liberation struggle to many in the outside world. Activists jailed in the infamous Maze prison engaged in hunger strikes and other forms of protest, and when Bobby Sands died, many viewed him as a martyr. The IRA, unlike the Protestant paramilitaries, took their campaign of terrorism to England, including a bombing that was intended to kill Prime Minister Margaret Thatcher as she attended her party's annual convention.

Neither side had the wherewithal to achieve their goal through violent means. Moreover, the IRA had to contend with the reality that the government of the Republic of Ireland was increasingly indifferent to their desire to end partition. At the same time, many Ulster nationalists became increasingly disenchanted with the British government due to its recurrent efforts to find a power-sharing compromise. Some began to argue on behalf of the idea that Northern Ireland ought to become an independent nation – neither British nor Irish. The intractability of the conflict led to recurrent waves of violence punctuated by uneasy calms. Since "the troubles" began, over 3,600 people have been killed (Holland 1982; Ignatieff 1993; *The Economist* 1998).

Current efforts at conflict resolution have their origin in the 1985 Anglo-Irish Agreement, initiated by the Thatcher government. For the first time, the Republic of Ireland was to have a consultative role in peace negotiations. Protestants were predictably hostile toward any attempt at bringing the Irish government into the process, while not surprisingly, Catholic sentiment was more favorable. However, extremists on both sides attempted to scuttle the process by renewed terrorist campaigns. They succeeded in provoking the Thatcher government to clamp down on the violence by a strong show of military might. For the next decade, renewed peace efforts were put on hold.

Labour Prime Minister Tony Blair began a new round of talks in 1997, which not only included the Irish Prime Minister Bertie Ahern and the UK Secretary of State for Northern Ireland Mo Mowlam, but also included former US Senator George Mitchell as the chair of the peace talks. Parties from both sides of the divide were involved, and they succeeded in obtaining ceasefire agreements from the paramilitaries. On April 10, 1998, the Belfast Agreement (popularly known as the Good Friday Agreement) was signed. The essence of the agreement is the implementation of an arrangement of consociational democracy (Lijphart 1977; Reynolds 1999/2000). The essence of this approach, as Michael Hechter (2000: 136) puts it, is to have ethnic group leaders "participate in decision-making as a cartel."

The centerpiece of the agreement involves the commitment on the part of all parties to resolving political differences solely through democratic and peaceful means. The agreement calls for the establishment of a council to develop channels of cooperation between Northern Ireland, the Republic of Ireland, and the British-Irish Council to ensure harmonious relations between the British and Irish governments. The Agreement calls for the establishment of a Northern Ireland Assembly, thus creating a devolved political structure not unlike that in Scotland and Wales. At this writing, such issues as police reform, demilitarization, and the decommissioning of weapons are being worked out (O'Hearn et al. 1999). The Agreement grants to the people of Northern Ireland the right to choose their collective future, with the British and Irish governments expressing a willingness to "recognize the legitimacy of whatever choice is freely exercised by a majority of the people of Northern Ireland with regard to its status, whether they prefer to continue to support the Union with Great Britain or a sovereign united Ireland" (*Belfast Agreement* 1998: 2). At this point it is unclear which choice will be made and whether either will ultimately be accomplished democratically and peacefully. Skeptics would concur with Hechter's (2000: 137) contention that, "By promoting group as against individual rights, consociationalism tends to inhibit intergroup cooperation."

The Basque comparison

If Catalonia resembles Scotland and Wales, the Basque region of Spain manifests a form of nationalism with consequences that parallel the experience of Northern Ireland. Although the Basque region does not contain two competing nationalisms, as Northern Ireland does, it has been the site of an ongoing campaign of terror by militant nationalists intent on severing ties with the Spanish state (Medrano 1988; Shafir 1995). The terrorism is the work of Euskadi ta Askatasuna (ETA), which can be translated as "Basque Homeland and Freedom." Since 1968, ETA has been responsible for around 800 deaths.

Like its Catalonian counterpart, Basque nationalism has deep historical roots, can trace its contemporary origins to the nineteenth century, suffered from extreme repression during the Franco dictatorship, and remains a potent factor in the democratic transition since the death of Franco. However, there are significant differences between Basque and Catalonian nationalism, reflecting in no small part the cultural distinctiveness of the Basques. The Basques can be conceived as the indigenous peoples of the area, predating the arrival of such peoples as the Gauls and Iberians. Thus, they are a non-Aryan race and the Basque language, known as Euskera, is one of the very few non-Indo-European languages alive in Europe today (Edles 1999: 322–5).

Although never an independent nation, the Basques succeeded in maintaining a considerable degree of self-rule under a system known as the Fueros, which meant that governance was structured around local laws and charters. This system was threatened in the late nineteenth century, coincidental with the industrialization of the Basque region and the immigration of non-Basques into the region in search of jobs. Out of this situation, the Basque National Party (PNV) was founded in 1893. The party reflected a nationalist vision rooted in the past, not the future. Its primary preoccupations were with the purity of the Basque race and the survival Euskera. Shaped by traditionalist Catholicism, it was also hostile to secularizing trends in Spanish culture. Linked to this cultural conservatism, the PNV was also antisocialist and anticommunist (Grugel 1990: 100–3).

At the eve of the Spanish Civil War, the Republic passed a statute of autonomy. This proved to be short-lived, for when the Franco regime came to power, not only was regional autonomy abolished, but in addition a concerted effort to crush Basque nationalism commenced, including a prohibition on the use of Euskera and other cultural expressions. A consequence of the decades-long repression of nationalist aspirations was the growing conviction among some nationalists that violence was justified and necessary. At the same time, opposition to the right-wing regime pushed nationalists politically leftward. ETA emerged in the 1960s as the Basques' paramilitary parallel to the IRA. It began a campaign of violence, including the sensational assassination of Prime Minister Luis Carrero Blanco in 1973, in its separatist bid to forge the independent nation of Euskadi. Guibernau (1999: 134) writes that, viewing themselves as a colonized country, "ETA understood its activities as part of a revolutionary war, a war of liberation which they compared to that of Cuba, Algeria, or Angola."

In the transition to democracy, the new Spanish government sought to find ways of ending the violence and addressing the grievances and the aspirations of Basque nationalists. In 1980, the Statute of Guernica made provisions for the establishment of self-government, which included the creation of a regional parliament with powers over such internal matters as education, policing, and taxation. The gambit of the Spanish government, like the British *vis-à-vis* Scotland and Wales, is to grant greater levels of regional autonomy in order to ward off the demands of separatists (Funes 1998).

Here as well, the ultimate outcome – autonomy or separatism – cannot be known at present. Basque nationalists are divided on the matter. This split is reflected in the different platforms of the main nationalist parties vying for support. On the one hand, the PNV, with the largest electoral constituency, advocates a moderate nationalism and a centrist politics within the framework of the Spanish state. Likewise, the more leftist Euskadiko Ezquerra (EE) favors autonomy rather than outright independence. On the other hand, the Marxist Herri Batasuna (HB) is the largest of the more militant separatist parties. HB operates as the legitimate political wing of ETA in a manner similar to the relationship between Sinn Féin and the IRA. In 1998 it merged with other leftist nationalist parties into a coalition known as Euskal Herritarrok (EH). Around the same time, ETA agreed to a ceasefire. While some observers thought this might mean an end to the decades-long terrorist campaign and the beginning of a negotiated settlement, more recently new terrorist acts have been committed. Thus, like Northern Ireland, the future of the Basque region remains clouded.

The Empire Strikes Back

Approximately 12,000,000 Africans were forced into slavery during the colonial era, and the British were one of the major European powers responsible for and benefiting from this human trade. Africans served as a crucial source of labor in Britain's colonies in the Americas and they added to the profitability of the British economy – directly in the case of business interests in cities such as London, Liverpool, and Bristol that were actually involved in the slavery, and indirectly insofar as they helped to improve the material well-being of the middle classes in general (Walvin 2000: 84–99). Along with this involvement in slavery, the dramatic expansion of colonial holdings by the nineteenth century meant that, "the sun never set on the British Empire." A crucial awareness took root that although its overseas possessions were overwhelmingly occupied by nonwhites, Britain itself was considered to be a white nation. While blacks and Asians were evident in British cities during the nineteenth and first half of the twentieth century, their numbers were quite small and they tended to be clustered in a select number of port cities, including Cardiff, Swansea, Bristol, Liverpool, and London.

During this same period, emigration levels from Britain rose as waves of economic migrants along with political and religious dissidents left for British colonies, especially in North America, Australia, New Zealand, and South Africa. This is not to suggest, however, that immigrants weren't entering the country. They were. By far the largest immigrant group in the nineteenth century and into the first half of the twentieth was the Irish. During much of this time, they were colonials migrating to the metropole – sometimes permanently, but frequently to meet temporary labor demands. Given their proximity to Britain, the Irish played a role not unlike that of Mexicans in the United States. They also suffered from considerable discrimination. In addition to the Irish, other immigrant groups included Jews, Gypsies, Russians, and Italians (Holmes 1988: 56–73). These ethnics tended to be among the poorest members of the working class, and they could be found concentrated in neighborhoods such as London's East End. Hostility to the newcomers – and in particular anti-Semitism – led to the passage of restrictive immigration legislation, beginning with the Aliens Act in 1905 and followed by a more expansive act passed in 1919. Despite the nation's less than tolerant response to immigrants, newcomers continued to arrive well into the twentieth century, including Germans fleeing Nazi Germany and, after the war, Displaced Persons from eastern Europe. During this time, relatively few people of color – from British colonies or elsewhere – could be found among the immigrants.

The development of a multiracial Britain

This situation began to change significantly during the economic recovery that got underway after the Second World War, as waves of immigrants from its colonies or former colonies entered Britain. At least symbolically, the beginning of this migratory movement occurred in 1948 when the *Empire Windrush* arrived at Tilbury Docks with 492 Jamaican passengers aboard. This marked the beginning of a small but steadily growing stream of new nonwhite immigrants. The new arrivals came overwhelmingly from British Commonwealth nations, and thus they possessed the British passports that gave them ready access to the empire's hub (Davison 1964). While the controversies over the nations without states discussed above raised questions about what it means to be British, these questions acquired even greater significance as a consequence of the arrival of these new immigrants (Colley 1992). Their impact on the contemporary ethnic make-up of Britain is portrayed in table 4.

The vast majority of the newcomers can be divided into three major groups, based on their points of origin: the Caribbean, the Indian subcontinent, and Africa. The Caribbean contingent began to arrive in Britain in part due to

Table 4   Ethnic groups in Britain

Group	1998	2020 (Projection)
African	354,000	700,000
African-Caribbean	797,000	1,000,000
Bangladeshi	232,000	460,000
Chinese	167,000	250,000
Indian	945,000	1,200,000
Irish	2,092,000	3,000,000
Pakistani	567,000	1,250,000
Various	601,000	1,000,000
White other than Irish	50,986,000	49,000,000
Total	56,741,000	57,860,000

Source: Labor Force Survey, UK Office for National Statistics, 1998.

the entry restrictions placed on them by the passage of the McCarran–Walter Act in the United States that denied their ability to enter this nearby nation (Grosfoguel 1997). With this destination effectively cut off, Britain became the main immigrant destination of English-speaking West Indians. While by far the largest numbers were from Jamaica, constituting about a half of the immigrants from the region, a wide range of countries were involved, including Antigua, Barbados, Belize, Dominica, Grenada, St. Kitts, St. Lucia, and Trinidad and Tobago. Throughout the 1950s, the majority of nonwhite immigrants came from the West Indies. According to the 1991 census, about a half million British blacks trace their backgrounds to the Caribbean (Peach 1991, Goulbourne 1998: 42–3).

The end of colonial India resulted in the 1947 partition of India into a Hindu-dominated India and a Muslim-controlled Pakistan, which in turn was composed of two geographically distinct regions, East and West. Around the same time, the island nation of Ceylon off the coast of India also gained its independence. Subsequent political developments in the region led to East Pakistan achieving its independence from the dominant West in 1972, becoming the nation of Bangladesh. In the same year, Ceylon renamed itself Sri Lanka. Thus, immigrants from the Indian subcontinent come from four countries: India, Pakistan, Bangladesh, and Sri Lanka. They include Muslims, Sikhs, and Hindus. The earliest arrivals were mainly young men from rural backgrounds with low literacy levels who came to Britain either as a result of service in the British military or with the hope of being able to accumulate sufficient assets to restore the wealth and status of their families back home (Holmes 1988). However, many did not return, and in fact they became the beachhead for a chain of migration that would grow in the 1960s into a large immigration stream. Later arrivals included a growing segment of more highly educated professionals and businesspersons.

When speaking of immigrants from Africa, it's important to distinguish between blacks and Indians. The former contributed relatively small numbers, generally from such west African nations as Nigeria, Ghana, and Sierra Leone. However, of particular significance to the politics of British immigration during the 1960s and 1970s were Indians forced out of east Africa by political events and who became in the process, in the phrase of Paraminder Bhachu (1985), "twice migrants." Diasporic Indians settled in many places in Africa, where they established themselves as "middle-men minorities," entrepreneurs whose clienteles were often the most impoverished sectors of the African community. In some postindependence nations in east Africa, nationalistic policies were implemented that called for the "Africanization" of the local economies. What this amounted to was a challenge to the livelihoods of the Indian communities. The first campaign occurred in Kenya in 1966, which resulted in the flight of Indians to several destinations, including Canada and India; many Indians holding British passports opted for the United Kingdom. Similar campaigns subsequently were undertaken in Malawi and Tanzania, but as Harry Goulbourne (1998: 44) observes, "by far the most dramatic exodus of Asians from East Africa was from Uganda in 1972, as a result of the expulsion of Asians, citizens and non-citizens alike, by the dictator Idi Amin."

The earlier stream in the 1950s expanded considerably from the 1960s forward due to the combined impact of these three components. While some new arrivals came, at least in part, for political reasons, as a whole this was overwhelmingly a labor migration: people moving to the industrial heartland where they concluded that there were greater economic opportunities than they could find at home (Solomos & Back 1995a). The earliest arrivals tended to be young men, often unskilled and illiterate, who hoped to accumulate assets capable of restoring the economic well-being and social status of their parents in the homeland. They viewed themselves as temporary laborers or sojourners, not intent on remaining abroad, but instead hoping to return home with needed capital. However, by the 1960s a pattern of voluntary chain migration was firmly in place and, moreover, complementing the unskilled workers were skilled professionals and businesspersons (Holmes 1988). Dependants also began to arrive, and with family reunification came the emergence of ethnic communities.

Cultural differences between these communities and the host society provoked an immediate anti-immigrant response in all quarters of British society. Indeed, as Christian Joppke (1996: 478) writes, "In the 1950s, 'no blacks, no dogs' signs were not rare sights in houses and shop windows across Britain." Not only did these new arrivals raise anew the question of what it means to be British in an increasingly multicultural society. They did so by also raising the specter of race (Rich 1986). In his perceptive account of British race relations, *'There Ain't No Black in the Union Jack'* (1987), the cultural sociologist Paul Gilroy traces the shifting responses on the part of the host society to the new people of color, focusing on the various reformulations of the category of "other" that have arisen since mid-century.

In fact, there is much that the new immigrants share with their established British counterparts, due to the impact of colonial administration on such matters as politics, education, and work, and as a consequence of the role of Christian missionary efforts during the colonial era. While British colonial administrators did not demand the assimilation of the colonized into English culture, as for example their French and Portuguese counterparts did, they did succeed in inculcating much about British culture, law, and politics (Goulbourne 1998: 38–9; see also Banton 1983). However, at the same time, what Ann Swidler (1986) calls the "cultural tool kits" of the new ethnics reflect differences, at times profound differences, from the host society's culture. The new immigrants operate with what Gilroy (1993), in a reference to W. E. B. DuBois, refers to as "double consciousness": they occupy a cultural space that straddles both their old world and the new world they have come to inhabit.

During the first phase of immigration, nonwhite immigrants were uniformly referred to as black, reflective of the fact that the host society tended to treat all in a similar fashion (Modood 1988). However, more recently there has been considerably more recognition of immigrant diversity on the part of the British public. Thus, there is a greater tendency to define groups in terms of national origin: Indian, Pakistani, Bengali, Jamaican, Trinidadian, and so forth. Likewise, there is a greater awareness of religions differences within and among these groups: Muslims, Hindus, and Sikhs, for example. Two pan-ethnic labels have emerged out of this and gained common currency, blacks (or Afro-Caribbeans) and Asians. The former refers not only to immigrants from Commonwealth nations in the Caribbean, but to blacks from Africa and elsewhere. However, since the vast majority of blacks are from the West Indies, a term that is often used as a virtual synonym for black is Afro-Caribbean. The term Asian has become the pan-ethnic label for those immigrant groups from the Indian subcontinent. Sometimes it is also meant to include the Chinese, who have come primarily from the former British colony of Hong Kong.

Although fewer than 100,000 immigrants had entered the country by 1960, racial tensions nonetheless escalated. Some commentators at the time contended that race relations in Britain were beginning to resemble those in the United States, particularly in the Deep South (Rex & Moore 1967b: 19). There was considerable evidence that housing and employment discrimination were rampant. Working-class youth engaged in sporadic attacks on immigrants. Isolated incidents became more common as immigrants – and in particular West Indians – were accused of exacerbating the housing shortage, competing with whites for jobs, and contributing to such social problems as prostitution (Holmes 1988: 259). Violence escalated into full-blown riots in 1958 in Nottingham and London's Notting Hill (Layton-Henry 1984: 35–8). An outgrowth of the violence was the creation of such white nationalist organizations as the White Defence League.

In addition to the fact that immigrants confronted racist barriers to housing, jobs, education, health and social services, and political participation, they also confronted a growing chorus of public opinion calling for immigration restriction. The Labour Party, under the leadership of Hugh Gaitskell, sought to take the high road by promoting racial harmony (Banton 1962). The leadership of both the Labour and Liberal parties opposed the Commonwealth Immigrants Act of 1962, but failed to prevent its passage. It was intended to slow the rate of immigration, doing so by imposing a voucher system that gave priority to people who had jobs waiting for them or who possessed particular skills that were in short supply. However, the Conservative Party was not alone in supporting such legislation. In fact, when Labour returned to power, and it was clear that the Act had not stemmed the tide of immigration, it abolished the third category of voucher, which was essentially a first-come-first-serve system.

The political divisiveness of the immigration question could be seen vividly in the 1964 parliamentary election in Smethwick, a small industrial city in the Birmingham area, where the infamous unofficial slogan employed by the Conservative Party's candidate was, "If you want a nigger for a neighbour, vote Labour" (quoted in Solomos & Back 1995a: 53).

In 1968 Parliament passed a considerably more restrictive, Labour-government sponsored Commonwealth Immigrants Act. In part a response to the east African "crisis," its intentions were clearly racist. Under a policy known as *partiality*, it limited New Commonwealth black and Asian access to Britain, without similarly limiting the ability of Old Commonwealth whites from places such as South Africa and Rhodesia from settling. The Immigration Act of 1971 and the Nationality Act of 1981 served to further block primary immigration from New Commonwealth nations (Mason 1995: 28–30; Joppke 1996: 479).

The political left in Britain, particularly the leadership of both the Labour Party and the Trade Union Congress, viewed the immigration question in terms of the legacy of British colonial rule. They sought to facilitate the transformation of former colonies into independent nations within the British Commonwealth, while arguing that immigrants needed to be viewed as workers with similar concerns as British-born workers. The socialism of the two institutions shaped their antiracist stance. Labour was instrumental in promoting the Race Relations Acts of 1965 and 1968, which began with the assumption that racial harmony was a common good. Labour also played a key role in establishing the Commission for Racial Equality in 1976 (Banton 1985). It's not surprising that when immigrants – both blacks and Asians – began to become involved in politics, they gravitated to the Labour Party (Anwar 1986). Since a majority of nonwhite immigrants entered the country as formal citizens, they were equipped with the rights and privileges of established residents. This situation made possible a faster introduction into the arena of British politics than immigrants to most other liberal democracies.

One of the dilemmas for both the party and trade union organizations was that many white rank-and-file members, manifesting racist sentiments, were hostile to the new immigrants, whom they saw as competitive threats in the workforce, unwelcome newcomers in their neighborhoods, and contributing to the enfeebling of British culture (Freeman 1979). These views played into the hands of the political right (Messina 1996). Perhaps nowhere was the perspective of the established political right more baldly presented than in Conservative MP Enoch Powell's 1968 "Rivers of Blood" speech in which he painted a picture of a nation overrun by the "coloured population" that would soon make the white British majority "strangers in their own country" (quoted in Solomos & Back 1995a: 60). Powell became the lightning-rod for the anti-immigration movement within Britain's political establishment. He was also, it should be noted, removed from his post in the shadow cabinet for his remarks. This was a reflection of the consensus in the political establishment, across the ideological spectrum, that the course Britain had set itself on involved limiting immigration while promoting racial harmony: "good race relations" were seen as requiring "strict immigration control" (Joppke 1996: 479).

At the same time, fringe groups on the extreme right emerged, the most significant being the neofascist National Front. It operated at one level as a political party, running slates of candidates for local elections. The front gained notoriety when it won a parliamentary seat in the working-class dockland area of the Isle of Dogs (Richmond 1994: 167–8). The Front functioned on a murkier level as well, wherein it was closely connected to violent skinhead gangs. An extremist culture developed, replete with rock bands, websites, and the like. Whether organized or unorganized, neofascist skinheads were responsible for countless acts of violence and for encouraging, when not engaged themselves, in what became known as "Paki-bashing." One manifestation of this culture could be seen in the escalation of hooliganism in British soccer. Indeed, the fans from some teams such as London's Millwall were known for their avowed racism (Back, Crabbe, & Solomos 1999).

One of the most persistent negative stereotypes of blacks, and Caribbeans in particular, is that they are inclined to engage in criminal activities and especially those associated with drugs. Acting on these stereotypes, the police enacted vigorous policing campaigns in many black neighborhoods, in the process escalating tensions between the communities and the authorities. Community leaders complained about intimidation, false arrests, and beatings, but elicited little response from police officials. In 1981, the tensions between blacks and the police exploded into full-blown riots in several locales, beginning in London's Brixton area and spreading to other cities, including Bristol, Liverpool, Manchester, Birmingham, and Wolverhampton.

The Conservative Party under Margaret Thatcher expressed relatively little sympathy for minorities in Britain, and was harsh in its criticisms of lawbreakers. The Tories also made it clear that they would continue to seek ways to control the flow of immigration. At the same time, the government had to walk a fine line insofar as it sought to disassociate itself from the racism of the extreme right. In a campaign poster from 1983, the Conservative Party staked out its vision a colorblind society: a young black male in a business suit contains the caption, "Labour Says He's Black. Tories Say He's British" (Gilroy 1987: 57–9). The Labour Party, pushed by its left wing, challenged this position and undertook a campaign against racism. This campaign was particularly evident in the work of the Greater London Council, under the leadership of the leftist Ken Livingstone (Gilroy 1987: 136–51; see also Small 1994; Solomos & Back 1996). Since the 1980s, politics in Britain has become more centrist and less polarized. This was especially the case with the advent of Prime Minister Tony Blair's "Third Way." By this point, the differences within the immigrant population had coalesced in the British mindset into a distinction between two above-noted pan-ethnic groups: blacks and Asians.

Black Britain

The 1991 Census for the first time asked residents to classify themselves according to ethnic group. As a consequence, the results of that census provide far more accurate information about the ethnic composition of the British people than earlier counts. At that time, all blacks represented only 1.6 percent of the total population, which meant that there were approximately 880,000 blacks (Owen 1992: 2). It is assumed that little has changed in terms of overall percentage and that the overall number has grown only modestly in the ensuing decade. Thus, we can assume that there are somewhere around a million blacks in Britain, the majority of which were born outside of the country.

A comparison with the United States can be instructive. Unlike their American counterparts, blacks in Britain are relative newcomers. They represent a smaller percentage of the nation's total population than black Americans: less than 2 percent in contrast to 12 percent. Blacks in Britain are heavily concentrated in the southeastern region of the nation, with over half of all Afro-Caribbeans residing in London and sizeable enclaves located in the West Midlands (Small 1994: 63–4; Austin 1995; Mason 1995: 35–7). In an early study of the initial settlements of blacks, John Rex and Robert Moore (1967) discovered considerable conflict and competition between blacks and whites over housing and persistent patterns of discrimination. The result was that blacks tended to be both more overcrowded than whites and more likely to live in substandard accommodations. Despite changes in the ensuing decades, these disparities persist.

Black residential enclaves can be found in major cities: Brixton, Hackney, and Peckham in London, Handsworth in Birmingham, Moss Side in Manchester, and Toxteth in Liverpool. Nonetheless, there is far less residential segregation in Britain than the United States, though there is evidence of white flight from neighborhoods as blacks move in. However, there is nothing approaching the hypersegregation found in major American cities (Massey & Denton 1993). A telling example is the inner-city neighborhood of Brixton in south London. Brixton is sometimes referred to as London's Harlem. However, unlike New York's Harlem, which is predominantly black, Brixton is a genuinely multiracial neighborhood. The minority population – which includes both blacks and, in smaller numbers, Asians – amounts to no more than 30 percent of the total population (Small 1994: 64). At the same time, a visit to Brixton Market reveals the imprint of Afro-Caribbean culture on the area: this is both a multiracial community and a center for black British culture.

The relatively small size of the black population in Britain helps to account for the fact that blacks are less segregated, not only residentially, but also in other arenas of social life, such as in schools and the workplace. Black students tend to attend integrated schools and the workforce is similarly multiracial. Moreover, a consequence of high levels of black–white interaction is that in the more intimate levels of social life there is greater contact between the races than in the United States. Comparing intermarriage rates in the two countries can reveal the lower level of social distance most vividly: while only 3 percent of blacks marry nonblacks in the US, the figure is 25 percent in Britain (Small 1994: 48, 161–2).

As Afro-Caribbeans struggle to obtain an economic foothold in their new homeland, they confront the classical problems associated with poverty, unemployment, discrimination, low wage rates, and the like (Model 1999). They are over-represented in the ranks of the unskilled working class (Brown 1992). In terms of economic niches, males are well represented in the transportation and communications sectors, while women are concentrated in healthcare (Anwar 1995: 274). Blacks report lower levels of self-employment than other groups. At the same time, a black middle class has emerged, and has continued to grow (Small 1994: 144; Ratcliffe 1999).

However, since most middle-class job opportunities are located in the professional sector of the economy, educational attainment plays a major role in upward mobility (Gillborn 1990). Here there is reason for concern about the future since blacks have not fared as well as other groups in the classroom. In a study conducted by the Institute of Education, they are the lowest performing group in Government Certificate of Secondary Education (GCSE) standardized test results. Few obtained Advanced (A) Level qualifications, settling instead for obtaining Ordinary (O) Level qualifications. Blacks have higher rates of academic failure than the general student population. In addition, blacks are far more likely to be expelled or suspended from school for behavioral problems. Some educationists have expressed fears that in some inner-city neighborhoods a black underclass is developing (Salmon 1996).

An ethnic community has emerged, replete with a range of institutions that provide needed services to blacks. These include mutual aid societies, political organizations, cultural organizations, churches, and the like. The general ideological orientation of ethnic institutions encourages practices that assist in the integration of blacks into British society. In other words, there is an acculturationist character to them. At the same time, in serving the particular needs of a racial minority population confronting discrimination and poverty, they have served to articulate a sense of what it means to be black in Britain (Kalilombe 1997). In the political arena, blacks have achieved a presence in the Labour Party via the creation of Black Sections in the party organizational structure. The election of three black members to the House of Commons in 1987 reflects the willingness of blacks to exercise their rights of citizenship in their efforts to find avenues for incorporation into British society, while simultaneously promoting a greater multicultural sensibility in the nation.

Despite evidence of improving attitudes towards blacks and gains in their socioeconomic status, it is clear that racism has not disappeared. The racist assault and murder of black student and aspiring architect Stephen Lawrence in 1993 was a reminder to the nation that, as Ian Hargreaves (1996) put it, "We have not put the racist devil behind us." The murder, of course, revealed the persistent problem posed by racist extremists. However, in addition, the fact that whites in the neighborhood where the crime was committed erected a wall of silence that protected the perpetrators, while the police failed to aggressively pursue the case, vividly pointed out that racism also took varied institutional forms (Goulbourne 1998: 149–51).

The Asian community

Asian immigrants occupy a somewhat different social location in contemporary British society. In some respects, these immigrants look like a success story, and insofar as they do, they bear a similarity to recent Asian immigrants in the United States, who are sometimes portrayed as the so-called "model minority," which is to say that they are thought to bring with them values such as industriousness and commitment to family that have helped many of them to make a rather successful economic adjustment to their new circumstances. While there is a tendency to overstate the level of economic success that has been achieved, in fact this segment of the new immigrant population is doing better economically than blacks. At the same time, Asians have a higher unemployment rate than whites, tend to be located in the lower-paying sectors of the economy, and continue to confront discrimination in hiring and promotion practices (Brown & Gay 1985). Language barriers also play a role in explaining economic disadvantage (Mason 1995: 57–8). It is also important to note that there are differences among the Asian groups in terms of their economic circumstances. Indians in general are doing better than their South Asian counterparts are, with Bangladeshis at the other end of the spectrum, experiencing the highest levels of unemployment and poverty.

Some Asians have found success in niche economies. Thus, many Indians, and particularly Sikhs, own small newsstands, convenience shops, and restaurants. They have also found similar niches in public-sector jobs, such as in the post office. In some instances, enclave economies that link entrepreneurs in Britain to their homeland in transnational economic alliances have developed. This can be seen quite clearly in the Bengali community centered on Brick Lane in London's East End, noted particularly for the numerous leather wholesalers in the area. Asians have a higher rate of self-employment than blacks or whites, with Bangladeshis having a lower rate than either Indians or Pakistanis (Mason 1995: 56). Paralleling this propensity to self-employment, these two groups also have the highest rates of home ownership of any groups, including whites. At the same time, there is evidence that they reside in substandard housing and in overcrowded conditions compared to whites (Brown 1984: 96).

In terms of educational attainment, Asians are doing comparatively well. In spite of language barriers and cultural differences, Asians as a whole are high achievers on standardized tests, and the number who go on to do A Level work and who continue on to university study is rising. In the Institute of Education study noted above, Indian students were found to be "the most highly qualified students in British schools and colleges," a situation researchers attribute in part to a "cultural commitment to education and family support" (Salmon 1996: 5). The value Asians place on higher education suggests that they are preparing their children, not for roles in the ethnic niche or enclave economies, but for careers in the larger society. As such, there is a clear acculturalist thrust to their orientation toward education and employment. This can be seen by the fact that many Asian families are overcoming traditionalist values about the roles of women and are increasingly coming to see the value of higher education for all of their children, regardless of gender.

At the same time, it is important to note that Asian groups are far more culturally distinctive than their black counterparts. This in no small part is due to the fact that they are largely non-Christian. One of the complex features of these groups is that their ethnic identities and their religious identities are intimately connected. Sometimes these identities are mutually reinforcing, while at other times this is not the case. Jessica Jacobson (1997), for example, found that among young British Pakistanis, there is a tendency to distinguish their ethnic from their religious identity. The former, in their view, referred to their place of origin and thus was particularistic in nature, while the latter was universal. However the various ethnic communities define this interrelationship, it is clear that for all of them regardless of religious tradition – Muslims, Hindus, and Sikhs – religious institutions have proven to be among the most important community-building institutions. Thus, wherever ethnic enclaves have emerged, mosques, temples, and gurdwaras have been established. This effort at transplanting their religious heritages into the context of an implicitly Christian nation suggests that in the cultural realm of social life, many Asians are intent on religious retention rather than acculturation. At the same time, they have sought to combat discrimination and in so doing have learned to work with the host society in various ways to accommodate their religious and cultural values in a new societal context (Modood 1994, 1997b, 2000).

The tensions between Muslims and the host society have been greater than in the case of the other Asian religions. The example of the Council of Mosques in the Midlands city of Bradford, a major center for British Muslims, is instructive in this regard. Established in 1981, it serves as an umbrella organization for local Muslims, whose mosques reflect the caste, ethnic, and sectarian divisions within the Asian community as a whole. The Council provides unity amidst this diversity. At one level, it functions as a civil rights organization, working with local authorities in combating racism and promoting multiculturalism. In this capacity, it became a vehicle for political involvement.

In one engagement that generated considerable controversy, the Council worked with the local educational authority to provide *halal* food in schools for Muslim schoolchildren. Critics claimed that the willingness on the part of the schools to do so amounted to a capitulation to special interests. The situation became more heated when animal rights activists objected to the policy on the grounds that because *halal* food preparation forbids the stunning of animals prior to slaughter, it amounted to condoning cruelty to animals. Many in the Asian community viewed their critics as racists, and challenged them in the court of public opinion, in the end prevailing, as the Bradford Council voted to provide *halal* meat in the schools (Lewis 1997: 112–14). This is an example of the ways that Asian Muslims have sought to insert themselves into the social and political realms of the host society in an effort to achieve mutual accommodation that permits the retention of valued aspects of their religious belief system.

Reconciling Muslim beliefs and values with the prevailing cultural values of the host society requires deft negotiation. The case of Salman Rushdie's *Satanic Verses* offers a particularly graphic illustration of this point. The novel was deemed by many Muslims as blasphemous due to its unflattering portrayal of the Prophet Muhammad. The book had been criticized by Muslims in India, who invoked a law that forbid the publication of works deemed to "insult or outrage the religious feelings of any class" (Ruthven 1990: 87). Iran's fundamentalist leader Ayatollah Khomeni issued a *fatwa*, which called for a death sentence for the author and his publishers. Many Muslims in Britain thought they could prevent the publication of the novel, and when that didn't happen, they engaged in public demonstrations against its appearance in bookstores. When many Muslims in Britain voiced support for the *fatwa*, Rushdie was forced to go into hiding, where he remained for years under constant police protection. The Muslim community came under considerable criticism as a result, with the blanket indictment of Islamic fundamentalist being hurled at what is, in fact, a highly diverse community – one clearly divided over this particular issue. The inability of many Muslims, including the leadership of the Bradford Council, to embrace Western ideals regarding freedom of expression and tolerance is indicative of a tension between illiberal traditional religious values and the liberal values of a modern democratic state (Parekh 2000: 298–304; see also Nielsen 1992 and Lewis 1997).

Generational tensions also are in evidence, pitting the desire of parents to instill traditional values and behaviors into children against lives that have been profoundly shaped by growing up in British society. Gender issues constitute a particularly significant realm of conflict surrounding topics such as traditional patterns of male authority, premarital sex, and arranged marriages. In each of these areas, there is evidence that members of the younger generation appear to occupy a transitional space somewhere between the value world of their parents and that of British society at large (Hennink et al. 1999; Alexander 2000). In this regard, Muslims are not alone, as similar tensions exist within the Hindu and Sikh communities as well.

There is evidence to suggest that many among the second generation remain committed to their ethnic and religious heritages (see, for example, Raj 2000). However, it is also the case that they are interested in and identify with aspects of British society (Lyon 1997). They, for example, share with white Britons fervent allegiances to particular soccer teams and they have similar interests in popular music (Back 1996). As is typical with the second generation in settler nations, they are engaged in a complex process of negotiating the construction of identities composed of elements from the old world and the new. At this point, the outcome of this process is indeterminate, but it is certain that the acculturation of the third generation and beyond will signal a new orientation towards the culture of their ancestors. Complicating the situation, a series of race riots in the summer of 2001 pitting Asians against whites – in Bradford, Oldham, and Burnley – points to the fact that such acculturation occurs within a society where extremist racism continues to cast its shadow.

The Future of Multi-ethnic Britain

In an article in *The New York Times*, journalist Warren Hoge (2001: A1) described Leicester as a city that "defines diversity and tolerance." An industrial city of about 300,000 located in the east Midlands, it has become home to a growing number of African Caribbean and south Asian immigrants since the 1970s. Demographic predictions suggest that it will become Britain's first city with a nonwhite majority within a decade. The article observed that during the initial settlement period immigrants confronted considerable hostility and overt discrimination, with local-government officials actually taking out newspaper advertisements telling the first newcomers – Indians arriving from east Africa – that housing, schools, and social services were already strained and thus they urged those thinking about coming to Leicester to think about other alternatives. Members of the National Front and skinheads marched and hurled verbal abuse at newcomers, and "Paki Go Home" graffiti was a common sight.

However, in the ensuing quarter of a century, it would appear that a corner had been turned and race relations have become in recent years considerably more constructive and positive. The second generation, in particular, appears inclined to view their home as one that appreciates its multicultural character. The new Asian residents, instead of being perceived as taking jobs from whites, are now viewed as playing a major role in the economic revitalization of the city, particularly in terms of commercial development and renewing derelict residential neighborhoods. Hoge (2001: A10) notes that "A typical sight in Leicester are Gothic churches with stone crosses or Victorian-period red brick mills and factory buildings now converted to Muslim community halls, Sikh and Hindu temples or small business centers." Reasons cited for the progressive improvement of ethnic relations are the role of local government officials in working with the new immigrants, and their willingness to use the police to control right-wing extremists.

A closer examination of the situation reveals a rather more complicated picture. While the situation for Asians may well suggest considerable improvement, such is not necessarily the case for the Afro-Caribbean community. Blacks are not doing as well economically, being more likely to have lower-paying jobs, experience higher levels of unemployment, and reside in council housing. In addition, they have considerably less political clout. Relationships with the police are often strained. A recent survey found that blacks are 11 times more likely to be stopped by the police than whites – reflecting the power of the stereotypical association of blacks with crime (Hoge 2001: A10).

In many respects Leicester can be seen as a microcosm of contemporary multi-ethnic Britain. Ethnic relations in that community are increasingly being shaped by the framework established by laws passed since the 1960s that sought to combat discrimination while promoting intergroup harmony. The most important law, one that replaced its 1965 and 1968 predecessors, was the Race Relations Act of 1976 (RRA). These laws collectively were designed to provide mechanisms for combating discrimination in employment, housing, and public services. The RRA added to this an effort to confront more indirect or institutional forms of discrimination. It should be recalled that the first of these laws emerged at the same time that tighter immigration policies went into effect, the message of Parliament being that they wanted to effectively limit the number of new immigrants, while expressing a willingness to find ways to assist in the integration of immigrants already in the country. In short, highly restrictive immigration laws were coupled with the state's management of liberal race relations policies. For instance, the purpose of the Race Equality Councils (RECs) that were created in the 1990s – replacing similar organizations known as Community Relations Councils – was to provide immigrant communities with locally based organizations that could respond to particular needs and problems, and serve as liaisons with governmental bodies.

The underlying ideal-typical model of ethnic relations embodied in the RRA and the RECs was not to seek an assimilation in which differences disappeared as immigrants "became British." Rather it was that of a multicultural society in which a respect for tolerance and an appreciation of diversity were to be central. Christian Joppke (1996: 481) depicts the character of British race-relations policy in the following way:

> Official multiculturalism has expressed itself in a multitude of legal provisions, such as partially exempting Hindus and Muslims from Britain's strict marriage rules, allowing Sikh boys to wear turbans and Asian girls to wear *shalwar* (trousers) at school, or – curiously – excusing Sikhs from wearing crash helmets on motorcycles provided they are wearing turbans. A short walk along East London's Brick Lane or Southall's South Road conveys authentic images of Islamabad or the Punjab, with Muslim, Hindu, and Sikh men, women, and children in their traditional dresses, the sight of Mosques, and exotic smells and oriental music from the bazaars and teahouses. Clearly there is no presumption for these ethnic groups to become "British" in any other sense than ownership of a British passport.

While there may be no presumption, there is evidence to suggest that being British means more to members of ethnic minorities than simply being the holder of a passport. In a study directed by Tariq Modood (1997b: 328–31), minority group members were asked both whether they thought of themselves as British, and whether they thought of themselves as members of particular ethnic communities. Not surprisingly, the overwhelming majority of respondents – Afro-Caribbean, African, Indian, Pakistani, Bangladeshi, and Chinese – contended that "in many ways" they thought of themselves as members of the ethnic group. At the same time, excluding the Chinese, slightly under two-thirds of respondents stated that, "In many ways I think of myself as British." Thus, a majority of ethnics can be seen as engaged in a strategy of acculturation, wherein they are attempting to add a sense of being British onto their ethnic identity rather than engaging in an either/or strategy.

Moreover, as Ruud Koopmans and Paul Statham (1999: 690) point out, British ethnic minorities not only engage in defensive actions against racism, but also make "a sizeable number of claims for extensions of minority rights" and thus they play an important role "in the overall public discourse on migration and ethnic relations." Insofar as this is the case, they are making claims about the nature of British citizenship and about their role in the process of reshaping what it means to be British in a multicultural and multiethnic society.

T. H. Marshall (1964) has pointed out that conceptions of citizenship are linked to particular notions of national consciousness. Changes in one lead to changes in the other. In this light, the debates underway over what it means to be British have particular relevance. On one end of the debate are those who seek to view Britishness as unchanging and exclusive – a perpetual reminder that "there ain't no black in the Union Jack." This position is not only found in the extreme fringes of British politics, but among more mainstream conservatives as well. In terms of the latter, it found expression in Lord Norman Tebbit's cricket test of loyalty, wherein he proposed that one could determine whether or not a person is really capable of being British depending on whether in international cricket matches she or he cheers on the British side or the team from their country of origin. This jingoistic "test" raises the issue of dual or divided loyalties, implying that at least some immigrant groups can't be truly British. Such is the case only if one is opposed to a reconfiguration of national consciousness in a fashion that accords with multiculturalism.

At the other end are those who refuse to embrace a British identity. This can be seen both among the nation without state nationalists in Scotland and Wales who refuse to consider the prospect of being Scottish or Welsh as well as being British. It can be seen in the irredentism of Irish republicanism in Northern Ireland. It is also evident among the most marginalized members of the Afro-Caribbean community, who – bitter over their treatment in Britain – opt to view themselves as a marginalized diaspora people. Finally, such an antipathy to Britishness can be found among the more fundamentalist elements of the south Asian community, and particularly among Islamic fundamentalists. They, too, view themselves as exilic peoples, residing in a society whose liberal values are seen as antithetical to their own religious beliefs.

In the middle are those who seek to foster a new multicultural sensibility that accords respect and tolerance for diversity, while simultaneously seeking to redefine what it means to be British, and in so doing establishing the basis for a shared culture. In 2000, the Runnymede Trust published a report produced by its Commission on the Future of Multi-Ethnic Britain that sought to articulate what this middle ground might look like. Chaired by Bhikhu Parekh, the report sketches a "vision of a relaxed and self-confident multicultural Britain with which all of its citizens can identify," and argues programmatically that Britain needs to develop both as a "community of citizens" and as a "community of communities" (Parekh 2000b: xv).

In addition to assessing what needs to be done to combat racism and remedy social inequalities, the report devotes attention to "rethinking the national story" and to exploring "identities in transition" (Parekh 2000b: 14–39). That these are sensitive matters that evoke considerable controversy can be seen by the response to the report's release. Both the press and the electronic media were riveted by the assertion in the report that "Britishness . . . has systematic, largely unspoken, racial connotations," or to be more specific, that "Britishness and whiteness go together like roast beef and Yorkshire pudding" (Parekh 2000b: 38, 25). This statement was frequently misrepresented to say that Britishness had racist connotations. What the authors intended was quite evident: to move away from an historic association of Britishness with whiteness toward a more inclusive, multi-ethnic understanding of national identity. It is a call for the promotion of civic assimilation into a liberal democracy that has to adapt from a heretofore singular focus on individual rights and protections to one in which groups, too, are accorded rights and protections. At the same time, it is cognizant of the need for channels of intercultural evaluation, which are needed to determine when illiberal group practices ought to be permitted and when they ought to be banned by a liberal democratic society. While this challenge is not unique to Britain, what makes this case distinctive is the fact that the issues are laid out more clearly, with a greater appreciation of the virtues of multiculturalism, than, as we shall see in the following chapter, in either Germany or France.

CHAPTER FIVE

Germany, France, and Shifting Conceptions of Citizenship

This chapter and the preceding one are designed to provide a comparative framework for assessing the potential future of multi-ethnicity in the liberal democracies of western Europe. We turn to the two nations that along with Britain constitute the largest countries in the region: Germany and France. Like Britain, Germany and France have long histories of importing labor from other countries – especially from eastern and southern Europe, but also involving other areas of the globe – during periods of labor shortages. In spite of this fact, Germany has generally been viewed as a labor exporting, rather than importing, nation. This is due to the fact that so many of its own citizens have opted at various historical junctures to migrate to settler states during the nineteenth and early twentieth centuries. In contrast, France suffered from persistent labor shortages, and thus the French were considerably less inclined to emigrate than their German counterparts. Moreover, these shortages made necessary labor recruitment from neighboring nations.

Again like their island counterpart, since 1945 Germany and France have become major immigrant-receiving nations. Indeed, they are the two largest immigrant-receiving nations of continental Europe. According to Demetrios Papademetriou (1997–8: 16) Germany is at the moment home to as many foreigners on a per capita basis as is Canada (more, if we include the expatriate Germans – *Spätaussiedler* and *Aussiedler*), while the per capita level of immigrants in France is comparable to that of the United States. Thus, it is clear that in the late twentieth and early twenty-first century, immigration is as significant a phenomenon in these nations as it is in the historic settler states discussed in chapters 2 and 3.

This chapter offers a comparative analysis of these two nations. As will become evident, Germany and France have operated until very recently with rather different conceptions about what it means to be, respectively, German and French, and linked to that what the appropriate criteria are for defining citizenship. In the former case, a "blood-and-soil" nationalism led to the establishment of an ethnically defined understanding of citizenship, while in the former, the ideals of the French Revolution informed a republican version of a civic citizenship in which, in theory, anybody who embraced the values of the republic was eligible for citizenship. Not surprisingly, these two different notions of citizenship have had profound implications for immigrants and go some way in accounting for the historical particularities of each nation. Rogers Brubaker, in *Citizenship and Nationhood in France and Germany* (1992: 81), described the contrast between the two nations in the following way:

> The central difference between French and German ascription rules turns on the significance attached to birth and prolonged residence in the territory. While French citizenship is ascribed, at birth or majority, to most persons born on French territory of foreign parents, German citizenship is ascribed only on the basis of descent. Birth and prolonged residence in Germany have no bearing on citizenship status. French citizenship law automatically transforms most second- and third-generation immigrants into citizens; German citizenship law allows immigrants and their descendants to remain foreigners indefinitely.

That being said, the similarities between Germany and France are sometimes striking. Both have experienced considerable opposition to immigration policies and to the immigrants themselves. Right-wing political parties in both countries have actively sought to stem the tide of immigration, while extremists have been responsible for disturbingly high levels of racist violence. Immigrants have confronted considerable prejudice and discrimination, and often live in socially isolated enclave communities. The shock of cultural differences – particularly evident in the role that Islam currently plays in both societies – has led to tensions and has raised concerns in some quarters about whether or not immigrants are capable of being incorporated into these nations (Vertovec & Peach 1997).

Further convergence in terms of rethinking definitions of citizenship is currently underway, in no small part as a consequence of the increasingly important role being played by the transnational European Union. Both Germany and France have been major promoters of the EU, in contrast to Britain, where a powerful sector of Euroskeptics exists in both the Tory and Labour parties (Schmidt 1999). At the end of the chapter, we shall turn to the implications of the EU for national identities and on what it means in the twenty-first century to speak about a European identity in relationship to speaking about particular national identities.

Germany: Blood and Soil Citizenship versus Multiculturalism

The labor migrants and political refugees who have settled in Germany since the end of the Second World War reflect a major change in German migration patterns and raise important questions about the contemporary meaning of citizenship. Linked to this legal issue is the question, "Who is a German?" (Cahn 2000). Comprehending these questions requires at the outset locating these current developments in the context of history, particularly the history of Germany in the industrial age.

Industrialization and the emergence of modern Germany

In this regard, we begin with the simple fact that Germany was from the early-nineteenth century until 1885 primarily a nation of emigration rather than immigration. The main destinations of Germans, leaving their country as labor migrants and to a more limited extent as political refugees or religious exiles, included first and foremost the United States. Indeed, Germans were to become the second largest immigrant group in the United States after the English. Other significant destinations included Canada, Australia, and various nations in South America, in particular Argentina (Esser & Korte 1985). During this period, unlike most other European nations, Germany maintained rather liberal emigration policies (Sassen 1999: 54). Actually, this statement needs to be qualified insofar as Germany did not actually become a unified nation until 1871, so when referring to Germany before that time it is something of a shorthand for several relatively autonomous principalities. The liberality of emigration policies was in no small part due to a recognition that German industrialization lagged behind that of nations such as Britain, and thus during this period it experienced a labor surplus rather than a shortage. Emigration was viewed as a way of reducing the pressures of and alleviating the potential problems created by this surplus.

This situation would change near the end of the nineteenth century as a unified German state with an ascendant capitalist class sought with only limited success to wrest control of the economy from the landowning aristocrats with their feudalistic worldview (Glassman et al. 1993: 87–95). German economic development during the last few decades of the nineteenth century resulted in an increased demand for workers. This led to a decline in emigration, and to new patterns of internal migration. German agricultural workers departed rural areas in search of industrial jobs. When the supply of German labor was demonstrably insufficient to meet demand, immigration proved to be the solution. The immigrants during this time were chiefly Poles and other Slavs from the east. They were principally employed in the agricultural sector east of the Elbe River, which was controlled by the great landowning class known as the Junkers. Though the presence of these workers benefited the German economy, they nonetheless confronted intense ethnocentric hostility. Slavic workers were viewed as culturally and morally inferior to Germans, and came to represent, along with Jews, the paradigmatic instances of the "Other" in German society – outsiders destined for perpetual marginality.

Germany's liberal emigration laws were countered by the passage of highly restrictive immigration policies. This was in no small part a reflection of the nation's understanding of what it meant to be German – and thus who was and who was not eligible for full incorporation into German society, which included determining who did and who did not qualify for citizenship. Germany was the ideal-typical model of the *jus sanguinis* principle, which in essence fuses ethnicity and citizenship by its understanding of German identity and collective membership as being rooted in "blood and soil," or in other words, descent (Richter 1998). One's lineage or bloodline determines membership. As a consequence, immigrants with differing ancestries stand outside the pale. Germany was not the only European nation to embrace this view: Sweden and Switzerland are two other European countries that have operated with the principle of *jus sanguinis*.

In order to prevent immigrant workers from seeking to establish permanent residence in Germany, the immigration policies enacted near the end of the nineteenth century were designed to ensure that they would be treated as *Gastarbeiter* ("guestworkers") that would never be eligible for citizenship. The government instituted strict controls over immigrants. Work permits for particular jobs were required; lacking one, an immigrant could be deported. To prevent workers from taking up permanent residence, they were forced to depart Germany each year from November 15 to April 1. The laws were designed to ensure that workers did not attempt to settle permanently, and in particular they sought to prevent family settlement from occurring. Immigrant workers were initially forbidden to switch from agricultural work to industrial work, the latter being reserved for Germans. However, over time the demand for labor in Germany's expanding industrial sector gradually necessitated a relaxation of this prohibition (Esser & Korte 1985). Nevertheless, subsequent legislation was passed that clearly sought to marginalize non-Germans and prevent their incorporation into either the economy or the society at large. For instance, a further restriction on foreign workers was enacted in 1899, which required German language skills as a prerequisite for senior positions. This was followed by the 1908 passage of the Reichsvereinsgesetz, paragraph 12 of which made German the official language of all organizations.

The dilemma confronting Germany was clear. On the one hand, it needed immigrant workers, but on the other hand it was unwilling to consider that they might become a part of the nation. The Citizenship Law of 1913 established the ethnic basis of citizenship that would become the basis of German notions of citizenship for the next 86 years. A reflection of the xenophobia built into the idea of *jus sanguinus* can be seen in the statement made by a government official in summarizing the rationale for the proposed legislation during the Reichstag debate. He said, "The march of nations goes from East to West, and on this march of nations, the [Eastern] masses . . . meet the German Reich with its rule of law, economic prosperity, and free institutions . . . [A restrictive citizenship policy] is in the national interest, because it erects a barrier to the stream of foreigners flooding our country from the East" (quoted in Joppke 1996: 467–8). In the years immediately preceding the First World War, the number of immigrants in Germany exceeded 1,250,000 (Sassen 1999: 58). When the war began, the need for immigrant workers became acute. While many workers sought to leave Germany, the state, facing an acute labor shortage, undertook efforts to force immigrant workers to remain in the country in order to work in the war effort.

In the interwar years levels of immigration were quite low, but anti-immigrant sentiment remained a significant feature both during the Weimar Republic and the Nazi era. The political right wing was particularly hostile to foreigners, relying on racist stereotypes and blood-and-soil German nationalism to justify their stand. Those on the political left were more ambivalent. This can be seen in the Social Democratic Party, which on the one hand urged an internationalist solidarity of the working class, but on the other hand was concerned about the impact of immigration on the high level of welfare rights guaranteed to workers, and willing to concede to the nationalism of the working class by demanding that preferences for jobs be given to German workers over foreign workers.

The Nazi era

The Nazi seizure of power represented the triumph of a racist ideology in which Aryans were depicted as the master race whose destiny it was to conquer the world and in the process control the fates of the inferior races. The most unfortunate consequence of this ideology for immigrant workers occurred with the passage in 1938 of the Aliens Decree, which prohibited foreign workers from leaving the country, while imposing police controls over their freedom of movement within it (Homze 1967). In addition, as Ewa Morawska (2000: 1069) has pointed out, "The Nazis boosted their national economy by deporting about 9 million East Europeans to forced labor in German agriculture and industry."

However odious this was, obviously, the most obscene aspect of Nazi race ideology dealt, not with immigrants, but with the strangers within: Jews (along, it should be noted, with Rom, or gypsies, and homosexuals). Building on a long history of anti-Semitism, the Nazi propaganda machine devoted itself to convincing the public that Jews were internal enemies and were responsible for Germany's economic problems. The genocidal intent of the Final Solution represented the absolute nadir of German nationalism's translation of racist ideology into practice.

At the end of the war, German racism had given the altogether prevalent racism throughout Europe and the Americas a bad name. To the extent that fascism and racism were seen as going hand-in-hand, both during and after the war, antifascism came to be seen as synonymous with antiracism. Struggling with how to make sense of the Nazi past and how to prevent it from reoccurring has been a major preoccupation of the Germans during the second half of the twentieth century. For example, when the American historian Daniel Goldhagen published his controversial *Hitler's Willing Executioners* (1997), his book tour throughout Germany was a major event. He argued that the reason for the success of the genocidal campaign was that anti-Semitism was such a characteristic feature of the collective consciousness of the German people that ordinary people, far from not knowing about the assault on German Jewry or distancing themselves from it, took an active part in the holocaust (see Finkelstein 1998 for a critical assessment of the Goldhagen thesis).

The West German miracle and immigration

After the Second World War and as a consequence of the Cold War that followed quickly on its heels, Germany was divided into the capitalist and democratic Federal Republic of Germany (West Germany) and the Soviet-bloc nation of the German Democratic Republic (East Germany). The latter, like its other Warsaw Pact allies, was destined over the next four decades to lag behind the West in terms of industrial development. Moreover, its totalitarian political system denied people the basic freedoms characteristic of liberal democracies, including the freedom of movement by citizens. Given the political climate and economic conditions, many East Germans sought to migrate to the West. To prevent them from doing so, the communist authorities constructed a fortress-like border system, including the infamous Berlin Wall.

In contrast, West Germany experienced a postwar economic boom that made it the "economic miracle" of western Europe (Heilig et al. 1990). Labor shortages were evident early on, as a result of war losses and what would become a persistently low fertility rate throughout the nation. Thus, once again the demand for labor intensified. In the first decade after the war, this demand was met in part by the arrival of 11,000,000 people of German ancestry who either had been expelled from eastern parts of the Reich that had been lost as a consequence of defeat or who were refugees from East Germany. Because these immigrants were of German ancestry, they were immediately granted citizenship. Although the adjustment of these newcomers was not easy, over time they were assimilated into the larger society (Castles & Miller 1993: 103).

However, the booming economy demanded more labor power. This time, Slavic immigrants could not meet the demand because the iron curtain had made the free movement of workers from the Warsaw Pact nations impossible. While immigrants have arrived from many different nations, including Italy, Spain, Portugal, Morocco, Algeria, and Tunisia, the two most important contributors have proven to be Turkey and the former Yugoslavia. These were the "guestworkers" who played a crucial role in making the economic development of Germany possible. Realizing the need for workers, the German government played an active role in recruiting guestworkers. They entered into recruitment agreements not unlike the bracero program in the United States except that in the latter case the program only involved one country. The German Federal Labor Office, by contrast, signed agreements with a number of countries, beginning with Italy in 1955 and again in 1965; and followed by Morocco in 1963; Greece, Spain, Portugal, and Turkey in 1964; Tunisia in 1965; and Yugoslavia in 1968 (Hildyard 1996: 134). Even during the period of heaviest recruitment of guestworkers, these workers were denied the legal right of permanent residence. The common length of stay for these contract foreign workers was initially one year, though that changed over time. In order to prevent employment competition between foreign and domestic workers, a system of work permits was developed. Extensions were granted, leading to the right to permanent residence (though not nationalization) after 5 or 8 years.

During the first phase of this policy, most of the workers came from southern Europe, but as the economies of this region began to grow, and along with it the demand for labor, this changed. By the late 1960s, Turkish workers constituted the largest group, and this despite the fact that the nations of the European Community, including Spain, Portugal, and Greece, were accorded privileged status in terms of rights of entry. Indeed, EC workers were granted the same privileges as German workers. Stephen Castles and Mark Miller (1993: 104) have described the key factors that shaped the growth of the Turkish community:

> The Turkish government hoped to relieve domestic unemployment and obtain foreign exchange through remittances. The migrants themselves sought an escape from poverty, unemployment, and dependence on semi-feudal landowners. There was an expectation that money earned and skills gained abroad would encourage economic development [in Turkey]. The Turkish government also hoped to gain access to the European Community.

Until relatively recently, the treatment of these new arrivals taken as a whole was not unlike that experienced by Slavs in an earlier period. The nation was unprepared to view them as potential fellow citizens. Instead, they were defined as temporary residents who would eventually return to their respective homelands. In short, the principle of *jus sanguinus* remained in effect. However, there were differences between the post-Second World War era and the first half of the twentieth century. Under the provisions of the Basic Law of 1949, the newly democratic nation attempted to both maintain its self-understanding as an ethnonational community – or *Volk* nation – rather than an immigrant land, while simultaneously repudiating the more odious features of Nazi race laws. The new guestworkers were denied the rights to citizenship, but were ensured certain basic human rights, including freedom of faith, conscience, creed, and expression as well as the right to establish private schools and to petition the government. They acquired the same social and industrial rights as Germans, being entitled, for example, to equal pay and to trade union rights. They were also entitled to rent subsidies, unemployment benefits, and to child allowances. Somewhat strangely, they were not permitted to found their own political parties, but could join existing parties even though they were not permitted to vote or run for elective office (Klusmeyer 2000: 5–6; see also Lepsius 1985).

From the 1950s to the early 1970s, guestworkers continued to be actively recruited as the needs of the German economy dictated. Though they lived lives apart from the German population – seen as being in but not of the nation – there was relatively little open hostility displayed toward them. This was chiefly due to the fact that low unemployment rates and economic good times permitted the German population to be tolerant. In part, it reflected an effort on the part of policy-makers to avoid the ugly racism of the past. The new workers entered the lower tier of what increasingly became a split labor market, performing the unpleasant, unskilled and low-paying jobs that German workers avoided. Thus, there was little direct competition between German and immigrant workers, another factor explaining the relative tranquility of the initial encounter.

This situation began to change in the early 1970s, as a consequence of the OPEC oil embargo and stalling of economic growth that resulted in increasing unemployment rates. Recruitment efforts ceased and instead the government began to encourage their guests to exit. Though there were some discussions about the viability of deporting guestworkers, the government's commitment to liberal democratic principles and to a number of international agreements did not permit it to seriously entertain this prospect (Castles & Miller 1993: 105). Relatively few guestworkers returned home, and in fact the actual number of immigrants in Germany increased during the 1970s as a result of the entry of the families of immigrant workers. By 1973, the number of immigrants reached 2,600,000.

The average stay for guestworkers had reached almost 10 years; workers avoided returning home, even for visits, because they feared that if they did so, they might not be permitted to reenter Germany. As a consequence of the end to labor recruitment and a new child allowance policy, family reunification became a growing phenomenon. A new generation – the off-spring of the guestworkers – was born on German soil and began to grow up with little or no contact with their parents' homelands. In the Turkish case, family reunification meant that between 1974 and 1980, the number of children under the age of 16 grew by almost 130 percent, accounting for nearly 40 percent of the total immigrant population (Abadan-Unat 1995: 280).

By 1982 the foreign population had reached 4,600,000. Despite this steady rise in the non-German population, the West German government still maintained as official policy the claim that Germany was not an immigrant country, and it persisted in viewing their immigrant workers as temporary residents (Katzenstein 1987: 239–40). At the same time, it was forced to begin to confront the prospect of a category of permanent residents who were not citizens. A stark question confronted the nation: Should there be efforts to integrate immigrants into the fabric of German society, or should they be encouraged to remain in self-contained and segregated ethnic enclaves? Given some of the peculiarities of the German political system, no singular answer to this question was forthcoming. Thus, each provincial government – or *Landesregierung* – was responsible for establishing education policies for immigrants. Some, including the conservative and anti-immigrant Bavarian government, opted for segregating immigrant children in their school system. While this may have appeared to be a multicultural approach to immigrant adjustment, in fact it was the reverse since the Bavarian authorities hoped that by maintaining the homeland language and culture, they were preparing the immigrants to return home. Others, such as Berlin, chose an immersion form of assimilation in which children attended ethnically integrated classes that were taught only in German. Still others sought a middle road that encouraged assimilation, but also allowed for the retention of homeland languages at least in the transition period (Abadan-Unat 1995: 280). At the same time, the provision of some social services (but not health or education) is contracted out to three charitable organizations, affiliated with the Catholic Church, the Evangelical Church, and the Social Democratic Party. Immigrant communities are assigned to one of these particular charities, thereby reinforcing ethnic distinctions (Joppke 2000: 13).

Though no comparable economic miracle took place in East Germany, it, too, suffered from labor shortages as a result of losses during the war and lower birth rates afterwards. To compound the problem, East Germany also had to confront the loss of part of its labor force due to the emigration of millions to the West (Heilig, Buttner, & Lutz 1990). East Germany did not publicly mention its labor problems, because to do so would have cast suspicions on the regime's ability to manage the economy. But nevertheless it did create a guestworker system of its own. In this instance, East Germany relied on immigrants from Third World nations, especially those with communist governments. Most of these *Vertragsarbeiter* came from Cuba, Mozambique, Angola, and Vietnam. The East German authorities contended that these workers from developing nations were there in order to facilitate "socialist rationalization," which meant in effect that the workers were there to acquire industrial skills that they could take home with them. While this was in part true, it is also the case that these foreigners were instrumental in filling in the gaps in the nation's workforce.

As in West Germany, the immigrants had to live with severe restrictions. Single workers were allowed into the country, not families. What made the situation even worse for these guestworkers was the fact that they were not permitted to send many durable goods home. Since the East German currency was worthless outside the country, this meant that these guestworkers were not able to establish a system of remittances comparable to that in West Germany (Heilig et al. 1990). To give an idea of how consequential the matter of remittances is, it is estimated that during the 1980s Turkish workers in West Germany sent somewhere between $1.5 and $2 billion per year back to relatives in the homeland (Castles & Miller 1993: 105).

Reunification

During the 1980s, the number of immigrants grew compared to the preceding decade. In part this was a South–North movement of asylum seekers from various countries in Africa, Asia, and South America (Castles & Miller 1993: 106). The fall of the Berlin Wall in 1989 signaled the collapse of communism and set the stage for the reunification of Germany, which took place in 1990. The sweeping changes in eastern Europe as communism collapsed in all of the Warsaw Pact nations and in the independent communist nation of Yugoslavia had an impact on immigration. Political and economic turmoil resulted, with some nations making a relatively successful transition to democracy and to market economies – such as Hungary and Poland – while others continue to live with the ghosts of their recent past. Many new labor immigrants from the East sought to leave the economic insecurity of their homelands for the possibilities they envisioned in Germany. Moreover, the number of political asylum seekers increased, particularly as a result of the collapse of Yugoslavia and the ethnic violence that occurred it its wake.

One of the groups to enter Germany in significant numbers from various points in eastern Europe was the *Aussiedler*. These people could claim citizenship rights immediately upon entry into Germany under the terms of *jus sanguinis* because they were ethnic Germans. Their ancestors had left Germany generations earlier for nations such as Russia, Poland, and Romania, and often lacked a familiarity with contemporary German culture and the German language. Castles and Miller (1993: 107) write that while these particular immigrants "are highly privileged compared to other migrants," because of their rural backgrounds and the culture shock they experienced once in an urban industrial setting, they "have considerable problems of social adaptation and labour market entry." Though they come from more urban industrial backgrounds, similar problems of adjustment have occurred among former East Germans who have migrated to the West. One of the most serious problems that the newly reunified nation confronts is attempting to rebuild the decrepit economy that communism bequeathed the nation.

One of the demographic realities the nation as a whole faces is that without continued immigration the German population will decline. Some projections suggest it would fall from 80,000,000 in the mid-1990s to 70,000,000 in 2030. The German population is aging and has a low fertility rate. Figure 4 illustrates the fact that, despite the need for population growth, immigrants remain a decidedly small part of the population. German ethnics constituted 94.1 percent of the population, with Turks representing 2.5 percent, and all other groups the remaining 3.4 percent – within which Serbo-Croatians, Italians, Russians, Greeks, Poles, and Spanish are among the largest groups. Immigration can counter this trend, but if it does so, given the higher fertility rates of immigrants compared to Germans, the newcomers will end up comprising a larger portion of the overall population than their current 6 percent level (Wingen 1997; Martin 1994).

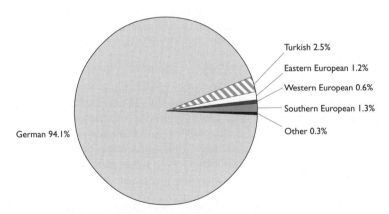

Turkish 2.5%

Eastern European 1.2%

Western European 0.6%

Southern European 1.3%

Other 0.3%

German 94.1%

Figure 4   Ethnic groups in Germany, 1990s
Source: Levinson 1998.

Yugoslavs and Turks

The two largest ethnic groups in Germany, immigrants from the former Yugoslavia and Turks, have established ethnic communities, replete with a wide array of institutions, including religious organizations, mutual aid societies, cultural and educational associations, political organizations, soccer clubs, and the like. Both ethnic communities are divided along religious and political lines. In the former case, Roman Catholic Croats, Orthodox Serbs, and Muslims from Bosnia (many of whom entered the country as political refugees and not as typical labor migrants) remain actively concerned about political events in their wartorn homeland. Likewise, in the Turkish case, secularists coexist with Muslims, and Turks with members of the Kurdish minority. The Kurdish political struggle to carve out a homeland in eastern Turkey (extending into Syria and Iraq) has led to conflict between Kurds and Turks in Germany and elsewhere in western Europe. Here, too, one sees the active involvement of immigrants in politics at home as well as efforts to influence German political opinion (Østergaard-Nielsen 2000).

But these ethnic communities do not simply concern themselves with their homelands. They are also, in a wide variety of ways, working to improve their economic and social situations within the German context. For example, they have taken advantage of the opportunities that are afforded by German law for obtaining educations and job training programs (Faist 2000). They have also lobbied public officials about such matters as Muslim religious instruction in state-funded schools. Turks in particular have become active in local Foreigners' Councils, forums that despite their limited power, constitute a mechanism whereby immigrants can express a collective political voice (Yalçin-Heckmann 1997: 102–5).

The Turkish presence is perhaps the most noticeable, in part because it is the largest group and in part because the cultural differences are the most pronounced. Eva Østergaard-Nielsen (2000: 25) describes the scene in the following way:

> There are numerous [Turkish] taxi drivers, an abundance of Turkish restaurants and cafeterias, and Turkish newspapers at newsstands. While the restaurants and taxis are patronized by all, the Turkish coffee houses, discos, pop events, mosques, and Koranic schools reflect the self-containment of Turkish communities. Travel agencies, driving schools, banks, and import-export firms headed by Turkish citizens and intended for Turkish citizens are, as such, advertised only in Turkish media.

The social distance between Turks and Germans is pronounced. In part this is seen in the occupational location of Turks, who tend to occupy the most unskilled sectors of the economy, with lower wages not only in comparison to Germans but to other immigrant groups as well (Schmidt 1997). Though upward social mobility is occurring, it is doing so slowly, and Turks continue to confront higher levels of unemployment than the national average. In part, social distance can be seen in residential segregation. Though Turks do not live in the hypersegregated enclaves of some inner-city blacks in the United States, residential segregation exists, reflecting the class location of Turks at the bottom of the social hierarchy. In those cities with large concentrations of Turks, ethnic neighborhoods, such as Berlin's Kreuzberg, have arisen. During the early years of settlement, the leadership of the ethnic community often reinforced the social isolation of the community.

Christian Joppke (1996: 474) contends that the earliest leaders tended to be rather orthodox Marxist-Leninists who were preoccupied with homeland political issues, and thus did not devote much attention to matters of immigrant adjustment. Their role in the community was relatively short-lived, giving way to religious leaders as more and more Turks embraced Islam. An indication of the significance of religion can be seen by the fact that the three mosques in Germany in the 1960s had grown to about 1,500 by the 1990s. Many Turks – though it is difficult to know with any precision how many – were attracted to Islamic fundamentalism. Joppke (1996: 474) quotes from a flyer distributed by a fundamentalist organization known as the Association of Koran Schools, which urged the faithful to avoid social contact with non-Muslims because behind the surface veneer lurks "an ugly communist face, a Christian missionary, or a Jewish agent." Thus, both political and religious extremists from the first generation played a role in reinforcing the social isolation of Turks in Germany. This situation is changing as the second generation – born in and far more familiar and comfortable with Germany – is taking the reins of community leadership. On the whole, they are less inclined to left-wing militancy and to fundamentalism, and far more likely to pursue a pragmatic course that is intended to assist immigrants in the process of incorporation into German society. This shift is connected to the emergence of a Turkish middle class. Thus, one sees at the moment the proliferation of professional organizations of Turkish businesspersons, lawyers, and the like (Joppke 1996: 475). These and similar organizations are intent on remedying problems in the ethnic community while attempting to help its members define themselves as a part of a multicultural Germany.

The demise of ethnocultural exclusionism?

As the discussion above suggests, Germany differs from Britain in terms of its definition of citizenship and its orientation toward the incorporation of immigrants. Ruud Koopmans and Paul Statham (1999: 691) have described the German case as "ethnocultural exclusionist," in contrast to the British case, which they define as "multicultural pluralist." While these terms accurately characterize the differing national responses to ethnic diversity during much of the past half-century, changes are underway in Germany as the nation haltingly moves closer to the British model. As it does so, however, it is meeting considerable resistance.

In recent years, Germany has witnessed considerable prejudice and discrimination, including violence, directed at foreigners. Racist hostility toward immigrants is seen in its most virulent form in the extreme right, which includes the overlapping groups associated with neo-Nazism and skinheads. While no immigrants have been immune, people of color have most frequently been the targets of racist attacks. In 1991, one of the most publicized incidents occurred in Hoyerswerda, involving a mob attack on a building housing asylum seekers. This set in motion a series of similar attacks in Rostock, Moellen, Solingen, and Madgeburg directed at Turks, Asians, and Africans (Pettigrew 1998: 96). After a decline in such activities after 1992, by the turn of the century, the number of anti-immigrant and anti-Semitic hate crimes once again rose dramatically. In 2000 approximately 14,000 hate crimes were reported (AP Worldstream 2001).

Anti-immigration sentiment is high. A national poll conducted in 1992 found that 78 percent of Germans felt that immigration was the nation's most pressing problem, compared with only 20 percent who felt that German reunification was. A substantial 90 percent contend that there are either "too many" or "a lot" of foreigners in the country, and a majority of respondents believe that their presence is not good for Germany (Simon & Lynch 1999). To appreciate something of the everyday nature of discrimination, an enterprising reporter disguised himself as a guestworker and proceeded to try to drink in bars and cafes in Frankfurt. On numerous occasions he was refused service and thrown out of the establishment (Pettigrew 1998: 89). It should be noted that anti-immigrant views were more prevalent in eastern Germany. Thus, a poll published in *Der Spiegel* in 1998 found that 55 percent of respondents in the East thought that foreigners lived in the country at the expense of Germans, while only 38 percent in the West thought so (Kim 1998).

In the political arena right-wing politicians have exploited this sentiment. This could be seen when a splinter party was formed after breaking ranks from the conservative Christian Social Union: the far-right Republikaner party, led by a former SS member, experienced limited electoral successes in the late 1980s and early 1990s. However, when the right-of-center Kohl government intensified its anti-immigrant platform, it managed to draw support from Republikaner supporters. The National Democratic Party (NPD), an even more sinister extremist organization, managed during the latter years of the 1990s to attract thousands of neo-Nazis. At the same time, mainstream conservative parties, such as the Christian Democrats and the Bavarian Christian Social Union, have intensified their calls for reducing immigration. With their leadership divided over the issue, they have also balked at taking action against the NPD, despite considerable evidence that it is a front for violence-prone extremists (Culp 2000). On the other hand, progressive voices in Germany have sought to counter the extreme right and to shift public opinion into a position of greater acceptance of immigrants. At the time of writing, the governing Social Democratic Party has taken action to outlaw the NPD. Under the terms of the German constitution, political parties can be banned if they can be proven to be a threat to the democratic social order. If the SDP succeeds in banning the NPD, it would be the first time in over 40 years that a party has been banned. Buoyed by public opinion polls that say that 78 percent of Germans think the government has not done enough to deal with violent right-wing groups, they have also begun a campaign to combat racism. They are supported by less progressive business interests who are concerned about the unwillingness of firms to invest in the economic revitalization of eastern Germany due to the unrest in the region.

Since the 1980s, pressure from the political left has prompted the nation to rethink its historic exclusionary immigration policies. When the right-of-center Christian Democrats remained in power, there was little likelihood that immigration policies would be revised. However, when the Social Democrats entered office in a coalition with the Green Party in 1998, a concerted effort was undertaken to liberalize German immigration law. On May 7, 1999, by a 2-to-1 margin the German Parliament voted to replace their citizenship policies with one more congruent with the policies of the European Union and with the policies of many other liberal democracies. The change represented official recognition for the first time of the fact, in Chancellor Gerhard Schröder's words, "that the immigration to Germany that has taken place over past decades is irreversible" (quoted in Klusmeyer 2000: 17).

The new law grants the right of citizenship to immigrant children born on German soil. Until age 23, they are permitted to possess two passports, but when they reach that age, they must decide whether to renounce their other citizenship in favor of German citizenship or give up the right to be a German citizen. The law also liberalized naturalization policies for foreign-born immigrants, including reducing the residency requirement from 15 years to 8. Political theorist Seyla Benhabib (1999: 7) has concluded that, "The German Social Democratic–Green coalition, with the help of the Free Democratic Party, is moving toward a multiethnic, multilingual, multifaith democratic polity."

This can be seen in German public radio's production of foreign-language programs. One manifestation of this general trend can be seen in the workings of Berlin's fourth public radio station, Sender Freies Berlin, commonly knows as Radio Multikulti. Seeking to provide a voice to the 440,000 immigrants residing in that city, the station's programming is divided into German-language programs and programs in "the languages of the world city."

There are time slots for programs in Turkish, Roma, Albanian, Arabic, Kurdish, Persian, Polish, Russian, Vietnamese, Italian, Spanish, and Greek, and after the break-up of Yugoslavia, separate programs were produced for Serbs, Croats, Slovenians, Bosnians, and Macedonians. The explicit rationale for the station is to encourage the integration of immigrants into German society (Vertovec, forthcoming).

Nonetheless, despite these recent developments, some commentators have a less sanguine sense of what the future holds in store than Benhabib's assessment. Claude Cahn (2000), for example, contends that changing the laws is merely a first step in a much larger task of redefining what it means to be a person who qualifies for citizenship and one who does not. The unresolved question is whether or not Germany will in the end abandon its traditional understanding of national identity based in pursuit of the ideal of an ethnonational community, or will seek to reaffirm this particularistic vision of nationality (Schuck & Münz 1998; Lehmann & Wellenreuther 1999). On the one hand, this particular conception of citizenship is deeply rooted in German history; on the other hand, the role of the European Union in shaping the citizenship policies of its constituent states is forcing the Germans to consider the implications of what it means to be a multicultural society.

France: Republican Ideals versus the Realities of Race

The ideology of French nationalism stands in stark contrast to the German version. Gérard Noiriel (1996) has referred to *le creuset français* – the French melting pot – to describe the prevailing assimilationist ideology of the nation. Since the French Revolution, the French have harbored the idea that anyone could become a citizen provided they embrace the ideals of the republic. In other words, rather than basing citizenship on an ethnocultural model, the French opted for a *jus soli* understanding of membership in the polity. Individuals could become French citizens either by conversion (giving up one's past affiliations and affirming an allegiance to France) or by territorial birthright. Brubaker (1992) points out that the French case is not pure given the fact that there is an element of *jus sanguinis* in their code. However, he argues that the *jus soli* conception of civic peoplehood is clearly dominant. Insofar as this is the case, the French notion of citizenship resembles the American understanding (Horowitz 1992).

Making modern France

The idea of assimilation could be seen before the advent of wide-scale immigration. In the nineteenth century, it also referred to the process of incorporating the rural peasantry into the nation. As Eugen Weber has shown in *Peasants into Frenchmen* (1976), prior to the emergence of the modern state, the peasantry often identified themselves in reference to their villages, regions, and regional dialects, but not in terms of the nation as a whole. The task of developing a modern nation-state involved in part a concerted effort to reduce the salience of these local identities while simultaneously enhancing the salience of a more encompassing French identity. As the melting-pot metaphor suggests, the process of incorporation meant that groups were expected to replace their local identities with a national identity, rather than preserving them in a multicultural context. The implications were clear for the main ethnic groups located within the nation: Bretons, Occitans, Corsicans, Basques, and Catalans – the last two, clearly, straddling the boundaries of two nations (DeCouflé 1992; Applegate 1999).

The international significance of the revolutionary ideals of liberty, equality, and fraternity was such that republican France became an important destination for political refugees fleeing oppressive regimes. During the nineteenth century, most of these refugees originated from various points in Europe, while in the twentieth it included a growing number of individuals from colonial nations, not surprisingly especially from French colonies. In the first half of the twentieth century, asylum seekers created small ethnic communities. These included Jews fleeing pogroms in eastern Europe and the rise of the Nazis in Germany, anti-Bolshevik Russians fleeing from that nation's revolutionary upheavals, and Armenians fleeing the genocidal assault on them by Turkish authorities (Hargreaves 1995: 10).

Labor migrations proved to be consequential in industrializing France. During the nineteenth century, it was the most important immigrant-receiving nation in Europe (Dignan 1981; Noiriel 1990). The majority of labor immigrants during this era came from elsewhere in Europe, especially from Italy, but also including Spain, Portugal, and Poland. For the most part, these immigrants did not experience much hostility because their labor was needed and many clearly defined themselves as sojourners intent on returning home whenever the economic situation permitted (Freeman 1979). Thus, they did not engender a serious debate about the best ways of incorporating the newcomers into the host society. Moreover, their levels were always quite low, never exceeding 3 percent of the population.

Nonetheless, the limits of French openness were evident during economic downturns. In terms of governmental policies, this contributed to a revision of the Nationality Law in 1889 that permitted the government to deny the naturalization of immigrants deemed to be "undeserving" or "undesirable" (Noiriel 1996: 63). Such legislative changes reflected shifts in public attitudes about foreigners. For example, during the economic slump of the early 1890s, anti-Italian sentiment intensified, especially in southern France where Italian immigrants were highly concentrated. Attacks on immigrants increased in frequency, the most violent of which took place in Aigues-Mortes in 1893 when 8 immigrants were killed and scores were injured (Hargreaves 1995: 7–8). Similar attacks occurred in 1901, when residents of the mining community of La Mure went on what they referred to as "bear hunts," forcing immigrant workers and their families to flee their homes, which were ransacked and the belongings of the immigrants burned (Corbett 1994: 194).

The levels of immigration increased in the early decades of the twentieth century, particularly in the 1920s, as a consequence of the labor shortages brought about by manpower loses as a result of the First World War and linked to the closing of the US to mass immigration. Reflecting the economic necessity of foreign labor, the government liberalized their immigration policies during this decade (Noiriel 1996: 64). By 1931, foreigners as a percentage of the total population reached what was until that point an all-time high of 6.6 percent. When the Depression struck, once again anti-immigrant hostility surfaced. In this instance, the government responded to anti-immigrant agitation by making naturalization more difficult, excluding immigrants from public-sector jobs, and enacting repatriation policies. The Depression and the Second World War combined to reduce the levels of immigrants in France, so that by 1954 the figure was 4.1 percent (INSEE 1992). This was soon reversed by the new waves of immigrants to arrive in France in the latter part of the twentieth century.

Contemporary immigration in France

Like Germany, Britain, and the rest of the EU nations, France experienced labor shortages after the Second World War. In response to this situation, it became an active recruiter of migrant workers from the mid-1950s to the early 1970s, as reflected in figure 5. Immediately after the war in 1945, the basis for subsequent policies was laid down. However, only part of the postwar discussions about immigration revolved around the need for labor; another part revolved around the need for population growth in the face of a declining birth rate. By unlinking residence permits from work permits, the government opened up the doors to jobseekers who had not yet been hired and to families. This encouraged immigrants to view themselves as permanent settlers rather than labor sojourners.

Alec Hargreaves (1995: 11) notes that "No ethnic quotas were laid down in the 1945 ordinance, but in implementing these formal regulations, successive governments sought as far as possible to encourage European rather than African or Asian immigrants." This suggested that as French republican ideals came face to face with the prospect of non-Western immigrants arriving in large numbers – where cultural and racial differences converged

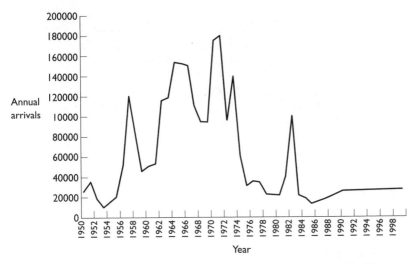

Figure 5   Annual arrivals of permanent foreign workers in France, 1950–99
Source: INSEE 1999.

– the French were capable of the same xenophobia as has been evident in the other liberal democracies discussed herein.

The two-decade period between the mid-1950s and mid-1970s represents the zenith of immigration in French history. Philip Ogden (1995: 292) writes that during these years "the total foreign population doubled and the role of foreign labor was at an all-time peak." As figure 6 indicates, two regions contributed the largest numbers of immigrants: the Iberian peninsula and the north African Maghreb region. In terms of the former, immigrants from Portugal constitute the largest group, while the level of Spanish residents in France was about a third of its peninsular neighbor. Both of these nations lagged behind the rest of western Europe economically, and continued to live under the authoritarian political regimes of Salazar and Franco. Thus, emigrants left their nations often as the result of an admixture of economic and political motives. Given the proximity of these nations to France, many immigrants viewed themselves as temporary laborers, and even after settlement were able to maintain ties to home with relative ease. The Portuguese are fairly widely distributed geographically, while Spaniards are heavily concentrated in southern France and in the Paris metropolitan region. For both groups, female employment is high, chiefly because many women have found employment in domestic service. Portuguese males have found a niche in the construction industry, while many Spanish males work in the agricultural sector (Hargreaves 1995: 76–7).

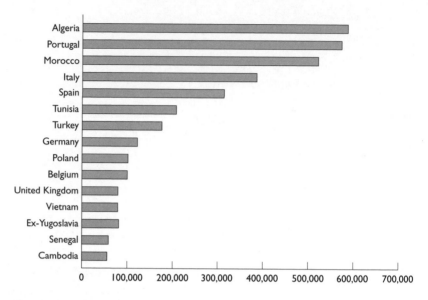

Figure 6 Immigrants in France, 1999
Source: INSEE 1999.

   Three nations from the Maghreb became important sources of immigration, as a whole providing the largest number of contemporary immigrants.
Of the three, Algerians were the largest group, followed by Moroccans and
Tunisians. Moreover, the struggle for Algerian independence had profound
consequences for political stability in France, playing a major role in the collapse of the Fourth Republic in 1958 (Cerny 1980; MacMaster 1997). Algeria remained a colony of France until it finally won its independence in 1962.
In part because of the sizeable French population in Algeria, the French were
particularly resistant to granting independence, despite the growing militancy within the colony calling for an end to French rule. A reflection of the
distinctive character of the relationship of France to Algeria can be seen by
the fact that Algeria was typically referred to as *l'autre France* (i.e., the France
across the Mediterranean), and the colony was declared to be an integral
part of France. This meant that all of the residents of Algeria, whether they
were of European or African descent, were considered to be French nationals, and thus that all Algerians were permitted to move freely between the
two nations.

   During the independence struggle, many French nationals living in Algeria repatriated to France. These people, commonly known as *pieds-noirs*, were
culturally French and did not look physically different from their counter-

parts in France. Thus, they were able to blend into the population with relative ease, even though many of them had lived all of their lives outside of France. Related to this particular migratory movement, a group of Algerians known as *harkis* also fled to France. This term refers to Algerians who fought on the side of the French during the independence struggle. After the French defeat, the triumphant nationalists executed many of these former French allies, but thousands managed to escape along with tens of thousands of others who were sympathetic to the French cause (Hargreaves 1995: 13, 78).

Independence did not stop the flow of Algerians. Indeed, shortly after independence the French and Algerian governments entered into the Evian Agreement, which was intended to provide a formal mechanism for labor recruitment. Within two years, the French sought to rescind the agreement, claiming that too many Algerians were arriving without work slots for them, and were thus contributing to social disorder (Freeman 1979: 83). This did not, however, stop the flow of migrants into France. It is estimated that during the five years after independence the number of immigrants from Algeria had reached 400,000 (Oberhauser 1991: 435). Algerians are concentrated in the Paris conurbation, Lyon, Marseille, and in a number of older industrial cities that have confronted rising unemployment rates since the 1970s as a result of deindustrialization.

Moroccans and Tunisians began to arrive in France in significant numbers somewhat later than Algerians did. Moroccans found employment in the auto industry and coal mines – two industries that have experienced considerable downsizing in recent years. This has led to the fact that Moroccans suffer comparatively high unemployment rates. They have also settled on the island of Corsica where they have found work in agriculture. The Tunisians, because they arrived last and at a time when jobs in old industries were at a nadir, tended to locate in central cities where they joined the Portuguese in the construction industry and found work as unskilled manual laborers in a variety of settings (Hargreaves 1995: 79).

Italy in the postwar era, long a source of labor in France, continued to contribute substantial numbers of immigrants. As did their predecessors, they continued to settle in southern France, as well as in the Paris region. Italians can be found in both industrial and agricultural settings. However, given the fact that the Italian economy has improved in recent decades, fewer Italians have been inclined to seek work in France, and many already in France have opted to return to their homeland. Nonetheless, they remain a significant part of the ethnic mix in contemporary France.

In addition, almost 340,000 immigrants from "Departements d'Outre-Mer" and "Territoires d'Outre-Mer" (DOM-TOM) arrived during this period. These immigrants were from some of the few overseas colonies or territories that France still controlled in the postcolonial era. Four nations from the

DOM-TOM provided the bulk of this segment of the immigrant population: the Caribbean nations of Guadeloupe, Martinique, and French Guyana and the island of Reunion in the Indian Ocean. On a smaller scale, immigrants from former French-speaking colonies in sub-Saharan Africa and from Congo (formerly a Belgian colony, but whose official language is French) have also contributed to the overall ethnic mix. Asians, including emigrants from Vietnam and other nations in southeast Asia as well as Turks, have joined them. The net result was that in contrast to the nineteenth and early twentieth centuries, where the overwhelming majority of immigrants were from Europe, such was not the case during the second half of the twentieth. With the arrival of Africans and Asians, the nation confronted a racial diversity heretofore unknown. Likewise, particularly with the immigrants from the Maghreb, it had to deal with an Islamic presence. This diversity would set the stage for developments on the political and cultural front for the remainder of the century.

As with the rest of the EU nations, France ceased to actively recruit foreign workers by the early 1970s, when economic changes brought about by the restructuring of the manufacturing sector and the negative impact of the oil embargo reduced the demand for labor (Islam 1994). In 1974 the conservative government of Valéry Giscard d'Estaing enacted legislation to suspend further immigration. This did not apply to members of the EU, who are guaranteed free movement across borders in the member states. It also did not rule out certain categories of skilled and professional workers where the demand remained high, and under the provisions of international treaties signed by the French the ban did not apply to refugees. Nonetheless, the intent was clear: France wanted to halt the influx of immigrants. But it did not stop here.

The conservative government also wanted to reduce the number of foreigners in the nation via a campaign of voluntary repatriation that involved monetary inducements to leave. While it was primarily directed at non-EU nations, in fact very few Third World immigrants took up the offer. In contrast, many Spanish and Portuguese immigrants did so due to the fact that the dictatorships that had ruled their respective nations had fallen, democratic regimes were in place, and the economic climate had also improved. In addition, an attempt designed to prevent family reunification was scuttled due to the protests of human rights groups. The result of these measures taken together was that, for the last quarter of the twentieth century, the size of the foreign population did not change appreciably (Oberhauser 1991: 441; Hargreaves 1995: 19–22).

The confluence of race and religion had a pronounced effect on attitudes of the public-at-large and on policy-makers. The French saw themselves as an assimilationist nation, but they were, simply put, unprepared for the presence of large numbers of people of color and similarly large numbers of Muslims. Alec Hargreaves (1995: 26–7) summarized the situation well in the following passage:

> The seeming invisibility of past generations of immigrants and of those who are today descended from them is often regarded as proof of the success with which they have been incorporated into French society. Immigrants who have settled in France during the post-war period, and more particularly those who have come to the fore during the past twenty years, are often felt to threaten this tradition. It is widely claimed that people of Third World origin are much harder to "integrate" than Europeans. Far from disappearing without a trace, they have actually increased in visibility at a time when successive governments have been claiming that immigration is at an end. . . . the fear is that immigration is leading remorselessly to the formation of permanently distinct minorities within French society.

The impact of the National Front on the politics of immigration

The far right wing remained on the margins of the political systems of the western European nations during the first several decades after the Second World War (Veugelers 2000: 22). However, more recently a number of extremist parties have begun to be a troubling force in a number of countries, including Austria's Freedom Party (founded by Nazi sympathizer Jörg Haider), Belgium's Vlaams Blok, Britain's National Front, Germany's Republikaners, the Netherlands' Centrum Party, and Switzerland's National Action Against the Swamping of the People and Homeland. The oldest and along with the Freedom Party the most politically successful is France's Front National (FN). Founded in 1972 by the charismatic racist Jean-Marie Le Pen, it attracted members of the extremist fringes of neofascism and right-wing nationalism. During the founding period, the party preached a distinctly backward-looking message, including nostalgia for the Vichy era, anti-Semitism, and anger for the "loss" of Algeria. For example, Le Pen's fondness for the Vichy government is linked to his revisionist reading of the Holocaust, which he has described as no more than "a point of detail" (quoted in Corbett 1994: 194). As such, during its first decade, the party never managed to obtain one percent of the vote.

However, when it turned its attention to the question of contemporary immigration, it very quickly became a potent force in French politics (Husbands 1991; Weber 1996). The FN harped on the presumed threat to French culture and to "traditional values" posed by the presence of large numbers of foreigners. A classic instance of scapegoating, it was also insistent that the problems of unemployment and housing shortages were a consequence of immigration. Foreigners were depicted as a drain on government treasuries, causing for example a social security deficit. Moreover, crime, delinquency, drug use, and other forms of antisocial behavior were attributed to the immigrant "invasion."

John Veugelers (2000: 22) contends quite correctly that, "The FN's transformation from a marginal to an established party has altered the political dynamics of the Fifth Republic." By the early 1970s, incidents of racist violence against north Africans increased (Freeman 1979: 95). Tapping into this growing anti-immigrant sentiment, the FN began to make inroads into the political bases of the established parties. This was clearly evident in the case of the right, as both Gaullist and non-Gaullist parties on this end of the political spectrum began to adopt an increasingly anti-immigrant rhetoric in an effort to ward off the challenge of the party. This is vividly evident in Giscard d'Estaing's contention that the newcomers were so culturally distinctive that they could not be assimilated and in his characterization of their presence as amounting to that of an "invasion" (Nair 1996: 76). But the FN also managed to tap into the electoral base of the political left, particularly the Communists, whose working-class constituents in declining industrial regions exhibited growing levels of xenophobia in the face of the threat of job losses. However, this working-class base should not be overstated. The main sources of support for the FN are among small-business owners and craftspersons. Thus, its growth is chiefly due to its ability to draw votes from other right-of-center parties (Pettigrew 1998: 93).

Opposition to the FN came from not only from students and civil rights organizations, but also from the Catholic Church. The most visible and media-savvy challenge to the party was SOS-Racisme, founded in 1984 by Harlem Désir as a multi-ethnic movement promoting tolerance and acceptance. The organization attracted celebrities that helped to popularize its slogan: *Touche pas à mon pote* ("Hands off my buddy"). Nevertheless, the FN has become an entrenched part of the political system. Since the 1980s it has managed to attract between 10 to15 percent of the vote in national elections. It, for example, won 35 seats in the National Assembly in 1986, while a decade later the party obtained 15 percent of the vote in the presidential election, and in some local contests reached levels of 30 to 40 percent. In 1997, it won control of the mayor's office in Vitrolles, defeating the Socialist candidate. And not only is its electoral appeal holding steady at around 15 percent, but according to opinion polls, larger percentages of the public are sympathetic to various positions of the FN (Wieviorka 1995b; Valls-Russell 1996; Jeambar 1997).

When Socialist François Mitterrand was elected to the presidency, the overt hostility toward immigrants exhibited by the previous government ceased, and indeed his administration promised that it would be committed to combating racism and the impact of discrimination while improving the economic and political situation of immigrant communities. The goal of the Mitterrand administration was to assist in the integration of immigrants into French society (Ireland 1994: 61). However, it should be noted that this was to be accomplished without the infusion of new immigrants. No effort was made to undo the restrictive immigration policies forged in the preceding decade. The net result was that the government pursued a policy that Sami Nair (1996: 76) has appropriately referred to as "integration with closure."

Sensing an electoral minefield, the Socialist government never made the immigration issue one of its central concerns. When center-right governments returned to power, for a short time between 1986 and 1988 and then again in 1993, various efforts were undertaken – at the initiation of the anti-immigrant Interior Minister Charles Pasqua – to make deportation easier, asylum requirements more stringent, and to push for reforms of the Nationality Code that were designed to make it more difficult to become a citizen by eliminating the *droit du sol*, which meant that the children of immigrants would no longer automatically become citizens, but must officially state their intention to do so.

Multiculturalism as an ethnonational problem

Across the mainstream political spectrum, the very idea of multiculturalism remains problematic due to the continuing impact of the French republican version of the melting pot. While hostility to the preservation and enhancement of ethnic groups is most evident in the xenophobia of the political right, in different form its problematic nature can be seen on the left as well. With an emphasis on the desirability of a common French value system and a unitary idea of "Frenchness," the integrationist ideal leaves little room for the preservation of ethnic identities. Thus, the notion that anyone can become French provided that they embrace the nation's culture and model themselves after the French means that the expectation is that ethnic identities will disappear. Moreover, there is little room for considering group identities in a nation where integration is perceived to occur at the individual level.

While the preceding discussion has highlighted this problem in relation to recent immigration, the opposition to multiculturalism can also be seen in the ways the nation has responded to its ethnonationalist communities: the Bretons, Corsicans, Occitans, and Basques (who, like their Catalonian counterparts, see their homeland as straddling the French and Spanish borders). Nationalist movements in Brittany and Corsica have been the most consequential, though the relative influence of nationalists in both regions is less significant than that of the ethnonationalist movements in Britain or Spain.

Brittany, located on the northwest coast, has a historic and linguistic connection with the Celtic peoples of the British Isles. It was an independent dukedom until annexed by the French monarchy in 1532, and the French

Revolution further undermined its autonomy by killing many Bretons sympathetic to the monarchy and banning their language. The language ban – key to cultural preservation in the eyes of nationalists – was to remain in effect for over a century. Like the nationalist movements in the United Kingdom and Spain, the nineteenth- and early twentieth-century movement in Breton placed an emphasis on cultural matters (Rogers 1990).

Contemporary Breton nationalists have had to live down the movement's affiliation during the 1930s and 1940s with the political right, which included its willingness to collaborate with fascism. When the Union Démocratique Bretonne (UDB) was founded in the 1960s, it was quick to criticize preceding organizations and to stress its political differences with reactionary nationalism. It tried to indicate its openness by entering into political alliances with socialists and communists. The problem for the party during the years of socialist government was that the willingness of the government to at least pay lip-service to the idea of decentralization and to regionalization led to a decline in membership, and forced it to attempt to define itself in terms of "socialist autonomy" in an effort to differentiate itself from the French left. At the same time, it attempted to forge alliances with environmental organizations and trade unions.

Most Bretons appear to favor greater regional autonomy obtained through gradualist politics, rather than seeking outright independence. Although their grievances include economic considerations, in many respects their nationalism emphasizes the erosion of Breton culture, and as such it bears a resemblance to Welsh nationalism. Mainstream nationalists are intent on promoting the Breton language and celebrating Brittany's distinctive culture (McDonald 1989; Rogers 1990). That being said, a small militant fringe committed to independence emerged in the 1970s and resurfaced again two decades later. Two small and shadowy terrorist groups have engaged in bombings, usually directed at government buildings and public utilities, but including a bombing in 2000 of a McDonald's restaurant that killed an employee. The Brittany Combat Group is thought to have links with ETA, while the Revolutionary Breton Army has links with Basque, Corsican, and Northern Irish groups (McNeil 2000).

An island in the Mediterranean, Corsica has had a long history of foreign rulers, including the Romans and Vandals. It was at various times under the control of the Bishop of Pisa and the City of Genoa. French rule began in 1768, and despite various interruptions by the British in the late eighteenth century and by the Axis occupation during the Second World War, Corsica has remained French. Again a nationalist movement committed primarily to cultural preservation arose in the nineteenth century, though in considerably weaker form than in the other instances discussed herein. It did not begin to make significant inroads into the populace and thus did not seek to challenge the status quo until nearly a century later, beginning after the

Second World War, but picking up steam in the 1970s. The largest and most influential of several nationalist groups is the Union of Corsican People (UCP). Its appeal was based on its ability to both demand steps to protect the culture, including the Corse language, and to promote economic development. Unlike Brittany, which has a vibrant economy, Corsica confronted the reality that it was the poorest region in France. To fuel the nationalist fires, the French government relocated many *pieds-noirs* to Corsica in the wake of Algerian independence, leading to escalating tensions between Corsicans and newcomers (Savigear 1990: 86–9).

The mobilization of nationalists during the 1970s put increased pressure on the central government to respond. In 1982 the National Assembly formally defined Corsica as a region with a unique constitutional status. More concretely, this meant that a regional assembly was established and it was granted control over local economic, educational, and cultural matters. However, when a new bill was proposed in the early 1990s that granted even greater autonomy, conservatives in the French parliament balked at the very idea of referring to the island's native inhabitants as "le peuple Corse" ("the Corsican people") because to do so, they argued, was to suggest that they were not French. When the bill finally passed in 1992, it made clear that Corsica was "a territorial collectivity having a certain autonomy but forming an integral part of the French nation" (Corbett 1994: 203). While these measures appear to have placated the majority of nationalists, like Brittany, the region has a small violent extremist element that continues to demand independence.

Given the comparative weakness of ethnic nationalism in France, there is far less likelihood that a French Tom Nairn will soon write a book on *The Break-up of France*. On the other hand, calls for a French equivalent of devolution will likely persist in coming decades. Insofar as they do, they will raise issues about what it means to speak about multicultural France. However, as the following section will indicate, the real battles over multiculturalism are being raised as a result of recent immigration, and most acutely in relation to the presence of Muslims regardless of their nation of origin.

The Muslims of France

At present there are somewhere between 4 and 5 million Muslims in France, which translates into 7 to 8 percent of the population. While most of the Muslims originate from the Maghreb, they also come from sub-Saharan Africa, Turkey, and elsewhere. Wherever their origins, there is no doubt that Muslim immigrants confront considerably more prejudice and discrimination than their EU counterparts. In the occupational arena, they are over-represented in unskilled manual-labor jobs, particularly those that native

French avoid. Thus, they tend to occupy the bottom tiers of a dual labor market (Edwards et al. 1975). Unemployment rates are higher for Muslims than for French citizens and for EU immigrants. Linked to their economic location, Muslim immigrants have higher school dropout rates and lower levels of educational attainment than the general population.

As a consequence of their location in the economy, Muslims tend to live in substandard housing and experience far higher levels of overcrowding than other groups (Rudder 1992). In the early years of settlement, many immigrants lived in *bidonvilles* (shantytowns) located on the outskirts of cities and lacking such basic features as running water, sewage systems, and electricity. Living in such circumstances has by and large given way to the creation of ethnic neighborhoods located in the suburbs of major cities. Known as *banlieues*, these suburbs contain many high-rise housing projects catering to low-income people. Hargreaves (1995: 72–3) observes that in contrast to the image of suburbs as places where the more affluent live, the term *banlieues* has "become synonymous with areas of acute social disadvantages" and as such they are the "sociological equivalent of British and American inner-city areas." One of the factors contributing to residential concentration is the illegal quota on housing that many municipal governments have introduced, amounting to a form of institutional racial discrimination.

In such neighborhoods the manifestations of enclave economies are evident – as Muslims have begun to acquire businesses, especially those associated with catering and grocery stores. However, as a point of comparison, the *banlieues* more closely resemble ethnic neighborhoods in Britain than in the US, because in most of these locales, immigrants still represent a minority of the population. The hypersegregation characteristic of many American inner-city neighborhoods is not characteristic of French "ghettos" (Wacquant 1992).

While the salience of race in the new ethnic hierarchy needs to be considered, it dovetails with religion, or more specifically with the Islamic presence. Malcolm Anderson (2000: 55) observes that "The building of mosques, female circumcision and polygamy, the intrusion of religion into the public domain, all produce high levels of disquiet and sometimes indignation." That being said, there are more Muslims in France at the beginning of the twenty-first century than there are Protestants or Jews, and thus it is the nation's second largest religion.

The French response to this novel situation can be characterized as a dialectical swing between a tolerant acceptance of Islam and fearful resistance to its adherents practicing their faith. On the one hand, Milton Viorst (1996: 79) points to various examples of tolerance, such as the fact that employers often offer their Muslim employees time off for prayer, including time to make a pilgrimage to Mecca, while the government provides chaplains and food in accordance with Islamic dietary laws to Muslims in prison. On the other hand, fear of Islam tends to revolve around what is perceived to be the threat it poses to the secular traditions associated with the French state. Former Interior Minister Charles Pasqua has argued that "It is not enough to have Islam in France. There must now be a French Islam" (quoted in Viorst 1996: 80). Implicit in this rather odd declaration is the suspicion that Muslim immigrants are different from other immigrants, and the difference revolves around their presumed unwillingness to embrace the cultural values of the larger society, particularly those associated with pluralism and secularism. This suspicion was nowhere more evident than in the 1989 headscarf affair discussed in the introduction to this book. The controversy served to reinforce the conviction on the part of many Muslims that their religious freedom was being attacked, while for the right wing it meant that Muslims were incapable of becoming truly French. While Muslims argued that wearing the headscarfs was no different than Jews wearing yarmulkes and Roman Catholics wearing crucifix necklaces, their secular critics contended that the scarves were an open attempt to proselytize.

Tensions intensified in the aftermath of this protracted debate. In its wake, a riot broke out in suburban Lyon that Donald Horowitz (1992:15) points out was similar to the inner-city riots in 1960s America and in early 1980s in Britain. While the spark of the riot involved conflicts with the police, the underlying factor contributing to it revolved around a sense that French society was unwilling to accept the new immigrants and to assist them in combating all of the problems associated with work, housing, and the like – in addition to the religious question. For its part, the FN seized upon the conflict to press its anti-immigrant message. It had an impact on public opinion and on the reactions of the major political parties. This was the climate that led four years after the incident to the passage of the revised nationality law noted above requiring that the children of immigrants apply for citizenship rather than, as had been the case, being granted it automatically (Hargreaves 1995: 31).

The response of Muslim organizations has been mixed. There are several thousand Islamic organizations in France, differentiated along such lines as nationality, theology, generation, gender, and profession. They constitute a decentralized array of group affiliations that are generally independent of homeland control and manipulation by the French (Ireland 1994: 70). Many of these organizations function, at least in part, as civil rights organizations, intent on finding ways to redress the most pressing problems confronting the Islamic community. Not surprisingly there have been a wide variety of approaches to dealing with these problems, ranging from encouraging accommodation to French society to the militant rejection of integration.

Some in the former camp argue that religion's proper sphere is in the private realm (Diop 1997). For example, the Grand Mufti of Marseille, Soheib Bencheikh, has argued that for Islam to flourish in France, it is necessary for the faithful to reconcile themselves to the fact that they live as a minority religious community in a secular society, which is radically different from the situation in their homelands, where Islam is the dominant state-sanctioned religion (Truehart 1997). This idea of compromise is anathema to Islamic fundamentalists, such as the Union of French Islamic Organizations and the militants affiliated with the Armed Islamic Group (AIG), which was responsible for a wave of terrorist bombings in the late 1990s that left at least 7 people dead and nearly 200 injured.

Many in the Islamic community are only nominally attached to Islam. This is especially evident among the second generation, known as the *beurs*. While there is evidence of generational upward mobility, the *beurs* are frustrated by the difficulties they have encountered in breaking into white-collar professions. At the same time, many of them are not religiously observant, and in fact chafe at the demands made by the religious community. The tensions between the more secular and the religious quarters of the community is humorously depicted in Mahmoud Zemmouri's film, *100% Arabica*, which revolves around the battle of wills that transpires in a Parisian suburb between a conniving imam and two raï musicians. The latter reflect the ambiguous situation experienced by many in the second generation. They live between two cultural worlds, as is evident in their relationship to popular culture, as they have managed to blend Western rock music with the rhythms of traditional North African music. This hybridization of culture is similar to reggae, except that raï has not been embraced by French youth to the extent that reggae made its way into the youth culture of white North America and Britain. What this does suggest, however, is that a form of acculturation is underway on the part of a generation that sees France as its homeland, and is seeking to find ways to enter the mainstream without giving up aspects of their cultural background that they continue to find meaningful.

Germany, France, and the European Union

Of all of the nations discussed herein, Germany and France have had the most difficult time embracing the idea of multiculturalism. In the German case, it is due to the necessity of overcoming the blood-and-soil nationalism that has informed German identity for all of the modern era. The French, by comparison, would appear to be far more open to diversity. However, closer examination reveals a conception of republicanism that entails an aggressive version of assimilation as absorption, thus entailing the loss of one's ethnic past. In short, Germans have had to deal with a history in which foreigners remain forever foreigners, while the French have lived with the view that newcomers were capable of transforming themselves into Frenchmen and Frenchwomen by replacing their ethnic identities with that of the French citizen. Each nation has its own powerful ideological barrier that makes difficult the emergence of a notion of multicultural citizenship. Each nation also must deal with an organized resistance to the inclusion of newcomers in their midst – in the French case within the political party system, in the German case chiefly in the form of illegal hate groups. Despite these challenges, it is also the case that in both nations changes have occurred during the past two decades that constitute a recognition that the immigrants are "here to stay." There is a growing willingness, particularly on the part of the democratic left, to entertain the idea of forging a new conception of national identity and of what it means to be a citizen.

The idea of multicultural citizenship is being aided by the existence of the European Union. It is not that we have entered into a postnational world where transnational organizations such as the EU have usurped the prerogatives of nations. Rather, in the context of western Europe, it is simply that the EU has had to play a role in shaping a variety of national practices and policies in the interest of a coherent EU position. This role is clearly evident in the case of immigration policies, particularly as they involve citizens of EU nations. In regard to non-EU immigrants, nations retain sovereignty over immigration policies, though here, too, the EU is beginning to play a role, as with efforts aimed at creating uniform asylum policies (Soysal 1994; Sassen 1998).

The EU ought to be seen as part of the reason that its member states have begun to wrestle with a situation in which total exclusion and the forced repatriation of foreigners is not an option – politically and economically – and where coercive assimilation is not a solution because, as Rainer Bauböck (2000: 10) observes, "it is incompatible with a modern understanding of cultural liberties and is more likely to trigger resistance than compliance." Thus, it becomes increasingly clear that the task ahead for these two nations – and indeed the rest of western Europe – is to begin to make sense of what multicultural citizenship might mean within the particularities of their own national histories.

CHAPTER SIX

Multicultural Prospects and Twenty-first Century Realities

During the past half-century the advanced industrial liberal democratic nations of the world have become increasingly enmeshed in the information age that is helping to reconfigure an increasingly global network society (Castells 1997). The economies of these nations have been transformed by the expansion of transnational capitalism and by the emergence and increasing significance of regional and international economic entities designed to regulate capitalist development. The political systems, too, have been transformed by globalization, in part calling into question the future functions of the nation-state *vis-à-vis* transnational political organizations (Alienikoff & Klusmeyer 2001). Finally, the pace and intensity of cultural diffusion is unlike that of anytime in the past, and as a result, terms such as hybridity and creolization have gained considerable currency in attempting to account for situations in which tradition and modernity coexist and reciprocally influence each other. Regardless of whether their relationship is a symbiotic one or one characterized by tension and conflict, in combination they create the postmodern moment.

Within this framework, it is clear that the ethnic factor will play a crucially important role in shaping the social life of these nation-states well into the future. The shared conviction of modernization theorists and Marxists about the presumed inevitable decline and ultimate disappearance of ethnic identities and ethnic group affiliations has been seriously undermined by the events of the recent past and by some of the most pressing challenges confronting these nations at present. Each of the nations examined herein – and indeed all of the other advanced industrial liberal democracies – will continue to be characterized by a unique "ethnoscape" (Appadurai 1990) based on the particular constellation of ethnic groups and patterns of intergroup relations within it. As the case studies in the four preceding chapters reveal, there are two major ways in which the saliency of ethnicity manifests itself today. First, it does so as a consequence of the "turbulence of migration" (Papastergiadis 2000) that has led to the massive influx of people from the less-developed nations to the core nations of the capitalist world system. Secondly, it is the result of the resurgence of "ethnonationalism" (Connor 1994) among people who define themselves as being members of "nations without states" (Guibernau 1999).

All of the advanced industrial nations can be defined as multicultural insofar as they are more culturally diverse than they once were. That being said, there is considerable variation among these nations, both in terms of the level of diversity and the sources of diversity. The three historic settler states – the United States, Canada, and Australia – continue to be more heterogeneous than their nonsettler-state counterparts. On a continuum, the US and Canada are clearly the most ethnically heterogeneous nations, while Germany and Japan remain the least heterogeneous. Within this comparative perspective, what all of these nations share in common is the fact that they have experienced significant influxes of immigrants from the less-developed nations during the latter part of the twentieth century.

Ethnonationalism is a factor in some of these states, but not all. Clearly, the Québecois nationalists in Canada, the Scottish and Welsh nationalist movements and Northern Ireland's republicans in the United Kingdom, and the Basque and Catalan movements in Spain represent the most powerful ethnonational movements. In some instances, these movements hold out the possibility of the break-up of the nation-state at some time in the future. In all instances, they suggest the necessity on the part of these nations to find ways of accommodating the demands for greater autonomy brought by aggrieved ethnic nationalists. While France also contains ethnonationalist movements, they pose less of a threat to the integrity of the nation-state than their counterparts in the other three nations. Ethnonationalism is not a factor of any real consequence in the US, Australia, Germany, or Japan.

Related to but distinct from this type of ethnonationalism is the increasing political assertiveness of indigenous peoples who were the historic victims of colonialism and the resurgence of demands for cultural preservation. Although distinct minorities in their homelands, often living in geographic isolation from metropolitan centers and experiencing social marginalization, nonetheless these indigenous peoples constitute a part of the multicultural mix of four states: the US, Canada, Australia, and Japan. As is clear from the case studies, the American Indians, First Nation's peoples of Canada, Australian Aborigines, and the Ainu of Japan have suffered enormously as a result of colonial conquest. The depth of the social problems confronting these native peoples is a reflection of the extent to which the long assault on their cultures has undermined their ability to control their destinies. It is in this light that the politicized ethnicity of these indigenous peoples needs to be understood.

The United States stands alone as the nation with a large racial minority that is the result of the slave trade. African Americans are the only group in any of the nations examined herein that are nonvoluntary migrants. The distinctive features of the legacy of slavery, that "peculiar institution," the century-long form of racial oppression known as Jim Crow, and the long battle for justice that has shaped all of American history continues to frame the way ethnic identities and intergroup relations are defined for all of the nation's ethnic groups.

If, as Bhikhu Parekh (2000a: 6) suggests, multiculturalism ought to be understood as the normative – and one should add political – response to the reality of these forms of cultural diversity, it is clear that the nations reviewed in this book exhibit considerable variation in terms of their sense of what multiculturalism is and how far they are willing to go in embracing it. When and under what circumstances, one might ask, have nations been willing to consider the prospect of multiculturalism? One way of getting at this question is to first place into political context the multiculturalist project, as do Jon Stratton and Ien Ang (1998: 138) in the following way:

> Viewed historically, multiculturalism could be understood as the consequence of the failure of the modern project of the nation-state, which emphasized unity and sameness – a trope of identity – over diversity and difference. . . . multiculturalism valorizes diversity where the modern nation-state valorized homogeneity. When a government adopts an active policy of multiculturalism, it does so on the explicit assumption that cultural diversity is a good thing for the nation and needs to be actively promoted.

Only two of the countries examined in chapters 2 through 5 have actually formulated explicit political programs in which the state commits itself to sponsoring and actively encouraging multiculturalism as matters of official policy: Canada and Australia. As settler states, they have had to confront the impact of immigration – and with it cultural pluralism – throughout their histories, while their sense of national identity has not been inherently tied to a particular ethnic identity. Such is also true of the US, where multiculturalism has gained acceptance among sectors of the public at large – who no longer embrace the ideal of assimilation-as-amalgamation – but has not become a state-sponsored program. The other nation that has been most open to the idea of multiculturalism is Britain, and to a somewhat more limited extent, Spain. At the other end of the spectrum are France, Germany, and Japan, which have not only been averse to the prospect of multiculturalism as government policy, but where the desire persists to salvage what Stratton and Ang call the "modern project," and with it a unified and immutable sense of what it means to be French, German, or Japanese.

As the theoretical discussion in chapter 1 contends, in culturally pluralist societies where states are perceived to no longer have the right or the ability to mandate a version of assimilation that amounts to the loss of one's distinctive ethnic identity, multiculturalism has arisen as the contemporary, postmodern response to issues related to identity and belonging. Prior to the advent of multiculturalism, in all of these nations racialized ethnicity has been the major variable in determining patterns of inclusion and exclusion. Considerable energy has been expended in attempting to define which ethnic groups were thought to be capable of absorption into the body politic and which were not. The latter groups have historically been defined by the notion of the racial "other," people not eligible for full societal membership. However, when considering what Stanford Lyman (1997: 75) refers to as the "usable fictions" of peoplehood employed by these nations, differences are evident that serve to account, at least in part, for the varied responses to multiculturalism.

The national identities of the US, Canada, and Australia were influenced by their own unique historical trajectories after being founded. In each instance, the English were the dominant ethnic group shaping an emerging sense of peoplehood. However, in the US case the American Revolution necessitated a certain distancing from those origins. The melting-pot ideal and the creation of the new person that was to become the American was a way of accomplishing this task. As a consequence, the idea of national identity was predicated on the notion of the nation as a land of immigrants. Thus, ethnic identity and national identity were separated. This created the ideological space within which the nation has expanded its conception of peoplehood from the earlier most constrictive WASP version to one that included all European Americans (whites), and finally to the present where that version competes with a multicultural one that seeks to bring all members of the nation's racial pentagon into full societal membership.

Canadians, meanwhile, were from the beginning more open to a multicultural version of national identity due to the fact that the English had to recognize the French as another – even if subordinate – charter group. On a purely pragmatic level, the multicultural policies that have been in place now for several decades are in part a consequence of the realization by government officials and policy-makers that the nation's economy needs immigrants. This is one of the reasons that the state has maintained more liberal immigration policies than one might expect given the suspicions about current immigration levels expressed by a majority of the citizenry. In fact, the state has had to play a careful balancing act between meeting the demands of a postindustrial economy and being responsive to anti-immigrant sentiment.

A similar situation characterizes the current state of ethnic pluralism in Australia. What makes this case all the more remarkable is that, because its British roots have remained more central to the society, comparatively speaking, it has maintained a more constrictive sense of peoplehood for a longer time than either the US or Canada. In a matter of little more than a decade, the nation shifted from an explicitly white Australia policy, first to one promoting a somewhat more expansive version of assimilation. This led more recently to a very explicit version of multiculturalism that calls for the maintenance of ethnic identities over time while finding ways of incorporating all ethnic groups in Australia into the society via civic assimilation. Thus, despite the obvious differences, these settler states have managed to make use of the image of themselves as nations of immigrants to create the prospect of a more open, fluid, and dynamic sense of national identity – one that accords with the dictates of multiculturalism.

At the other end of the spectrum are Germany and Japan, the two nations that have most explicitly and persistently employed "blood ties" in defining their national identities. In other words, in these two examples, ethnic identity and national identity have historically been fused, thus making it extraordinarily difficult for a more inclusive sense of peoplehood to develop. This being the case, for multiculturalism to be possible in these societies, it is first necessary for them to shed this particularly limiting fiction of peoplehood.

In both nations there is evidence of limited success in efforts to do just that. In the German case, those on the political left who argue on behalf of an inclusive society have been most supportive of such changes, while those on the political right continue to argue that Germany is not a nation of immigrants and remain committed to preserving a traditionalist *Volksgemeinschaft*. The European Union has been instrumental in forcing the nation to reconsider its policies on citizenship, and insofar as it has done so, it has assisted those on the left in seeking to invent a more inclusive version of German national identity that can replace the traditional "blood-and-soil" version. The recent liberalization of Germany's citizenship laws is a reflection of the extent to which the contemporary challenges to ethnic nationalism have succeeded in developing, in embryonic form, a multicultural alternative. At the same time, resistance to such developments, by the mainstream political right and by reactionary extremists, poses serious challenges to these developments. In comparison, the forces of exclusion in Japan continue to be more successful in resisting change, and thus it can be said that although Japan is becoming a multicultural society, it is a long way from embracing multiculturalism.

The British and French cases fall in between those nations committed in some fashion to multiculturalism and those most resistant to it. What is at some level surprising is that it is the British, and not the French, who appear more akin to the settler states, while the French are closer to the Germans. For the British, national identity is chiefly predicated on a sense of heritage deeply rooted in a shared history. This gives it an obdurate quality that would not seem to make it readily open to a more expansive understanding of what it means to be British. In particular, this poses problems for the inclusion of people of color into a nation where there "ain't no black in the Union Jack" (Gilroy 1987). Meanwhile, the republican ideals so integral to national identity in France would appear to be conducive to the forging of French multiculturalism. However, as the analyses of these two nations indicate, it is the British, and not their counterparts across the English Channel, who appear to be more open at the moment to multiculturalism.

While it is not entirely clear why this should be the case, I suspect that a key factor has to do with national minorities rather than with immigrants. One of the clear differences between the two nations revolves around the different impacts that ethnonationalism has had in each nation and the respective central governments' response to nationalist movements. The British have clearly confronted a more serious challenge to the integrity of the body politic, and have been forced to contend with the possibility that territorial boundaries may have to be reconfigured at some point in the future. They have confronted both violent and nonviolent campaigns and have responded by granting greater regional autonomy to Scotland and Wales via devolution and by seeking a peaceful and democratic solution to the conflict in Northern Ireland. All of this had necessitated a rethinking of what it means to be British – clearly with a view to finding ways of creating a national identity separate from ethnic identity.

If the gambit of devolution succeeds in keeping Britain whole, it will do so by encouraging people in Scotland and Wales to view themselves in ethnic terms as Scottish or Welsh while at the same time seeing themselves as British, or in other words as part of something larger and more heterogeneous than their particularistic ethnic identities. Parenthetically, as Tom Nairn (2000) has noted, this has also forced a reconsideration of what it means to be English. For if this new version of British identity is to succeed, the tendency to equate being English with being British will cease, as the English will have to be seen as but one of the constituent ethnic components of Britain. Though a comprehensive overview of Spain was not presented herein, insofar as the impact of immigration was not discussed, it should be noted that in many respects the situation in Spain during its democratic transition parallels that of Britain.

However, this does not mean that immigrants in either nation have discovered that they are readily welcomed as potential new additions to either of these nations. Rather, racialized ethnicity continues to cast its shadow. This was evident, for example, in the media and public response to the Runnymede Trust's study on *The Future of Multi-Ethnic Britain* (Parekh 2000b). Although the overall thrust of the report was remarkably positive, contending that the nation had made significant strides in moving towards a more tolerant and inclusive multicultural society, it mentioned in passing that the term "English" carried with it racial connotations. This provoked an outcry that suggested more than anything else that many were ill-prepared to recognize the fact that there was at the very least an implicit racial character underlying what it meant to be English (and British).

In the case of France, ethnonationalist movements have not been as consequential as they have been in Britain and Spain, and the government has not – except in the geographically and politically unique case of Corsica – been pressed to grant greater regional autonomy or to seriously contemplate granting independence to one of its nationalist minorities. For this reason, France's ethnonationalist minorities have not managed to force the nation to rethink the connection between ethnic identity and national identity. The French melting pot has not been seriously challenged from within. To the extent that this is the case, there is even less willingness among the public at large or within government circles to address the issue of what might be involved in shedding the racialized ethnicity of what it means at present to be French. The fact that the forces of xenophobia have considerably more political clout in France due to the presence of the Front National in the political arena makes all the more difficult the kind of dialogue that at least is beginning to occur in Britain. For this reason – somewhat ironically given the republican ideals shaping French national identity – the French case more closely resembles the German than does the British.

Despite these differences, what all of these nations face is the reality of a multicultural future and the impossibility of returning to the status quo ante. For this reason they confront the task of finding ways of incorporating ethnic groups – be they ethnonational minorities, indigenous peoples, or recent immigrants – into full societal membership. As I argued in chapter 1, to do so in a manner that is supportive of multiculturalism means that assimilation ought to be viewed in terms of civic incorporation. In other words, what is essential is that members of ethnic communities are afforded the opportunities and the rights associated with citizenship. On the one hand, multiculturalism permits and may even encourage the continued involvement in one's ethnic group. On the other hand, citizenship becomes both a basis for belonging and the vehicle by which the members of ethnic groups – acting individually or corporately – become agents with voice in the democratic public sphere (Habermas 1994; Tambini 2001).

At the dawn of the twenty-first century, there is much that remains unclear regarding multiculturalism's prospects. Rather than predicting the dynamics of social change with the confidence of modernization and Marxist theorists of the recent past, we conclude with an appreciation of the contingent nature of a postmodern social world that must increasingly be understood in global terms. The viability and the contents of multiculturalism are open to various possibilities based on the outcomes of the vigorous debates that are currently taking place. Among the questions addressed in these debates are the following:

- What is the appropriate role of the state in combating racism and other forms of ethnic hostility?
- Should rights be seen solely in terms of individuals, or does multiculturalism also necessitate the articulation and implementation of group rights?
- Does the state have an obligation to ensure the preservation of particular ethnic cultures, and thus to be proactive, or is its duty limited to the defense of cultures from external threats?
- What is the proper response of the state to illiberal and intolerant practices on the part of minority ethnic groups: to tolerate all such practices, to prohibit them, or to establish criteria to determine which practices will be permitted and which will be prohibited?
- What does equality of opportunity mean and what are the obligations of the state in ensuring its realization?
- What does it mean to be a citizen in a liberal democracy today?
- Are there alternatives to current notions of citizenship that ought to be considered, including the idea of denizenship and the possibility of dual citizenship for transnational immigrants?
- What exactly does it mean to suggest that new, postnational ideas of citizenship are arising to either supplant or complement the idea of national citizenship, and what is the likelihood of these trends becoming significant phenomena in the foreseeable future?

This is not meant to be an inclusive list of questions. It is meant, however, to identify a number of the most critical issues that confront the liberal democracies of the advanced industrial nations. The particular answers to these and related questions will determine the extent to which any particular nation is prepared to define itself in multicultural terms and what the precise form and content of its version of multiculturalism will look like. The answers will be arrived at through the political process, and thus will depend on the ways that the particular configurations of power in each nation play out, either in favor of the voices of inclusion and cosmopolitanism or the voices of exclusion and parochialism. Making sense of all this is the challenge confronting twenty-first century sociology.

References

Abadan-Unat, Nermin. 1995. "Turkish Migration to Europe." Pp. 279–84 in Robin Cohen (ed.), *The Cambridge Survey of World Migration*. Cambridge: Cambridge University Press.

Abelmann, Nancy and John Lie. 1995. *Blue Dreams: Korean Americans and the Los Angeles Riots*. Cambridge, MA: Harvard University Press.

Alba, Richard D. 1985. *Italian Americans: Into the Twilight of Ethnicity*. Englewood Cliffs, NJ: Prentice-Hall.

—— 1990. *Ethnic Identity: The Transformation of White America*. New Haven, CT: Yale University Press.

—— 1998. "Assimilation, Exclusion, or Neither? Models of the Incorporation of Immigrants in the United States." Pp. 1–31 in Peter H. Schuck and Rainer Münz (eds.), *Paths to Inclusion*. New York: Berghahn Books.

—— 1999. "Immigration and the American Realities of Assimilation and Multiculturalism." *Sociological Forum*, 14(1): 3–25.

—— John R. Logan, Brian J. Stults, Gilbert Marzan, and Wenquan Zhang. 1999. "Immigrant Groups in Suburbs: A Reexamination of Suburbanization and Spatial Assimilation." *American Sociological Review*, 64(4): 446–60.

Alba, Victor. 1975. *Catalonia*. New York: Praeger.

Alienikoff, T. Alexander. 1998. "A Multicultural Nationalism?" *American Prospect*, 36(Jan./Feb.): 80–6.

Alienikoff, T. Alexander and Douglas Klusmeyer, eds. 2001. *Citizenship Today: Global Perspectives and Practices*. Washington, DC: Carnegie Endowment for International Peace.

Alexander, Claire E. 2000. *The Asian Gang: Ethnicity, Identity, Masculinity*. Oxford: Berg.

Allen, Theodore W. 1994. *The Invention of the White Race*, vol. 1, *Racial Oppression and Social Control*. London: Verso.

Anderson, Benedict. 1991. *Imagined Communities: Reflections on the Origins and Spread of Nationalism*. London: Verso.

Anderson, Elijah. 1990. *Streetwise*. Chicago: University of Chicago Press.

Anderson, Malcolm. 2000. *States and Nationalism in Europe Since 1945*. London:

Routledge.

Anthias, Floya. 1990. "Race and Class Revisited – Conceptualizing Race and Racisms." *The Sociological Review*, 38(1): 19–42.

Anwar, Muhammad. 1986. *Race and Politics: Ethnic Minorities and the British Political System*. London: Tavistock.

—— 1995. "'New Commonwealth' Migration to the U.K." Pp. 274–8 in Robin Cohen (ed.), *The Cambridge Survey of World Migration*. Cambridge: Cambridge University Press.

AP Worldstream. 2001. "German Government Applies to Top Court for Ban on Far Right Party." Jan. 30.

Appadurai, Arjun. 1990. "Disjuncture and Difference in a Global Cultural Economy." Pp. 295–310 in Mike Featherstone (ed.), *Global Culture: Nationalization, Globalization, and Modernity*. London: Sage.

—— 1996. *Modernity at Large: Cultural Dimensions of Globalization*. Minneapolis: University of Minnesota Press.

Applegate, Celia. 1999. "A Europe of Regions: Reflections on the Historiography of Sub-National Places in Modern Times." *American Historical Review*, 104(4): 1157–82.

Apter, David. 1969. *The Politics of Modernization*. Chicago: University of Chicago Press.

Archdeacon, Thomas. 1990. "Hansen's Hypothesis as a Model of Immigrant Assimilation." Pp. 42–63 in P. Kivisto and D. Blanck (eds.), *American Immigrants and Their Generations*. Urbana: University of Illinois Press.

Armstrong, John A. 1982. *Nations Before Nationalism*. Chapel Hill: University of North Carolina Press.

Austin, R. L. 1995. "Inside Babylon: The Caribbean Diaspora in Britain." *Review of Black Political Economy*, Summer: 92–4.

Back, Les. 1996. *New Ethnicities and Urban Culture: Racisms and Multiculture in Young Lives*. New York: St. Martin's.

Back, Les, Tim Crabbe, and John Solomos. 1999. "Beyond the Racist/Hooligan Couplet: Race, Social Theory and Football Culture." *British Journal of Sociology*, 50(3): 419–42.

Bailyn, Bernard. 1967. *The Ideological Origins of the American Revolution*. Cambridge, MA: The Belknap Press of Harvard University Press.

Balsom, Denis. 1990. "Wales." Pp. 8–23 in Michael Watson (ed.), *Contemporary Minority Nationalism*. London: Routledge.

Banton, Michael. 1983. "The Influence of Colonial Status upon Black–White Relations in England, 1948–1958." *Sociology*, 17(3): 546–59.

—— 1985. *Promoting Racial Harmony*. Cambridge: Cambridge University Press.

—— 1987. *Racial Theories*. Cambridge: Cambridge University Press.

—— 2001. "Progress in Ethnic and Racial Studies." *Ethnic and Racial Studies*, 24(2): 173–94.

Barkan, Elliot. 1995. "Race, Religion and Nationality in American Society: A Model of Ethnicity – From Contact to Assimilation." *Journal of American Ethnic History*, 14(2): 38–75.

Barrett, Stanley R. 1987. *Is God a Racist? The Right Wing in Canada*. Toronto: University of Toronto Press.

Barth, Fredrik, ed. 1969. *Ethnic Groups and Boundaries: The Social Organization of Cul-*

ture Difference. Boston: Little, Brown, & Co.

Basch, Linda, Nina Glick Schiller, and Christian Szanton Blanc. 1994. *Nations Unbound: Predicaments and Deterritorialized Nation States.* Langhorne, PA: Gordon and Breach.

Bash, Harry. 1979. *Sociology, Race, and Ethnicity: A Critique of American Ideological Intrusions upon Sociological Theory.* New York: Gordon and Breach.

Bauböck, Rainer. 2000. "Multicultural Citizenship: Towards a European Policy." *Siirtolaisuus/Migration,* 4: 4–14.

Bauman, Zygmunt. 1998. *Globalization: The Human Consequences.* Cambridge: Polity.

Bean, Frank D. and Marta Tienda. 1987. *The Hispanic Population of the United States.* New York: Russell Sage.

Bean, Frank D. and Stephanie Bell-Rose. 1999. "Immigration and Its Relation to Race and Ethnicity in the United States." Pp. 1–28 in Frank D. Bean and Stephanie Bell-Rose (eds.), *Immigration and Opportunity.* New York: Russell Sage.

Beck, Ulrich. 2000. *What is Globalization?* Cambridge: Polity.

Beckett, Jeremy. 1995. "National and Transnational Perspectives on Multiculturalism: The View from Australia." *Identities* 1(4): 421–6.

The Belfast Agreement. 1998. London: The Stationary Office (April).

Benhabib, Seyla. 1999. "Germany Opens Up." *The Nation,* June 21: 6–7.

Bhachu, Parminder. 1985. *Twice Migrants: East African Sikh Settlers in Britain.* London: Tavistock.

Blank, Rebecca. 2001. "An Overview of Trends in Social and Economic Well-Being, by Race." Pp. 21–39 in Neil J. Smelser, William Julius Wilson, and Faith Mitchell (eds.), *America Becoming: Racial Trends and Their Consequences,* vol. 1. Washington, DC: National Academy Press.

Blassingame, John W. 1972. *The Slave Community: Plantation Life in the Antebellum South.* New York: Oxford University Press.

Bobo, Lawrence D. 2001. "Racial Attitudes at the Close of the Twentieth Century." Pp. 264–301 in Neil J. Smelser, William Julius Wilson, and Faith Mitchell (eds.), *America Becoming: Racial Trends and Their Consequences,* vol. 1. Washington, DC: National Academy Press.

Bodnar, John. 1985. *The Transplanted: A History of Immigrants in Urban America.* Bloomington: Indiana University Press.

Bogardus, Emory. 1933. "A Social-distance Scale." *Sociology and Social Research,* 17 (Jan.–Feb.): 265–71.

—— 1959. *Social Distance.* Yellow Springs, OH: Antioch Press.

Bonilla-Silva, Eduardo. 1997. "Rethinking Racism: Toward a Structural Interpretation." *American Sociological Review,* 62(3): 465–80.

—— 1999. "The Essential Social Fact of Race." *American Sociological Review,* 64 (6): 899–906.

—— 2000. "'This is a White Country': The Racial Ideology of the Western Nations of the World-System." *Sociological Inquiry,* 70(2): 188–214.

Bonime-Blanc, Andrea. 1987. *Spain's Transition to Democracy: The Politics of Constitution-Making.* Boulder, CO: Westview.

Borjas, George. 2000. "The Economic Progress of Immigrants." Pp. 15–49 in George Borjas (ed.), *Issues in the Economics of Immigration.* Chicago: University of Chicago

Press.

Bourne, Randolph. 1977. *The Radical Will: Selected Writings, 1911–1918.* New York: Urizen Books.

Bourque, Gilles and Jules Duchastel. 1999. "Erosion of the Nation-State and the Transformation of National Identities in Canada." Pp. 183–198 in Janet L. Abu-Lughod (ed.), *Sociology for the Twenty-first Century: Continuities and Cutting Edges.* Chicago: University of Chicago Press.

Bowcott, Owen. 1999. "Racism on the March in 'Europeans-Only' Norway." *The Guardian*, Sept. 30: 20.

Boyce, George. 1990. "Northern Ireland: The Nationalists." Pp. 38–51 in Michael Watson (ed.), *Contemporary Minority Nationalism.* London: Routledge.

Brand, Jack. 1990. "Scotland." Pp. 24–37 in Michael Watson (ed.), *Contemporary Minority Nationalism.* London: Routledge.

Breen, Richard. 2000. "Class Inequality and Social Mobility in Northern Ireland, 1973 to 1996." *American Sociological Review*, 65(3): 392–406.

Breton, Raymond. 1986. "Multiculturalism and Canadian Nation-Building." Pp. 27–66 in Alan Cairns and Cynthia Williams (eds.), *The Politics of Gender, Ethnicity, and Language in Canada.* Toronto: University of Toronto Press.

Breton, Raymond, Wsevolod W. Isajiw, Warren Kalbach, and Jeffrey G. Reitz. 1990. *Ethnic Identity and Equality: Varieties of Experience in a Canadian City.* Toronto: University of Toronto Press.

Breuilly, John. 1982. *Nationalism and the State.* Chicago: University of Chicago Press.

Brick, Howard. 2000. "Talcott Parsons's 'Shift Away from Economics,' 1937–1946." *Journal of American History*, 87(2): 490–514.

Brooke, James. 2000. "Sikhs on the Rise in British Columbia." *New York Times*, July 18: A8.

Broome, Richard. 1982. *Aboriginal Australians: Black Response to White Dominance, 1788–1980.* Sydney: Allen & Unwin.

Brown, Colin. 1984. *Black and White Britain: The Third PSI Survey.* Aldershot: Gower.

—— 1992. "'Same Difference': The Persistence of Racial Disadvantage in the British Employment Market." Pp. 46–63 in Peter Graham, Ali Rattansi, and Richard Skellington (eds.), *Racism and Antiracism: Inequalities, Opportunities, and Policies.* London: Sage.

Brown, Colin and Pat Gay. 1985. *Racial Discrimination: 17 Years after the Act.* London: Policy Studies Institute.

Brubaker, Rogers. 1992. *Citizenship and Nationhood in France and Germany.* Cambridge, MA: Harvard University Press.

—— 1996. *Nationalism Reframed: Nationhood and the National Question in the New Europe.* Cambridge: Cambridge University Press.

—— 2001. "The Return of Assimilation? Changing Perspectives on Immigration and Its Sequels in France, Germany, and the United States." *Ethnic and Racial Studies*, 24(3): 531–48.

Bulmer, Martin and Anthony M. Rees, eds. 1996. *Citizenship Today: The Contemporary Relevance of T. H. Marshall.* London: UCL Press.

Burman, Stephen. 1995. *The Black Progress Question.* Thousand Oaks, CA: Sage.

Burton, Frank. 1978. *The Politics of Legitimacy: Struggles in a Belfast Community.* London: Routledge and Kegan Paul.

Bush, Rod. 1999. *We Are Not What We Seem: Black Nationalism and Class Struggle in the American Century*. New York: New York University Press.

Cahn, Claude. 2000. "Who is a German?" *SAIS Review*, 20(1): 117–24.

Calhoun, Craig. 1997. *Nationalism*. Minneapolis: University of Minnesota Press.

Callinicos, Alex. 1993. *Race and Class*. London: Bookmarks.

Camic, Charles. 1989. "Structure After Fifty Years: The Anatomy of a Charter." *American Journal of Sociology*, 65(1): 38–107.

Carsten, I. L. 1994. "A History of Foreign Labor." *English Historical Review*, 110(433): 1027–8.

Castells, Manuel. 1997. *The Power of Identity*, vol. II of *The Information Age: Economy, Society and Culture*. Malden, MA: Blackwell.

Castles, Stephen and Mark J. Miller. 1993. *The Age of Migration: International Population Movements in the Modern World*. New York: The Guilford Press.

Cerny, Philip G. 1980. "The Political Balance." Pp. 1–25 in Philip G. Cerny and Martin A. Schain (eds.), *French Politics and Public Policy*. New York: St. Martin's.

Colley, Linda. 1992. *Britons*. New Haven: Yale University Press.

Collymore, Yvette. 2000. "Immigration is Red-Hot Issue in Australia." *Population Reference Bureau*, Quickfacts: 1–2.

Connor, Walker. 1993. "Beyond Reason: The Nature of the Ethnonational Bond." *Ethnic and Racial Studies*, 16(3): 373–89.

—— 1994. *Ethnonationalism: The Quest for Understanding*. Princeton, NJ: Princeton University Press.

Conzen, Kathleen Neils, David A. Gerber, Ewa Morawska, George E. Pozzetta, and Rudolph J. Vecoli. 1990. "The Invention of Ethnicity: A Perspective from the USA." *Altreitalie*, 3: 37–62.

Corbett, Edward. 1980. *Quebec Confronts Canada*. Baltimore: The Johns Hopkins University Press.

Corbett, James. 1994. *Through French Windows: An Introduction to the Nineties*. Ann Arbor: University of Michigan Press.

Cornell, Stephen. 1988. *The Return of the Native: American Indian Political Resurgence*. New York: Oxford University Press.

Cornell, Stephen and Douglas Hartmann. 1998. *Ethnicity and Race: Making Identities in a Changing World*. Thousand Oaks, CA: Pine Forge.

Cox, Oliver. 1948. *Caste, Class, and Race*. New York: Monthly Review Press.

—— 1987. *Race, Class, and the World System*, eds. Herbert M. Hunter and Sameer Y. Abraham. New York: Monthly Review Press.

Culp, Eric. 2000. "Racism is Top Issue in German Economy, Upcoming Elections." *Sunday Business*, Oct. 22: 1–2.

Darby, John. 1976. *Conflict in Northern Ireland: The Development of a Polarized Community*. Dublin: Gill and Macmillan.

Davis, F. James. 2000. "Black Identity in the United States." Pp. 101–11 in Peter Kivisto and Georganne Rundblad (eds.), *Multiculturalism in the United States*. Thousand Oaks, CA: Pine Forge.

Davison, R. B. 1964. *Commonwealth Immigrants*. London: Oxford University Press.

DeCouflé, André-Clément. 1992. "Historic Elements of the Politics of Nationality in France (1889–1989)." Pp. 357–67 in Donald Horowitz and Gérard Noiriel (eds.), *Immigrants in Two Democracies: French and American Experiences*. New York: New

York University Press.

de Crèvecoeur, J. Hector St. John. 1904 [1782]. *Letters from an American Farmer.* New York: Fox, Duffield.

Delanty, Gerard. 2000. *Citizenship in a Global Age.* Buckingham: Open University Press.

Department of Immigration and Multicultural Affairs, Australia. 2001. *Immigration, the Facts – Information Kit.* www.immi.gov.au

Devine, T. M. 1999. *The Scottish Nation: A History, 1700–2000.* New York: Viking.

Diez Medrano, Juan. 1995. *Divided Nations: Class, Politics and Nationalism in the Basque Country and Catalonia.* Ithaca, NY: Cornell University Press.

Dignan, D. 1981. "Europe's Melting Pot: A Century of Large-Scale Immigration into France." *Ethnic and Racial Studies,* 4(2): 137–52.

Diop, A. Moustapha. 1997. "Negotiating Religious Difference: The Opinions and Attitudes of Islamic Associations in France." Pp. 111–25 in Tariq Modood and Pnina Werbner (eds.), *The Politics of Multiculturalism in the New Europe: Racism, Identity and Community.* London: Zed Books.

D'Souza, Dinesh. 1995. *The End of Racism.* New York: The Free Press.

The Economist. 1997. "The Choice for Scotland and Wales." Sept. 6: 56–8.

—— 1998. "From Process to Procession." April 18: 19–28.

—— 1999. "The State of Scotland: A Nation Once Again?" May 1: 351.

—— 2000a. "The New Americans." March 11, Survey: 1–18.

—— 2000b. "A Sorry Tale." Sept. 9: 12–13.

Edles, Laura Desfor. 1999. "A Culturalist Approach to Ethnic Nationalist Movements." *Social Science History,* 23(3): 311–55.

Edwards, Richard, Michael Reich, and David Gordon. 1975. *Labor Market Segmentation.* Boston: D. C. Heath.

Edwards, Sian. 1999. "'Reconstructing the Nation': The Process of Establishing Catalan Autonomy." *Parliamentary Affairs,* 52(4): 44–62.

Elliott, Jean Leonard, ed. 1983. *Two Nations, Many Cultures.* Scarborough, Ont.: Prentice-Hall of Canada.

Ellison, Ralph. 1999. *Juneteenth.* New York: Random House.

Engels, Friedrich. 1959. "Why There is No Large Socialist Party in America." P. 458 in Lewis Feuer (ed.), *Marx and Engels: Basic Writings on Politics and Philosophy.* Garden City, NY: Doubleday.

Erickson, Charlotte. 1972. *Invisible Immigrants: The Adaptation of English and Scottish Immigrants in Nineteenth-Century America.* Coral Gables, FL: University of Miami Press.

Esser, Harmut and H. Korte. 1985. "Federal Republic of Germany." Pp. 165–205 in Tomas Hammar (ed.), *European Immigration Policy.* Cambridge: Cambridge University Press.

Evans, J. A. S. 1996. "The Present State of Canada." *The Virginia Quarterly,* 72(3): 213–25.

Evans, Richard. 1995. "All for One or Not at All?" *Geographical Magazine,* 67(6): 28–32.

Faist, Thomas. 1998. "Transnational Social Spaces Out of International Migration: Evolution, Significance, and Future Prospects." Archives Europ. Social., XXXIX (2): 213–45.

—— 1999. "Transnationalization in International Migration: Implications for the

Study of Citizenship and Culture." Transnational Communities Working Papers. University of Oxford.

—— 2000a. *The Volume and Dynamics of International Migration and Trans-national Social Spaces.* Oxford: Oxford University Press.

—— 2000b. "Social Citizenship for Whom? Young Turks in Germany and Mexican Americans in the United States." Pp. 421–36 in Peter Kivisto and Georganne Rundbland (eds.), *Multiculturalsim in the United States.* Thousand Oaks, CA: Pine Forge.

Farley, Reynolds. 1999. "Racial Issues: Recent Trends in Residential Patterns and Intermarriage." Pp. 85–128 in Neil J. Smelser and Jeffrey C. Alexander (eds.), *Diversity and Its Discontents.* Princeton, NJ: Princeton University Press.

Feagin, Joe R. 1991. "The Continuing Significance of Race: Antiblack Discrimination in Public Places." *American Sociological Review* 56(1): 101–16.

—— and Hernán Vera. 1995. *White Racism.* New York: Routledge.

Fenton, Steve. 1999. *Ethnicity: Racism, Class, and Culture.* London: Macmillan.

Finkelstein, Norman, G. 1998. *A Nation on Trial: The Goldhagen Thesis and Historical Truth.* New York: Metropolitan Books.

Fitzpatrick, Joseph. 1987. *Puerto Rican Americans.* Englewood Cliffs, NJ: Prentice-Hall.

Fix, Michael and Raymond J. Struyk, eds. 1993. *Clear and Convincing Evidence.* Washington, DC: Urban Institute.

Fleras, Augie and Jean Leonard Elliott. 1996. *Unequal Relations: An Introduction to Race, Ethnic, and Aboriginal Dynamics in Canada.* Toronto: Prentice-Hall of Canada.

Fletcher, Christine. 1998. "Citizens Without Rights: Aborigines and Australian Citizenship." *Australian Journal of Political Science,* 33: 455–6.

Foner, Eric. 1988. *Reconstruction: America's Unfinished Revolution, 1863–1877.* New York: Harper & Row.

Fong, Eric. 1996. "A Comparative Perspective on Racial Residential Segregation: American and Canadian Experiences." *The Sociological Quarterly,* 37(2): 199–226.

—— and Milena Gulia. 1999. "Differences in Neighborhood Qualities Among Racial and Ethnic Groups in Canada." *Sociological Inquiry,* 69(4): 575–98.

Fong, Timothy P. 1994. *The First Suburban Chinatown: The Remaking of Monterey Park, California.* Philadelphia: Temple University Press.

—— 2000. "The History of Asian Americans." Pp. 13–30 in Timothy P. Fong and Larry H. Shinagawa (eds.), *Asian Americans: Experiences and Perspectives.* Upper Saddle River, NJ: Prentice-Hall.

Fontaine, Louise. 1995. "Immigration and Cultural Policies: A Bone of Contention Between the Province of Quebec and the Canadian Federal Government." *International Migration Review,* 29(4): 1041–8.

Foster, Charles R., ed. 1980. *Nations Without a State: Ethnic Minorities in Western Europe.* New York: Praeger.

Foster, Roy. 1988. *Modern Ireland.* London: Penguin.

Francis, E. K. 1976. *Interethnic Relations: An Essay in Sociological Theory.* New York: Elsevier.

Freedland, Jonathan. 1999. "Nationalists Lose the Plot." *The Guardian,* Sept. 22: 21.

Freeman, Gary P. 1979. *Immigrant Labor and Racial Conflict in Industrial Societies: The French and British Experience, 1945–1975.* Princeton, NJ: Princeton University Press.

French, Howard W. 2000. "Still Wary of Outsiders, Japan Expects Immigration Boom." *New York Times*, March 14: A1 and A11.

Frideres, James S. 1996. *Native Peoples of Canada*. Scarborough, Ont.: Prentice-Hall of Canada.

Fuchs, Lawarence H. 1990. *The American Kaleidoscope: Race, Ethnicity, and Civic Culture*. Hanover, NH: Wesleyan University Press.

Funes, Maria J. 1998. "Social Responses to Political Violence in the Basque Country." *The Journal of Conflict Resolution*, 42(4): 493–510.

Füredi, Frank. 1998. *The Silent War: Imperialism and the Changing Perception of Race*. New Brunswick, NJ: Rutgers University Press.

Gallagher, A. M. and S. Dunn. 1991. "Community Relations in Northern Ireland: Attitudes to Contact and Integration." Pp. 7–22 in Peter Stringer and Gillian Robinson (eds.), *Social Attitudes in Northern Ireland*. Belfast: Blackstall Press.

Gans, Herbert. 1956. "American Jewry Present and Future." *Commentary*, 21(5): 422–30.

—— 1979. "Symbolic Ethnicity: The Future of Ethnic Groups and Cultures in America." *Ethnic and Racial Studies*, 2(1): 1–20.

—— 1992a. "Ethnic Invention and Acculturation: A Bumpy-Line Approach." *Journal of American Ethnic History*, 12(1): 42–52.

—— 1992b. "Second Generation Decline: Scenarios for the Economic and Ethnic Futures of Post-1965 American Immigrants." *Ethnic and Racial Studies*, 15(2): 173–92.

—— 1999. *Making Sense of America: Sociological Analyses and Essays*. Lanham, MD: Rowman & Littlefield.

Gellner, Ernest. 1983. *Nations and Nationalism*. Ithaca, NY: Cornell University Press.

Genovese, Eugene. 1969. *The World the Slaveholders Made: Two Essays in Interpretation*. New York: Pantheon.

Gershon, Shafir. 1995. *Immigrants and Nationalists*. Albany: State University of New York Press.

Gerstle, Gary. 1995. "Race and the Myth of Liberal Consensus." *Journal of American History*, 82(2): 579–86.

Geschwender, J. A. and N. Guppy. 1995. "Ethnicity, Educational Attainment and Earned Income Among Canadian-born Men and Women." *Canadian Ethnic Studies*, 27(1): 67–84.

Giddens, Anthony. 1990. *The Consequences of Modernity*. Stanford, CA: Stanford University Press.

Gies, David T. 1994. "The Rise of Europe's Little Nations: A Country in Spain." *The Wilson Quarterly*, 18(1): 70–6.

Gillborn, David. 1990. *"Race," Ethnicity and Education*. London: Unwin Hyman.

Gilroy, Paul. 1987. *"There Ain't No Black in the Union Jack": The Cultural Politics of Race and Nation*. Chicago: University of Chicago Press.

—— 1993. *The Black Atlantic: Modernity and Double Consciousness*. London: Verso.

—— 2000. *Against Race: Imagining Political Culture Beyond the Color Line*. Cambridge, MA: The Belknap Press of Harvard University Press.

Glassman, Ronald, William H. Swatos, Jr., and Peter Kivisto. 1993. *For Democracy*. Westport, CT: Greenwood Press.

Glazer, Nathan. 1975. *Affirmative Discrimination: Ethnic Inequality and Public Policy*.

New York: Basic Books.

Glazer, Nathan. 1993. "Is Assimilation Dead?" *The Annals of the American Academy of Political and Social Science*, 530(Nov.): 122–36.

—— 1997. *We Are All Multiculturalists Now*. Cambridge, MA: Harvard University Press.

—— and Daniel P. Moynihan. 1963. *Beyond the Melting Pot: The Negroes, Puerto Ricans, Jews, Italians, and Irish of New York City*. Cambridge, MA: MIT Press and Harvard University Press.

—— and ——, eds. 1975. *Ethnicity: Theory and Experience*. Cambridge, MA: Harvard University Press.

Gleason, Philip. 1964. "The Melting Pot: Symbol of Fusion or Confusion?" *American Quarterly*, 16(1): 20–46.

Glenn, Evelyn. 2000. "Citizenship and Inequality: Historical and Global Perspectives." *Social Problems*, 47(1): 1–20.

Glick Schiller, Nina, Linda Basch, and Christina Szanton Blanc. 1995. "From Immigrant to Transmigrant: Theorizing Transnational Migration." *Anthropological Quarterly*, 68(1): 48–63.

Gobineau, Arthur de. 1915 [1853–5]. *The Inequality of Human Races*. London: Heinemann.

Gold, Steven. 2000. "Transnational Communities: Examining Migration in a Globally Integrated World." Pp. 209–27 in Preet Aulakh and Michael Schecter (eds.), *Rethinking Globalization(s): From Corporate Transnationalism to Local Interventions*. London: Macmillan.

Goldhagen, Daniel J. 1997. *Hitler's Willing Executioners: Ordinary Germans and the Holocaust*. New York: Vintage.

Gordon, Milton. 1964. *Assimilation and American Life: The Role of Race, Religion, and National Origins*. New York: Oxford University Press.

Gorski, Philip. 2000. "The Mosaic Moment: An Early Modernist Critique of Modernist Theories of Nationalism." *American Journal of Sociology*, 105(5): 1428–68.

Goulbourne, Harry. 1998. *Race Relations in Britain Since 1945*. London: Macmillan.

Grant, Madison. 1916. *The Passing of the Great Race*. New York: Charles Scribner's Sons.

Greeley, Andrew. 1971. *Why Can't They Be Like Us? America's White Ethnic Groups*. New York: E. P. Dutton.

—— 1974. *Ethnicity in the United States: A Preliminary Reconnaissance*. New York: John Wiley & Sons.

Greeley, Andrew and William C. McCready. 1973. "The Transmission of Cultural Heritages: The Case of the Italians and the Irish." Pp. 209–35 in Nathan Glazer and Daniel P. Moynihan (eds.), *Ethnicity: Theory and Experience*. Cambridge, MA: Harvard University Press.

Greenfeld, Liah. 1992. *Nationalism: Five Roads to Modernity*. Cambridge: Cambridge University Press.

Grescoe, P. 1987. "A Nation's Disgrace." Pp. 127–40 in D. Colhurn et al. (eds.), *Health and Canadian Society*. Toronto: Fitzhenry and Whiteside.

Grosfoguel, R. 1997. "Colonial Caribbean Migrations to France, the Netherlands, Great Britain, and the United States." *Ethnic and Racial Studies*, 20: 595–609.

Grugel, Jean. 1990. "The Basques." Pp. 100–15 in Michael Watson (ed.), *Contempo-

rary Minority Nationalism. London: Routledge.

Guentzel, Ralph. 1999. "The Centrale de l'Ensignement du Quebec and Quebec Separatist Nationalism, 1960–1980." *Canadian Historical Review,* 80(1): 61–83.

Guibernau, Montserrat. 1999. *Nations Without States: Political Communities in a Global Age.* Cambridge: Polity.

Guindon, Hubert. 1960. "The Social Evolution of Quebec Reconsidered." *Canadian Journal of Economics and Political Science,* XXVI(4): 61–79.

Gurr, Ted Robert. 1993. *Minorities at Risk: A Global View of Ethnopolitical Conflicts.* Washington, DC: United States Institute of Peace Press.

Gutierrez, David G. 1995. *Walls and Mirrors: Mexican Americans, Mexican Immigrants, and the Politics of Identity.* Berkeley: University of California Press.

Gyory, Andrew. 1998. *Closing the Gate: Race, Politics, and the Chinese Exclusion Act.* Chapel Hill: University of North Carolina Press.

Habermas, Jürgen. 1994. "Citizenship and National Identity." Pp. 20–35 in Bart van Steenbergen (ed.), *The Condition of Citizenship.* London: Sage.

Hammar, Tomas and Kristof Tamas. 1997. "Why Do People Go or Stay?" Pp. 1–19 in Tomas Hammar, Grete Brouchmann, Kristof Tamas, and Thomas Faist (eds.), *International Migration, Immobility, and Development.* New York: Berg.

Handlin, Oscar. 1973. *The Uprooted.* Boston: Little, Brown & Co.

Hargreaves, Alec G. 1995. *Immigration, "Race," and Ethnicity in Contemporary France.* London: Routledge.

Hargreaves, Ian. 1996. "We Have Not Put the Racist Devil Behind Us." *New Statesman,* 128(4460): 52.

Harles, John C. 1997. "Integration Before Assimilation: Immigration, Multiculturalism and the Canadian Polity." *Canadian Journal of Political Science,* 30 (4): 711–36.

Harney, Robert F. 1978. *Italians in Canada: The Multicultural History of Ontario.* Toronto: Random House.

Harvey, David. 1989. *The Condition of Postmodernity.* Oxford: Blackwell.

Hawkins, Freda. 1989. *Critical Years in Immigration: Canada and Australia Compared.* Kingston and Montreal: McGill–Queen's University Press.

Hawkins, Mike. 1997. *Social Darwinism in European and American Thought, 1800–1945.* Cambridge: Cambridge University Press.

Hechter, Michael. 1975. *Internal Colonialism: The Celtic Fringe in British National Development.* Berkeley: University of California Press.

—— 2000. *Containing Nationalism.* New York: Oxford University Press.

Heilig, G., T. Buttner, and G. Lutz. 1990. "Germany's Population: Turbulent Past, Uncertain Future." *Population Bulletin,* 45(4): 28–9.

Helmes-Hayes, Rick and James Curtis, eds. 1998. *The Vertical Mosaic Revisited.* Toronto: University of Toronto Press.

Hennink, Monique, Ian Diamond, and Philip Cooper. 1999. "Young Asian Women and Relationships: Traditional or Transitional?" *Ethnic and Racial Studies,* 22(5): 867–91.

Herberg, Will. 1955. *Protestant–Catholic–Jew: An Essay in American Religious Sociology.* Garden City, NY: Doubleday.

Herrnstein, Richard J. and Charles Murray. 1994. *The Bell Curve: Intelligence and Class Structure in American Life.* New York: The Free Press.

Higham, John. 1970. *Strangers in the Land.* New York: Atheneum.

—— 1975. *Send These to Me: Jews and Other Immigrants in Urban America.* Baltimore: Johns Hopkins University Press.

—— 1999. "Cultural Responses to Immigration." Pp. 39–61 in Neil J. Smelser and Jeffrey C. Alexander (eds.), *Diversity and Its Discontents.* Princeton, NJ: Princeton University Press.

Hildyard, Nicholas. 1996. "Migrant Labor in the Global Economy." *The Ecologist*, 26(July/Aug.): 133–4.

Hiller, Harry H. 1991. *Canadian Society: A Macro Analysis.* Scarborough, Ont: Prentice-Hall of Canada.

Ho, Robert. 1990. "Multiculturalism in Australia: A Survey of Attitudes." *Human Relations*, 43(March): 259–72.

Hobsbawm, E. J. 1969. *Industry and Empire.* New York: Penguin Books.

—— 1990. *Nations and Nationalism Since 1780: Programme, Myth, Reality.* Cambridge: Cambridge University Press.

—— and Terence Ranger, eds. 1983. *The Invention of Tradition.* Cambridge: Cambridge University Press.

Hoge, Warren. 2001. "British City Defines Diversity and Tolerance." *New York Times*, Feb. 8: A1, A10.

Holland, Jack. 1982. *Too Long a Sacrifice: Life and Death in Northern Ireland.* New York: Penguin.

Hollinger, David. 1995. *Post-Ethnic America: Beyond Multiculturalism.* New York: Basic Books.

Holmes, Colin. 1988. *John Bull's Island: Immigration and British Society, 1871–1971.* London: Macmillan.

Homze, Edward L. 1967. *Foreign Labor in Nazi Germany.* Princeton, NJ: Princeton University Press.

Horowitz, Donald L. 1992. "Immigration and Group Relations in France and America." Pp. 3–35 in Donald L. Horowitz and Gérard Noiriel (eds.), *Immigrants in Two Democracies: French and American Experiences.* New York: New York University Press.

Houston, R. A. and I. D. Whyte. 1989. *Scottish Society, 1500–1800.* Cambridge: Cambridge University Press.

Hsu, Madeline Yuan-yin. 2000. *Dreaming of Gold, Dreaming of Home:* Transnationalsim and Migration between the United States and South *China, 1883–1942.* Stanford, CA: Stanford University Press.

Hughes, Everett C. 1943. *French Canada in Transition.* Chicago: University of Chicago Press.

Husbands, C. T. 1991. "The Support for the Front National: Analyses and Findings." *Ethnic and Racial Studies*, 14(4): 382–416.

Ignatieff, Michael. 1993. *Blood and Belonging: Journeys into the New Nationalism.* London: BBC Books and Chatto & Windus.

—— 1997. *The Warrior's Honor: Ethnic War and the Modern Conscience.* New York: Henry Holt and Company.

ILO/IOM/UNHCR. 1994. *Migrants, Refugees, and International Cooperation.* Geneva: UNHCR.

Inglis, Kenneth Stanley. 1974. *The Australian Colonists, 1788–1870.* Carleton, Vic.:

Melbourne University Press.

INSEE (Institut National de la Statistique de des Etudes Economiques). 1992. *Recensement de la Population de 1990: Nationalitiés, Résultats du Sondage au Quart.* Paris: INSEE.

Ireland, Patrick R. 1994. *The Policy Challenges of Ethnic Diversity: Immigrant Politics in France and Switzerland.* Cambridge, MA: Harvard University Press.

Isajiw, Wsevolod. 1979. *Definitions of Ethnicity.* Occasional Papers in Ethnic and Immigration Studies. Toronto: The Multicultural History Society of Ontario.

Islam, Shada. 1994. "Europe's Growing Fortress Mentality." *World Press Review,* 41(Oct.): 10–11.

Israel, Milton, ed. 1987. *The South Asian Diaspora in Canada: Six Essays.* Toronto: The Multicultural History Society of Ontario.

Jackson, John D. 1977. "The Functions of Language in Canada: On the Political Economy of Language and Society in Canada." Pp. 59–76 in W. H. Coons, D. M. Taylor, and M. Tremblag (eds.), *The Individual, Language and Society in Canada*, Toronto: The Canada Council.

Jacobs, Jane. 1980. *The Question of Separatism: Quebec and the Struggle Over Sovereignty.* New York: Random House.

Jacobson, David. 1996. *Rights Across Borders: Immigration and the Decline of Citizenship.* Baltimore: The Johns Hopkins University Press.

Jacobson, Jessica. 1997. "Religion and Ethnicity: Dual and Alternative Sources of Identity Among Young British Pakistanis." *Ethnic and Racial Studies,* 20(2): 238–56.

Jaret, Charles. 1999. "Troubled by Newcomers: Anti-Immigration Attitudes and Action During Two Eras of Mass Immigration to the United States." *Journal of American Ethnic History,* 18(3): 9–39.

Jaynes, Gerald David and Robin M. Williams, Jr. 1989. *A Common Destiny: Blacks and American Society.* Washington, DC: National Academy Press.

Jeambar, Denis. 1997. "A Black Day for France at the Polls." *World Press Review,* 44(May): 9–10.

Jenkins, Richard. 1997. *Rethinking Ethnicity: Arguments and Explorations.* London: Sage.

Johnson, Graham E. 1992. "Ethnic and Racial Communities in Canada and Problems of Adaptation: Chinese Canadians in the Contemporary Period." *Ethnic Groups,* 9: 151–74.

Jones, J. Gwynfer. 1994. *Early Modern Wales, c. 1525–1640.* London: Macmillan.

Jones, Maldwyn Allen. 1960. *American Immigration.* Chicago: University of Chicago Press.

Joppke, Christian. 1996. "Multiculturalism and Immigration: A Comparison of the United States, Germany, and Great Britain." *Theory and Society,* 25: 259–98.

—— 1999. "How Immigration is Changing Citizenship: A Comparative View." *Ethnic and Racial Studies,* 22(4): 629–52.

—— ed. 1998. *Challenge to the Nation-State: Immigration in Western Europe and the United States.* Oxford: Oxford University Press.

Kalilombe, Patrick. 1997. "Black Christianity in Britain." *Ethnic and Racial Studies,* 20(2): 306–24.

Kallen, Horace. 1924. *Culture and Democracy in the United States: Studies in the Group*

Psychology of the American People. Salem, NH: Ayer Company.

Karni, Michael, ed. 1981. *Finish Diaspora I: Canada, South America, Africa, Australia, and Sweden.* Toronto: Multicultural History Society of Ontario.

Katzenstein, Peter J. 1987. *Policy and Politics in West Germany: The Growth of a Semisovereign State.* Philadelphia: Temple University Press.

Kazal, Russell A. 1995. "Revisiting Assimilation: The Rise, Fall, and Reappraisal of a Concept in American Ethnic History." *The American Historical Review*, 100(2): 437–71.

Kedourie, Eli. 1985. *Nationalism.* London: Hutchison.

Kelley, Ninette and Michael Trebilcock. 1998. *The Making of the Mosaic: History of Canadian Immigration Policy.* Toronto: University of Toronto Press.

Kennedy, Ruby Jo Reeves. 1944. "Single or Triple Melting Pot? Intermarriage Trends in New Haven, 1870–1940." *American Journal of Sociology*, 49(4): 331–9.

Kim, Lucian. 1998. "German Special Squad Tackles Neo-Nazi Attacks, but Roots of Problem Remain." *Christian Science Monitor*, 90(r3), March 26: 7.

Kivisto, Peter, ed. 1989. *The Ethnic Enigma.* Philadelphia: Balch Institute Press.

—— 1990. "The Transplanted Then and Now: The Reorientation of Immigration Studies from the Chicago School to the New Social History." *Ethnic and Racial Studies*, 13(4): 255–81.

—— 1993. "Religion and the New Immigrants." Pp. 92–108 in William H. Swatos, Jr. (ed.), *A Future for Religion? New Paradigms for Social Analysis.* Newbury Park, CA: Sage.

—— 1995. *Americans All: Race and Ethnic Relations in Historical, Structural and Comparative Perspectives.* Belmont, CA: Wadsworth.

—— 2001. "Theorizing Transnational Immigration: A Critical Review of Current Efforts." *Ethnic and Racial Studies*, 24(3): 549–77.

Klusmeyer, Douglas. 2000. "Four Dimensions of Membership in Germany." *SAIS Review*, 20(1): 1–21.

Koopmans, Ruud and Paul Statham. 1999. "Challenging the Liberal Nation-State? Postnationalism, Multiculturalism, and the Collective Claims Making of Migrants and Ethnic Minorities in Britain and Germany." *American Journal of Sociology*, 105(3): 652–96.

Kosmin, Barry, Sidney Goldstein, Joseph Waksberg, Nava Lerer, Ariella Keysar, and Jeffrey Scheckner. 1991. *Highlights of the CJP 1990 National Jewish Population Survey.* New York: Council of Jewish Federations.

Kristeva, Julia. 1993. *Nations Without Nationalism.* New York: Columbia University Press.

Kymlicka, Will. 1995. *Multicultural Citizenship: A Liberal Theory of Minority Rights.* New York: Oxford University Press.

Lal, Barbara Ballis. 1990. *The Romance of Culture in an Urban Civilization: Robert E. Park on Race and Ethnic Relations in Cities.* London: Routlege.

Landry, Bart. 1987. *The New Black Middle Class.* Berkeley: University of California Press.

Layton-Henry, Zig. 1984. *The Politics of Race in Britain.* Boston: George Allen & Unwin.

Lega Nord. 1996. "Declaration of Independence and Sovereignty of Padania." http//:www.11151.4.58.42/eng/declar.htm.

Legendre, Camille. 1980. *French Canada in Crisis: A New Society in the Making?* London: Minority Rights Group.

Lehmann, Hartmut and Hermann Wellenreuther, eds. 1999. *German and American Nationalism: A Comparative Perspective.* New York: Berg.

Lepsius, M. Rainer. 1985. "The Nation and Nationalism in German." *Social Research,* 52 (Spring): 43–64.

Levack, Brian P. 1987. *The Formation of the British State.* Oxford: Clarendon Press.

Levine, Marc. 1990. *The Reconquest of Montreal: Language, Policy and Social Change in a Bilingual City.* Philadelphia: Temple University Press.

Levinson, David. 1998. *Ethnic Groups Worldwide.* Phoenix, AZ: Oryx Press.

Levitt, Peggy. 2001. *The Transnational Villagers.* Berkeley: University of California Press.

Lewis, Philip. 1997. "The Bradford Council for Mosques and the Search for Muslim Unity." Pp. 103–28 in Steven Vertovec and Ceri Peach (eds.), *Islam in Europe: The Politics of Religion and Community.* London: Macmillan.

Li, Peter, ed. 1990. *Race and Ethnic Relations in Canada.* Toronto: Oxford University Press.

Lian, Jason Z. and David Ralph Matthews. 1998. "Does the Vertical Mosaic Still Exist? Ethnicity and Income in Canada." *The Canadian Review of Sociology and Anthropology,* 35(4): 461–81.

Lie, John. 2001. *Multiethnic Japan.* Cambridge, MA: Harvard University Press.

Light, Ivan and Steven Gold. 2000. *Ethnic Economies.* San Diego, CA: Academic Press.

Lijphart, Arend. 1975. "The Northern Ireland Problem: Cases, Theories, and Solutions." *British Journal of Political Science,* 5: 83–106.

—— 1977. *Democracy in Plural Societies: A Comparative Exploration.* New Haven, CT: Yale University Press.

Lipset, Seymour Martin. 1963. *The First New Nation: The United States in Historical and Comparative Perspective.* New York: Basic Books.

—— 1990. *Continental Divide: Values and Institutions of the United States and Canada.* New York: Routledge.

Lipset, Seymour Martin and Gary Marks. 2000. *It Didn't Happen Here: Why Socialism Failed in the United States.* New York: W. W. Norton.

Lipsitz, George. 1998. *The Possessive Investment in Whiteness: How White People Profit from Identity Politics.* Philadelphia: Temple University Press.

Litwack, Leon. 1998. *Trouble in Mind: Black Southerners in the Age of Jim Crow.* New York: Alfred A. Knopf.

Liu, Xiao-Feng and Glen Norcliffe. 1996. "Closed Windows, Open Doors: Geopolitics and Post-1949 Mainland Chinese Immigration to Canada." *The Canadian Geographer,* 4: 306–19.

London, H. I. 1970. *Non-White Immigration and the "White Australia" Policy.* New York: New York University Press.

Loveman, Mara. 1999. "Is 'Race' Essential?" *American Sociological Review,* 64(6): 891–8.

Lower, Arthur M. 1977. *Colony to Nation.* Toronto: McCelland and Stewart.

Lyman, Stanford M. 1972. *The Black in American Sociological Thought.* New York: Capricorn Books.

—— 1974. *Chinese Americans.* New York: Random House.

—— 1997. *Postmodernism and a Sociology of the Absurd and Other Essays on the*

"Nouvelle Vague" in American Social Science. Fayetteville: University of Arkansas Press.

Lyon, Wenonah. 1997. "Defining Ethnicity: Another Way of Being British." Pp. 186–205 in Tariq Modood and Pnina Werbner (eds.), *The Politics of* Multiculturalism in the New Europe: Racism, Identity, and Community. London: Zed Books.

Mac an Ghaill, Máirtín. 1999. *Contemporary Racisms and Ethnicities: Social and Cultural Transformations.* Buckingham, UK: Open University Press.

MacAskill, Ewen and Gerard Seenan. 1999. "Climbdown by Heir Apparent After Gaffe Over 'Offensive' Union Flag." *The Guardian,* Sept. 24: 6.

MacEoin, G. 1974. *Northern Ireland: Captive of History.* New York: Holt, Rinehart, and Winston.

Macintyre, Stuart. 1999. *A Concise History of Australia.* Cambridge: Cambridge University Press.

MacMaster, Neil. 1997. *Colonial Migrants and Racism: Algerians in France, 1900–1962.* London: Macmillan.

Macmillan, Michael. 1990. "Quebec." Pp. 117–34 in Michael Watson (ed.), *Contemporary Minority Nationalism.* London: Routledge.

Maney, Gregory M. 2000. "Transnational Mobilization and Civil Rights in Northern Ireland." *Social Problems,* 47(2): 153–79.

Marger, Martin. 1989. "Factors of Structural Pluralism in Multiethnic Societies: A Comparative Case Study." *International Journal of Group Tensions,* 19: 52–68.

—— 1994. *Race and Ethnic Relations.* Belmont, CA: Wadsworth.

Marshall, T. H. 1964. *Class, Citizenship, and Social Development.* Garden City, NY: Doubleday.

Martin, Philip L. 1994. "Comparative Migration Policies." *International Migration Review,* 28(1): 164–9.

Martin, Philip and Jonas Widgren. 1997. "International Migration: A Global Challenge." Washington, DC: Population Reference Bureau.

Marx, Karl and Friedrich Engels. 1967[1848]. *The Communist Manifesto.* New York: Penguin.

Mason, David. 1995. *Race and Ethnicity in Modern Britain.* Oxford: Oxford University Press.

Massey, Douglas S. and Nancy A. Denton. 1993. *American Apartheid: Segregation and the Making of the Underclass.* Cambridge, MA: Harvard University Press.

McAdam, Doug. 1982. *Political Process and the Development of Black Insurgency, 1930–1970.* Chicago: University of Chicago Press.

McAllister, Ian. 1977. *The Northern Ireland Social Democratic and Labor Party.* London: Macmillan.

McClellan, Grant S., ed. 1977. *Canada in Transition.* New York: H. W. Wilson.

McCrone, David. 1992. *Understanding Scotland: The Sociology of a Stateless Nation.* London: Routledge.

McCrone, David, Stephen Kendrick, and Pat Straw, eds. 1989. *The Making of Scotland: Nation, Culture, and Social Change.* Edinburgh: Edinburgh University Press.

McDonald, Maryon. 1989. *"We Are Not French!": Language, Culture, and Identity in Brittany.* New York: Routledge.

McNeil, Donald G., Jr. 2000. "French McDonald's Bombed; Breton Terrorists Suspected." *New York Times,* April 20: A8.

Medrano, Juan Diaz. 1988. "The Effects of Ethnic Segregation and Ethnic Competition on Political Mobilization in the Basque Country." *American Sociological Review*, 59(6): 873–89.

Memmi, Albert. 2000. *Racism.* Minneapolis: University of Minnesota Press.

Meredith, Christopher. 1999. "Do We Really Want to Be Welsh?" *New Statesman*, 12(553): 9–10.

Messina, Anthony M. 1996. "The Not So Silent Revolution: Postwar Migration to Western Europe." *World Politics*, 69(1): 130–54.

Miles, Robert. 1982. *Racism and Migrant Labour: A Critical Text.* London: Routledge & Kegan Paul.

—— 1989. *Racism.* London: Tavistock.

—— 1993. *Racism After "Race Relations."* London: Routledge.

Mills, C. Wright. 1951. *White Collar: The American Middle Class.* New York: Oxford University Press.

—— 1959. *The Sociological Imagination.* New York: Grove.

Min, Pyong Gap. 1996. *Caught in the Middle: Korean Communities in New York and Los Angeles.* Berkeley: University of California Press.

Model, Susan. 1999. "Ethnic Inequality in England: An Analysis Based on the 1991 Census." *Ethnic and Racial Studies*, 22(5): 966–91.

Modood, Tariq. 1988. "'Black', Racial Equality and Asian Identity." *New Community*, 14(3): 397–404.

—— 1994. *Racial Equality: Colour, Culture, and Justice.* London: Policy Studies Institute.

—— 1997a. *Ethnic Minorities in Britain.* London: Policy Studies Institute.

—— ed. 1997b. *Church, State and Religious Minorities.* London: Policy Studies Institute.

—— 2000. "Anti-Essentialism, Multiculturalism, and the 'Recognition' of Religious Groups." Pp. 175–95 in Will Kymlicka and Wayne Norman (eds.), *Citizenship in Diverse Societies.* Oxford: Oxford University Press.

Moore, Joan and Raquel Pinderhughes, eds. 1993. *In the Barrios: Latinos and the Underclass Debate.* New York: Russell Sage.

Morawska, Ewa. 1994. "In Defense of the Assimilation Model." *Journal of American Ethnic History*, 13(2): 76–87.

—— 1999. "The Sociology and History of Immigration: Reflections of a Practitioner." Paper presented at the European University Institute, Florence, Italy, May 20.

—— 2000. "Intended and Unintended Consequences of Forced Migrations: A Neglected Aspect of East Europe's Twentieth Century History." *International Migration Review*, 34(4): 1049–87.

Morgan, Kenneth O. 1981. *Rebirth of a Nation.* Oxford: Oxford University Press.

Morris, Aldon D. 1984. *The Origins of the Civil Rights Movement: Black Communities Organizing for Change.* New York: The Free Press.

Moynihan, Daniel P. 1993. *Pandemonium: Ethnicity in International Politics.* New York: Oxford University Press.

Mulhern, Francis. 2000. "Britain After Nairn." *New Left Review*, 5 (Oct./Nov.): 53–66.

Murphy, Brian. 1993. *The Other Australia: Experiences of Migration.* Cambridge: Cambridge University Press.

Murphy, Simon. 1990. "Northern Ireland: The Unionists." Pp. 52–65 in Michael Watson (ed.), *Contemporary Minority Nationalism*. London: Routledge.

Murray, Dominic. 1986. "Educational Segregation: 'Rite' or Wrong?" Pp. 244–64 in Patrick Clancey (ed.), *Ireland: A Sociological Profile*. Dublin: Institute of Public Administration.

Myrdal Gunnar. 1944. *An American Dilemma: The Negro Problem and Modern Democracy*. New York: Harper and Brothers.

Nagel, Joane. 1996. *American Indian Ethnic Renewal: Red Power and the Resurgence of Identity and Culture*. New York: Oxford University Press.

—— 2000. "The Politics of Ethnic Authenticity: Building Native American Identities and Communities." Pp. 113–24 in Peter Kivisto and Georganne Rundblad (eds.), *Multiculturalism in the United States*. Thousand Oaks, CA: Pine Forge.

Nair, Sami. 1996. "France: A Crisis of Integration." *Dissent*, 43 (Summer): 75–8.

Nairn, Tom. 1977. *The Break Up of Britain*. London: New Left Books.

—— 1999. "The End of the Affair." *New Statesman*, Nov. 8: 50–2.

—— 2000. *After Britain*. London: Granta.

Neary, Ian. 1989. *Political Protest and Social Control in Pre-war Japan: The Origins of Buraku Liberation*. Atlantic Highlands, NJ: Humanities Press.

Nelson, Benjamin. 1949. *The Idea of Usury*. Princeton, NJ: Princeton University Press.

Newman, Saul. 1996. *Ethnoregional Conflict in Democracies: Mostly Ballots, Rarely Bullets*. Westport, CT: Greenwood Press.

Nielsen, Jens Kaalhauge. 1991. "The Political Orientation of Talcott Parsons: The Second World War and Its Aftermath." Pp. 217–33 in Roland Robertson and Bryan S. Turner (eds.), *Talcott Parsons: Theorist of Modernity*. Thousand Oaks, CA: Sage.

Nielson, Jørgen. 1992. *Muslims in Western Europe*. Edinburgh: Edinburgh University Press.

Noiriel, Gérard. 1990. *Workers in French Society in the 19th and 20th Centuries*. New York: Berg.

—— 1996. *The French Melting Pot: Immigration, Citizenship, and National Identity*. Minneapolis: University of Minnesota Press.

Novak, Michael. 1972. *The Rise of the Unmeltable Ethnics: Politics and Culture in the Seventies*. New York: Macmillan.

Oberhauser, Ann M. 1991. "International Mobility of Labor: North African Migrant Workers in France." *Professional Geographer*, 43: 431–45.

O'Brien, Conor Cruise. 1972. *States of Ireland*. London: Hutchinson.

Ogden, Philip E. 1995. "Labor Migration to France." Pp. 289–96 in Robin Cohen (ed.), *The Cambridge Survey of World Migration*. Cambridge: Cambridge University Press.

O'Hearn, Dennis, Sam Porter, and Alan Harper. 1999. "Turning Agreement to Process: Republicanism and Change in Ireland." *Capital and Class*, 69 (Autumn): 7–25.

O'Leary, B. and J. McGarry. 1993. *The Politics of Antagonism: Understanding Northern Ireland*. London: Athlone.

Oliver, Melvin L. and T. M. Shapiro. 1995. *Black Wealth/White Wealth: A New Perspective on Racial Inequality*. New York and London: Routledge.

Olzak, Susan. 1992. *The Dynamics of Ethnic Competition and Conflict*. Stanford, CA:

Stanford University Press.

O'Malley, Padraig. 1983. *The Uncivil Wars: Ireland Today.* Boston: Houghton Mifflin.

Omi, Michael A. 2001. "The Changing Meaning of Race." Pp. 243–63 in Neil J. Smelser, William Julius Wilson, and Faith Mitchell (eds.), *America Becoming: Racial Trends and Their Consequences*, vol. 1. Washington, DC: National Academy Press.

Omi, Michael A. and Howard Winant. 1994. *Racial Formation in the United States: From the 1960s to the 1980s.* New York: Routledge.

Ong, Aihwa. 1999. *Flexible Citizenship: The Cultural Logics of Transnationalism.* Durham, NC: Duke University Press.

Ongley, Patrick and David Pearson. 1995. "Post-1945 International Migration: New Zealand, Australia, and Canada Compared." *International Migration Review*, 29(3): 765–83.

Osmond, John. 1995. "Plaid Makes the Most of Labour's 'Fascism Jibe.'" *New Statesman and Society*, 8: 8.

Østergaard-Nielsen, Eva. 2000. "Trans-State Loyalties and Politics of Turks and Kurds in Western Europe." *SAIS Review*, 20(1): 23–38.

Øverland, Orm. 2000. *Immigrant Minds, American Identities: Making the United States Home, 1870–1930.* Urbana: University of Illinois Press.

Owen, David. 1992. *Ethnic Minorities in Britain: Settlement Patterns.* University of Warrick, Centre for Research in Ethnic Relations, National Ethnic Minority Data Archive, 1991 Census Statistical Paper No. 2.

Papademetriou, Demetrios. 1997–8. "Migration." *Foreign Policy*, 109: 15–31.

Papastergiadis, Nikos. 2000. *The Turbulence of Migration.* Cambridge: Polity.

Parekh, Bhikhu. 2000a. *Rethinking Multiculturalism: Cultural Diversity and Political Theory.* London: Macmillan.

—— 2000b. *The Future of Multi-Ethnic Britain*, Report of the Runnymede Trust Commission on the Future of Multi-Ethnic Britain. London: Profile Books.

Park, Robert E. 1950. *Race and Culture: The Collected Papers of R. E. Park.* Glencoe, IL: The Free Press.

Park, Robert E. and Herbert A. Miller. 1921. *Old World Traits Transplanted.* Chicago: University of Chicago Society for Social Research.

Parsons, Talcott. 1937. *The Structure of Social Action.* New York: McGraw-Hill.

—— 1967. *Sociological Theory and Modern Society.* New York: The Free Press.

—— 1971. *The System of Modern Societies.* Englewood Cliffs, NJ: Prentice-Hall.

—— 1975. "Some Theoretical Considerations on the Nature and Trends of Change of Ethnicity." Pp. 53–83 in Nathan Glazer and Daniel P. Moynihan (eds.), *Ethnicity: Theory and Experience.* Cambridge, MA: Harvard University Press.

—— 1977. *The Evolution of Societies.* Englewood Cliffs, NJ: Prentice-Hall.

—— 1993. *Talcott Parsons on National Socialism*, edited and introduced by Uta Gerhardt. New York: Aldine de Gruyter.

Partington, Geoffrey. 1997. *The Australian Nation: Its British and Irish Roots.* New Brunswick, NJ: Transaction.

Patterson, Orlando. 1982. *Slavery and Social Death: A Comparative Study.* Cambridge, MA: Harvard University Press.

—— 1997. *The Ordeal of Integration: Progress and Resentment in America's "Racial" Crisis.* Washington, DC: Civitas/Counterpoint.

—— 2000. "Ecumenical America: Global Culture and the American Cosmos." Pp.

465–80 in Peter Kivisto and Georganne Rundbland (eds.), *Multiculturalism in the United States*. Thousand Oaks, CA: Pine Forge.

Peach, Ceri. 1991. *The Caribbean in Europe: Contrasting Patterns of Migration and Settlement in Britain, France, and the Netherlands*, Research Papers in Ethnic Relations, No. 15. Coventry: Centre for Research in Ethnic Relations.

Pearson, David. 2001. *The Politics of Ethnicity in Settler Societies: States of Unease*. New York: Palgrave.

Pedraza, Silvia. 1992. "Cubans in Exile, 1959–1989: The State of the Research." Pp. 24–36 in D. J. Fernandez (ed.), *Cuban Studies Since the Revolution*. Gainesville: University Presses of Florida.

Pedraza-Bailey, Silvia. 1990. "Immigration Research: A Conceptual Map." *Social Science History*, 14(1): 43–67.

Perlman, Joel and Roger Waldinger. 1999. "Immigrants, Past and Present: A Reconsideration" Pp. 223–38 in Charles Hirschman, Philip Kasinitz, and Josh DeWind (eds.), *The Handbook of International Migration. The American Experience*. New York: Russell Sage.

Pettigrew, Thomas. 1998. "Reaction Toward the New Minorities of Western Europe." *Annual Review of Sociology*, 24: 77–103.

Pettman, Jan Jindy. 1997. "Race, Ethnicity, and Gender in Australia." Pp. 202–7 in Samuel P. Oliner and Phillip T. Gay (eds.), *Race, Ethnicity and Gender: A Global Prospective*. Dubuque, IA: Kendall/Hunt.

Phizacklea, Annie and Robert Miles. 1980. *Labour and Racism*. London: Routledge and Kegan Paul.

Porter, John. 1965. *The Vertical Mosaic: An Analysis of Social Class and Power in Canada*. Toronto: University of Toronto Press.

Portes, Alejandro. 1995. "Children of Immigrants: Segmented Assimilation." Pp. 248–80 in Alejandro Portes (ed.), *The Economic Sociology of Immigration*. New York: Russell Sage.

—— 1996. "Global Villagers: The Rise of Transnational Communites." *American Prospect*, 25 (March/April): 74–7.

——, Luis E. Guarnizo, and Patricia Landolt. 1999. "The Study of Transnationalism: Pitfalls and Promise of an Emergent Research Field," *Ethnic and Racial Studies*, 22(2): 217–37.

—— and Rubén Rumbaut. *Legacies: The Story of the Immigrant Second Generation*. Berkeley and New York: University of California Press and Russell Sage.

—— and Richard Schauffler. 1996. "Language and the Second Generation: Bilingualism Yesterday and Today." Pp. 8–29 in Alejandro Portes (ed.), *The New Second Generation*. New York: Russell Sage

—— and Min Zhou. 1993. "The New Second Generation: Segmented Assimilation and Its Variants." *The Annals of the American Academy of Political and Social Sciences*, 530(Nov.): 74–96.

Quinn, Herbert E. 1979. *The Union Nationale*. Toronto: University of Toronto Press.

Raj, Dhooleka Sarhadi. 2000. "Who the Hell Do You Think You Are? Promoting Religious Identity Among Young Hindus in Britain." *Ethnic and Racial Studies*, 23(3): 535–58.

Ramchavan, Subhas. 1982. *Racism: Non-Whites in Canada*. Toronto: Butterworths.

Ratcliffe, Peter. 1999. "Paradigms in Conflict: Racial and Ethnic Inequality in Contemporary Britain." *Innovation: The European Journal of Social Science*, 4(3): 212–33.

Reed, Stanley. 1999. "Could Scotland Turn into Tony Blair's Quebec?" *Business Week*, (April): 53–6.

Rex, John and Robert Moore. 1967a. *Race, Community and Conflict: A Study of Sparkbrook*. London: Oxford University Press.

—— 1967b. *Colonial Immigrants in a British City*. London: Routledge and Kegan Paul.

Reynolds, Andrew. 1999/2000. "A Constitutional Pied Piper: The Northern Irish Good Friday Agreement." *Political Science Quarterly*, 114(4): 613–37.

Rhea, Joseph Tilden. 1996. *Race Pride and the American Identity*. Cambridge, MA: Harvard University Press.

Rich, Paul B. 1986. *Race and Empire in British Politics*. Cambridge: Cambridge University Press.

Richmond, Anthony H. 1969. "Immigration and Pluralism in Canada." *International Migration Review*, 4(1): 5–24.

—— 1994. *Global Apartheid: Refugees, Racism, and the New World Order*. Oxford: Oxford University Press.

Richter, A. 1998. "'Blood and Soil': What It Means to be German." *World Policy Journal*, 15(4): 91–8.

Rickard, John. 1996. *Australia: A Cultural History*. London: Longman.

Rieder, Jonathan. 1985. *Canarsie: The Jews and Italians of Brooklyn Against Liberalism*. Cambridge, MA: Harvard University Press.

Robertson, Roland. 1992. *Globalization: Social Theory and Global Culture*. London: Sage.

Robertson, Roland and Bryan S. Turner (eds.). 1991. *Talcott Parsons: Theorist of Modernity*. Thousand Oaks, CA: Sage.

Roediger, David R. 1991. *The Wages of Whiteness: Race and the Making of the American Working Class*. New York: Verso.

Rogers, Vaughan. 1990. "Brittany." Pp. 67–85 in Michael Watson (ed.), *Contemporary Minority Nationalism*. London: Routledge.

Rose, Peter. 1997. *Tempest-Tost: Race, Immigration, and the Dilemmas of Diversity*. New York: Oxford University Press.

Rousseau, Mark O. 1999. "Ethnic Mobilization in Quebec, Federalism in Canada, and the Global Economy." *Research in Social Movements, Conflicts, and Change*, 21: 205–23.

Roy, Patricia. 1995. "The Fifth Force: Multiculturalism and the English Canadian Identity." *The Annals of the American Academy of Political and Social Science*, 538(March): 199–209.

Ruane, Joseph and Jennifer Todd. 1996. *The Dynamics of Conflict in Northern Ireland: Power, Conflict, and Emancipation*. Cambridge: Cambridge University Press.

Rudder, Véronique de. 1992. "Immigrant Housing and Integration in French Cities." Pp. 247–67 in Donald Horowitz and Gérard Noiriel (eds.), *Immigrants in Two Democracies: French and American Experiences*. New York: New York University Press.

Rumbaut, Rubén. 1996. "The Crucible Within: Ethnic Identity, Self-Esteem, and Segmented Assimilation Among Children of Immigrants." Pp. 119–70 in Alejandro Portes (ed.), *The New Second Generation*. New York: Russell Sage.

Rushton, J. Philippe. 1999. *Race, Evolution, and Behavior*. New Brunswick, NJ: Transaction.

Ruthven, M. 1990. *A Satanic Affair: Salman Rushdie and the Rage of Islam.* London: Chatto & Windus.

Salmon, Jon. 1996. "Indian Pupils Outclass All Other Groups." *The Sunday Times,* Sept. 1: 5.

Samuel, John T. 1990. "Third World Immigration and Multiculturalsim." Pp. 383–97 in Shiva S. Halli, Frank Trovato, and Leo Dreidger (eds.), *Ethnic Demography.* Ottawa, Ont.: Carleton University Press.

Sassen, Saskia. 1994. *Cities in a World Economy.* Thousand Oaks, CA. Pine Forge.

—— 1998a. *Globalization and Its Discontents: Essays on the New Mobility of People and Money.* New York: The New Press.

—— 1998b. "The *de facto* Transnationalizing of Immigration Policy." Pp. 49–85 in Christian Joppke (ed.), *Challenge to the Nation-State: Immigration in Western Europe and the United States.* Oxford: Oxford University Press.

—— 1999. *Guests and Aliens.* New York: The New Press.

Savigear, Peter. 1990. "Corsica." Pp. 86–99 in Michael Watson (ed.), *Contemporary Minority Nationalism.* London: Routledge.

Schermerhorn, R. A. 1978. *Comparative Ethnic Relations: A Framework for Theory and Research.* Chicago: University of Chicago Press.

Schlesinger, Arthur M., Jr. 1992. *The Disuniting of America: Reflections on a Multicultural Society.* New York: W.W. Norton.

Schmidt, Christoph M. 1997. "Immigrant Performance in Germany: Labor Earnings of Ethnic German Migrants and Foreign Guest-Workers." *Quarterly Review of Economics and Finance,* 37: 379–97.

Schmidt, Vivien A. 1999. "Discourse and (Dis)Integration in Europe: The Cases of France, Germany, and Great Britain." Pp. 167–97 in Stephen R. Graubard (ed.), *A New Europe for the Old?* New Brunswick, NJ: Transaction.

Schuck, Peter and Rainer Münz, eds. 1998. *Paths to Inclusion: The Integration of Migrants in the United States and Germany.* New York: Berghahn Books.

Sears, David O. 1994. "Urban Rioting in Los Angeles: A Comparison of 1965 with 1992." Pp. 237–53 in Mark Baldassare (ed.), *The Los Angeles Riots: Lessons for the Urban Future.* Boulder, CO: Westview.

See, Katherine O'Sullivan. 1986. *First World Nationalisms.* Chicago: University of Chicago Press.

Sennett, Richard. 1998. *The Corrosion of Character: The Personal Consequences of Work in the New Capitalism.* New York: W. W. Norton.

Shafir, Gershon. 1995. *Immigrants and Nationalists: Ethnic Conflict and Accommodation in Catalonia, the Basque Country, Latvia, and Estonia.* Albany: State University of New York Press.

Sherington, Geoffrey. 1980. *Australia's Immigrants, 1788–1978.* Sydney: Allen & Unwin.

Shigematsu, Stephen. 1993–94. "Multiethnic Japan and the Monoethnic Myth." *MELUS,* 18(4): 63–81.

Siggner, Andrew J. 1986. "The Socio-Demographic Conditions of Registered Indians." *Canadian Social Trends,* Winter: 2–9.

Simon, Rita J. and James P. Lynch. 1999. "A Comparative Assessment of Public Opinion Toward Immigrants and Immigration Policies." *International Migration Re-*

view, 33(2): 455–67.

Sklair, Leslie. 2001. *The Transnational Capitalist Class.* Oxford: Blackwell.

Skrentny, John David. 1996. *The Ironies of Affirmative Action: Politics, Culture, and Justice in America.* Chicago: University of Chicago Press.

Small, Stephen. 1994. *Racialised Barriers: The Black Experience in the United States and England in the 1980s.* London: Routledge.

Smith, Anthony. 1986. *The Ethnic Origins of Nations.* Oxford: Blackwell.

—— 1991. *National Identity.* London: Penguin.

Smith, David J. and Gerald Chambers. 1991. *Inequality in Northern Ireland.* Oxford: Clarendon Press.

Smith, Goldwin. 1991. *Canada and the Canadian Question.* Toronto: University of Toronto Press.

Smolicz, J. J. 1997. "Australia: From Migrant Country to Multicultural Nation." *International Migration Review* 31(Spring): 171–86.

Smooha, Sammy and Theodor Hunt. 1996. "Conflict-Regulation in Deeply Divided Societies." Pp. 326–33 in John Hutchinson and Anthony D. Smith (eds.), *Ethnicity.* Oxford: Oxford University Press.

Sniderman, Paul M. and Edward G. Carmines. 1997. *Reaching Beyond Race.* Cambridge, MA: Harvard University Press.

Sniderman, Paul M. and Thomas Piazza. 1993. *The Scar of Race.* Cambridge, MA: The Belknap Press of Harvard University Press.

Snipp, C. Matthew. 1989. *American Indians: The First of This Land.* New York: Russell Sage.

Sollors, Werner, ed. 1989. *The Invention of Ethnicity.* New York: Oxford University Press.

Solomos, John. 1986. "Varieties of Marxist Conceptions of 'Race,' Class, and the State: A Critical Analysis." Pp. 184–90 in John Rex and David Mason (eds.), *Theories of Race and Ethnic Relations.* Cambridge: Cambridge University Press.

Solomos, John and Les Back. 1995a. "Marxism, Racism, and Ethnicity." *American Behavioral Scientist*, 38(3): 407–20.

—— 1995b. *Race, Politics, and Social Change.* London: Routledge.

—— 1996. *Racism and Society.* New York: St. Martin's.

Soysal, Yasemin Nuhoğlu. 1994. *Limits of Citizenship: Migrants and Postnational Membership in Europe.* Chicago: University of Chicago Press.

—— 2000. "Citizenship and Identity: Living in Diasporas in Post-war Europe?" *Ethnic and Racial Studies*, 23(1): 1–15.

Spinner-Halev, Jeff. 1999. "Cultural Pluralism and Partial Citizenship." Pp. 65–86 in Christian Joppke and Steven Lukes (eds.), *Multicultural Questions.* Oxford: Oxford University Press.

Stampp, Kenneth M. 1956. *The Peculiar Institution: Slavery in the Ante-Bellum South.* New York: Alfred A. Knopf.

Steinberg, Stephen. 2000. "Affirmative Action and Liberal Capitulation." Pp. 287–94 in Peter Kivisto and Georganne Rundblad (eds.), *Multiculturalism in the United States.* Thousand Oaks, CA: Pine Forge.

Stratton, Jon and Ien Ang. 1998. "Multicultural Imagined Communities: Cultural Difference and National Identity in the USA and Australia." Pp. 135–62 in David Bennett (ed.), *Multicultural States: Rethinking Difference and Identity.* London:

Routledge.

Stull, Donald D., Michael J. Broadway, and Ken C. Erickson. 1992. "The Price of A Good Steak: Beef Packing and Its Consequences for Garden City, Kansas." Pp. 35–64 in Louise Lamphere (ed.), *Structuring Diversity: Ethnographic Perspectives on the New Immigration.* Chicago: University of Chicago Press.

Swain, Carol M. 2001. "Affirmative Action: Legislative History, Judicial Interpretations, Public Consensus." Pp. 318–47 in Neil J. Smelser, William Julius Wilson, and Faith Mitchell (eds.), *America Becoming: Racial Trends and Their Consequences,* vol. 1. Washington, DC: National Academy Press.

Swidler, Ann. 1986. "Culture in Action." *American Sociological Review,* 51(2): 111–25.

Swyripa, Frances. 1978. *Ukrainian Canadians.* Edmonton: University of Alberta Press.

Takaki, Ronald. 1989. *Strangers From a Different Shore: A History of Asian Americans.* Boston: Little, Brown.

Tambini, Damian. 2001. "Post-National Citizenship." *Ethnic and Racial Studies* 24(2): 195–217.

Taylor, Charles, with commentary by Amy Gutmann, Steve C. Rockefeller, Michael Walzer, and Susan Wolf. 1992. *Multiculturalism and "The Politics of Recognition."* Princeton, NJ: Princeton University Press.

Terry, Don. 1996. "In White Flight's Wake, a Town Tries to Keep Its Balance." *New York Times,* March 11, p. A6.

Thompson, Richard H. 1989. *Theories of Ethnicity: A Critical Appraisal.* New York: Greenwood Press.

Thomson, Dale. 1995. "Language, Identity, and the Nationalist Impulse: Quebec." *The Annals of the American Academy of Political and Social Science,* 538: 69–82.

Thornton, Russell. 1987. *American Indian Holocaust and Survival: A Population History Since 1492.* Norman: University of Oklahoma Press.

Tienda, Marta. 1999. "Immigration, Opportunity, and Social Cohesion." Pp. 129–46 in Neil J. Smelser and Jeffrey C. Alexander (eds.), *Diversity and Its Discontents.* Princeton, NJ: Princeton University Press.

Tizon, Orlando. 1999. "Congregation and Family: Changing Filipino Identities." Ph.D. dissertation, Loyola University.

Touraine, Alain. 1997. *What is Democracy?* Boulder, CO: Westview.

Trosset, Carol. 1993. *Welshness Performed.* Tucson: University of Arizona Press.

Trueheart, Charles. 1997. "Islam is Adjusting to Its Role as a Minority Religion in a Secular Continent." *Washington Post Foreign Service,* Wed., Dec. 24, P. A10.

Tuan, Mia. 1998. *Forever Foreigners or Honorary Whites? The Asian Ethnic Experience.* New Brunswick, NJ: Rutgers University Press.

Turner, Bryan S. 2000. "Introduction." Pp. 1–18 in Bryan S. Turner (ed.), *The Blackwell Companion to Social Theory.* Oxford: Blackwell.

US Census Bureau. 1999. *Statistical Abstract of the United States.* Washington, DC: US Government Printing Office.

US Census Bureau. 2001. "Diversity of the Country's Hispanics Highlighted." http://www.census.gov.

Valls-Russell, Janice. 1996. "Spring Hatred in France." *The New Leader,* 79 (Oct.): 3–4.

Verdery, Katherine. 1998. "Transnationalism, Nationalism, Citizenship, and Property: Eastern Europe Since 1989." *American Ethnologist,* 25(2): 291–306.

Vertovec, Steven. Forthcoming. "Fostering Cosmopolitanisms: A Conceptual Survey and a Media Experiment in Berlin." *Cultural Anthropology.*

Vertovec, Steven and Ceri Peach, eds. 1997. *Islam in Europe: The Politics of Religion and Community.* London: Macmillan.

Veugelers, John W. P. 2000. "Right-Wing Extremism in Contemporary France: A 'Silent Counterrevolution'?" *The Sociological Quarterly,* 44(1): 19–40.

Vidich, Arthur J. and Stanford M. Lyman. 1985. *American Sociology: Worldly Rejections of Religion and Their Directions.* New Haven, CT: Yale University Press.

Viorst, Milton. 1996. "The Muslims of France." *Foreign Affairs,* 75 (Sept./Oct.): 78–96.

Wacquant, Luc. 1992. "Banlieues Françaises et Ghetto Noir Américain: De l'amalgame à la Comparaison." *French Politics and Society,* 10(4): 81–103.

Waldinger, Roger. 2001. "Strangers at the Gates." Pp. 1–29 in Roger Waldinger (ed.), *Strangers at the Gates: New Immigrants in Urban America.* Berkeley: University of California Press.

Waldinger, Roger and Jennifer Lee. 2001. "New Immigrants in Urban America." Pp. 30–79 in Roger Waldinger (ed.), *Strangers at the Gates: New Immigrants in Urban America.* Berkeley: University of California Press.

Walvin, James. 2000. *Making the Black Atlantic: Britain and the African Diaspora.* London: Cassell.

Walzer, Michael. 1997. *On Toleration.* New Haven, CT: Yale University Press.

Warner, Stephen and Judith Wittner, eds. *Gatherings in Diaspora: Religious Communities and the New Immigration.* Philadelphia: Temple University Press.

Waters, Mary. 1990. *Ethnic Options: Choosing Identities in America.* Berkeley: University of California Press.

Watson, Michael, ed. 1990. *Contemporary Minority Nationalism.* New York: Routledge.

Weber, Eugen. 1976. *Peasants into Frenchman: The Modernization of Rural France, 1870–1914.* Stanford, CA: Stanford University Press.

—— 1996. "The Art of the Impossible." *The American Scholar,* 65(Winter): 91–8.

West, Cornel. 1993. *Race Matters.* Boston: Beacon.

Wieviorka, Michel. 1995a. *The Arena of Racism.* Thousand Oaks, CA: Sage.

—— 1995b. "Racism and Social Movements." Pp. 87–106 in Louis Maheu (ed.), *Social Movements and Social Classes: The Future of Collective Action.* Thousand Oaks, CA: Sage.

Wigley, Dafydd. 1996. "New Alliances." *New Statesman and Society,* 9: 18–19.

Williams, Gwyn A. 1982. *The Welsh in Their History.* London: Croom Helm.

—— 1985. *When Was Wales?* London: Black Raven Press.

Wilson, J. Donald. 1994. "Multiculturalism and Immigration Policy in Canada: The Last Twenty-five years." *Siirtolaisuus,* 2: 5–12.

Wilson, William Julius. 1978. *The Declining Significance of Race: Blacks and Changing American Institutions.* Chicago: University of Chicago Press.

—— 1996. *When Work Disappears: The World of the New Urban Poor.* New York: Alfred A. Knopf.

—— 1999. *The Bridge Over the Racial Divide: Rising Inequality and Coalition Politics.* Berkeley: University of California Press.

Wilson, V. Seymour. 1993. "The Tapestry Vision of Canadian Multiculturalism." *Canadian Journal of Political Science,* 26(Dec.): 645–69.

Winant, Howard. 1994. *Racial Conditions*. Minneapolis: University of Minnesota Press.
—— 1999. "Whiteness at Century's End." Pp. 23–45 in M. Wray (ed.), *The Making and Unmaking of Whiteness*. Durham, NC: Duke University Press.
—— 2000. "Race and Race Theory." *Annual Review of Sociology*, 26: 169–85.
Wingen, Max. 1995. "Immigration to the Federal Republic of Germany as a Demographic and Social Problem." *International Migration Review*, 29(3): 710–19.
Winks, Robin W. 1988. *The Relevance of Canadian History*. Lanham, MD: University Press of America.
Woo, Deborah. 1999. *Glass Ceilings and Asian Americans: The New Face of Workplace Barriers*. Walnut Creek, CA: Alta Mira.
Woodward, C. Van. 1974. *The Strange Career of Jim Crow*. New York: Oxford University Press.
Woolard, Kathryn Ann. 1989. *Double Talk: Bilingualism and the Politics of Ethnicity in Catalonia*. Stanford, CA: Stanford University Press.
Yalçin-Heckmann, Lale. 1997. "The Perils of Ethnic Associational Life in Europe: Turkish Migrants in Germany and France." Pp. 95–110 in Tariq Modood and Pnina Werbner (eds.), *The Politics of Multiculturalism in the New Europe: Racism, Identity, and Community*. London: Zed Books.
Yinger, J. Milton. 1994. *Ethnicity: Source of Strength? Source of Conflict?* Albany: State University of New York Press.
Zhou, Min. 2001. "Contemporary Immigration and the Dynamics of Race and Ethnicity." Pp. 200–42 in Neil J. Smelser, William Julius Wilson, and Faith Mitchell (eds.), *America Becoming: Racial Trends and Their Consequences*, vol. 1. Washington, DC: National Academy Press.

Index

Pettman, Jan, 104
Phillip, Arthur, 103
pied-noirs, 181
Plaid Cymru, 125, 127–9
Plessy v. Ferguson, 54, 64
pluralism, 37
 caste, 52–4
 coercive, 50–6
 predatory, 51–2
 sojourner, 54–6
 see also cultural pluralism
Poles, 16, 34, 48, 97, 157
politics of recognition, 36, 65, 92
polyethnic states, 117
Porter, John, 85, 91, 96
Portes, Alejandro, 32–3, 38, 41, 81
Portugal, 12
postethnic America, 37
postmodern era, 41–2
Powell, Enoch, 5, 143–4
prejudice, 85
Proposition 187, 80
Proposition 209, 67
Protestants in Northern Ireland, 132–6
prejudice, 85
Puerto Ricans, 76–7
Pujol, Jordi, 131

Québec, 8, 36
Québec Act of 1774, 87
Québecois nationalism, 10, 91–6, 187
Quiet Revolution, 92

race, 2, 9, 26
 against, 14–8
 declining significance of, 68
 relations, 26
 relations cycle, 27
Race Discrimination Act of 1975
 (Australia), 110
Race Equality Councils, 152
Race Relations Acts of 1965 and 1968
 (Britain), 143
Race Relations Act of 1976 (Britain),
 151–2
racial formation, 14
 new, 57–81

racial groups, 15
Racial Pride Movement, 65
racialization, 26
racism, 22, 28, 154
 end of, 68
Ranger, Terence, 9, 19
Reagan, Ronald, 70, 72
Red Power, 71, 100
regional cosmoses, 40
renaixenca, 130
Republican Party (US), 77
Republikaner Party (Germany), 168,
 177
reservation system, 51
Rex, John, 145
Rhea, Joseph T., 65
Richmond, Anthony, 99
right-wing activism, 6, 11, 72, 156,
 168–9
Rivera, Miguel Primo de, 130
Robertson, Roland, 24
Roediger, David, 16
Rom, 160
 see also gypsies
Ross, Edward Alsworth, 17
Royal Commission on Bilingualism and
 Biculturalism (Canada), 92
Royal Ulster Constabulary, 134
Runnymede Trust, 153, 191
Rupert's Land, 86
Rushdie, Salman, 149–50
Rushton, J. Philippe, 17
Rwanda, 26

Saudi Arabia, 3
Scandinavians, 16
Schröder, Gerhard, 6, 169
Scotland, 7, 26, 117–18, 123–7, 136
Scottish National Party (SNP), 124–9
Scottish Nationalist Party, 7, 11
Scottish Parliament, 7, 126
Second World War, 1, 11, 20, 24, 56,
 58, 72, 89–90, 97, 104, 108–9,
 118, 122, 124, 139, 157, 160,
 162, 172, 181
segregation, 62–3
 de facto, 63, 66